The Early Church
in Herefordshire

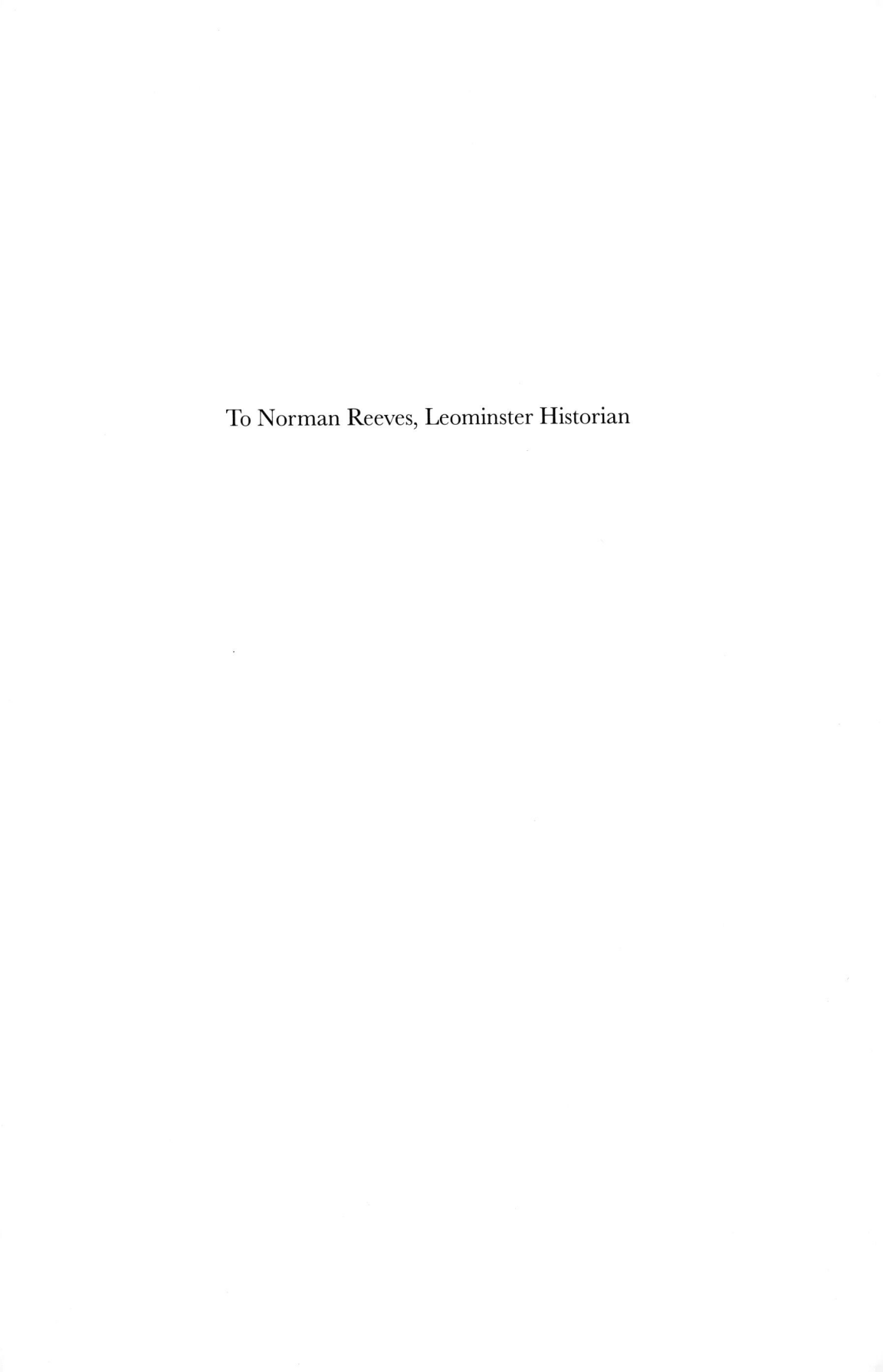

To Norman Reeves, Leominster Historian

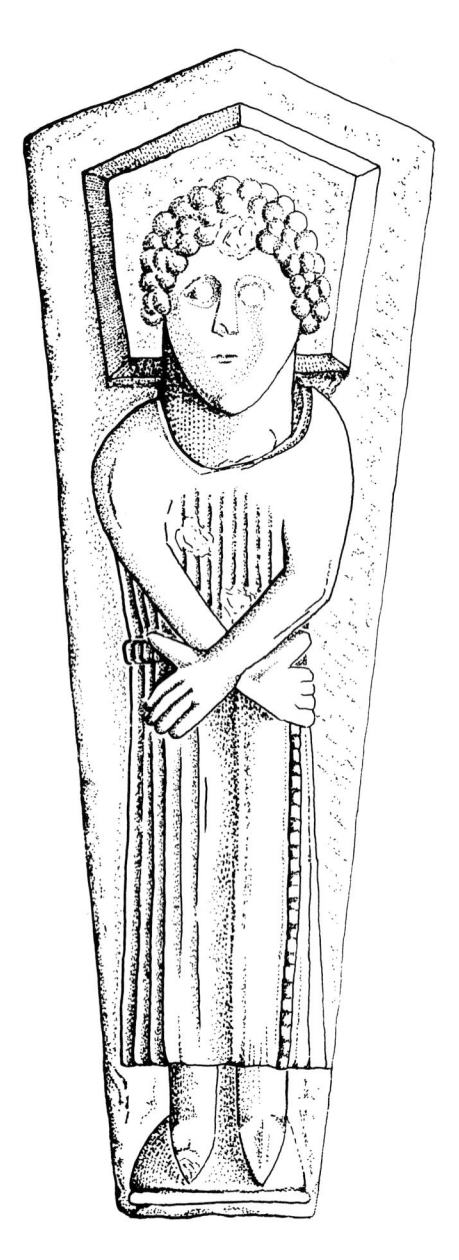

The Llangarron Figure

© *Copyright Herefordshire Archaeology*

HEREFORDSHIRE HISTORY

The Early Church in Herefordshire

Proceedings of a Conference
held in Leominster in June 2000

Edited by

Ann Malpas, Janet Butler, Arthur Davis, Sheila Davis,
Tony Malpas and Chris Sansom

Cover, graphic design and layout
by Arthur Davis

PUBLISHED FOR LEOMINSTER HISTORICAL SOCIETY
BY
LEOMINSTER HISTORY STUDY GROUP

LEOMINSTER HISTORY STUDY GROUP
Hillside, Kimbolton, Leominster, Herefordshire HR6 0JA

First published by Leominster History Study Group 2001
Copyright © The Contributors 2001

*All rights reserved. No part of this publication may be reproduced,
stored in a retrieval system, or transmitted in any form or by any means
electronic, mechanical, photocopying, recording or otherwise, without
prior permission in writing of the publisher.*

ISBN 0 9536314 1 9

Set in Baskerville and
printed by Orphans Press, Leominster.

Acknowledgements

Thanks are due to the following:

The British Library for permission to reproduce BL MS 478, f 11b, The Summer Canon (Colour plate 1) and also BL Harley MS 2253 f 132r, The Legend of St Etfrid (Fig 3) taken from Hillaby, J, 'Early Christian and Pre-Conquest Leominster' *Transactions of the Woolhope Naturalists' Field Club* XLV (iii) (1987) by courtesy of Joe Hillaby and the Woolhope Naturalists' Field Club
W D Turton and Leominster Museum for permission to use part of the Galliers Map, 1825 (Fig 6)
The Society of Antiquaries of London for permission to reproduce the illustration of the Wheel of Life painting in Leominster Church, in their *Proceedings* Volume XXVI, 2nd series, 1914 (Fig 21)
Hereford Museum for permission to reproduce the drawings of the Romano-British strap-end from Kenchester (Fig 23) and the photograph of the ecclesiastical handbell from Marden (Fig 31)
The Shropshire Records and Research Centre, for permission to reproduce the nineteenth century drawing of the Wroxeter Cross (Fig 33), after White, R and Barker, P, *Wroxeter: Life and Death of a Roman City*, Page 141, Tempus, Stroud, 1998, by courtesy of the authors and publishers
S J Plunkett for permission to reproduce the illustrations of ecclesiastical sculpture (Fig 1) from his Cambridge Ph D thesis (1984) *Mercian and West Saxon Decorative Stone-Sculpture: Styles and Patterns of Influence*
R Bryant for permission to reproduce the photograph of the Gloucester cross shaft (Fig 13)
The National Monuments and Record Centre, English Heritage, for permission to reproduce the plan of Leominster Priory Church from The Royal Commission of Historical Monuments of England, *An Inventory of the Historical Monuments of Herefordshire* III (North West) (Fig 19).

For help with the arrangements for the Leominster Conference

Joe Hillaby, Jean O'Donnell, Jim Tonkin and Ruth Richardson for leading conducted tours of Herefordshire churches, and also Keith Ray, Julian Cotton and Tim Hoverd, all of *Herefordshire Archaeology,* for site visits
Brother Bernard of Belmont Abbey for conducted tours of the Abbey
David Gorvett and Brian Redwood for arranging visits
Dominic Harbour and Claire Ashford for a special opening of the *Mappa Mundi* Exhibition
Margaret Bent for help and advice
Sandy Marchant for help and advice and exhibition judging
Kate Tudge of *Herefordshire Tourism* for financial and other support and publicity.

Contents

	Page
Acknowledgements	vii
Foreword The Bishop of Hereford, The Rt Revd John Oliver	x
Preface	2
1 The Anglo-Saxon Church in Herefordshire: Four Themes John Blair	3
2 The Legend of St Etfrid of Leominster Hugh Pawsey	14
3 The Early Church in Herefordshire: Columban and Roman Joe Hillaby	41
4 Echoes from the Stones John Harper	77
5 The Wheel of Life Painting in Leominster Priory Church Ann Malpas	89
6 Archaeology and the Three Early Churches of Herefordshire Keith Ray	99

	Page
Glossary	150
List of Illustrations	152
Index of churches and other places in Herefordshire referred to in this book	154
Index of Names	156

Foreword

It was a great pleasure for me to be present for part of the Conference on the Early Church in Herefordshire in June 2000 in Leominster. The sun shone, a large and enthusiastic attendance showed how great is the interest in this subject, and the qualities of the papers reflected the remarkable depth and range of expertise which happily exists in Herefordshire and beyond. I am very glad to commend this learned publication, impressive for its outstanding scholarship, which is fully and carefully backed-up by the comprehensive annotation, yet which is also remarkably accessible to the general reader.

Studying this book has added enormously to my understanding of the subject, as well as giving great enjoyment. John Blair, in his paper, looks forward to a future conference in the year 2100, by which time – he hopes – much more research will have been undertaken into the Minster Churches of Herefordshire, and he and Keith Ray both emphasise how much remains to be discovered. There is enormous potential for adding to our knowledge and understanding of the early centuries of the Christian faith in Herefordshire. I share their enthusiasm and their aspiration to see this work go forward, but meanwhile, I have been particularly glad to learn more about the British Church, which flourished in Herefordshire between the end of the Roman Occupation and the arrival of the Anglo-Saxons; about the uncertain beginnings of the Hereford Diocese and its earliest Bishops; about the remarkable evidence of the very Early Church, provided in particular by the Llangarron figure and the Llanveynoe standing cross; and about the patterns of worship in ministry which focussed on monastic foundations or on minster churches, and which we in this diocese are in some way re-creating in the 21st century through the development of our Ministry Teams; about Offa's enthusiasm for creating an Archbishopric in Lichfield – an issue which has interestingly been very tentatively revived as one possible solution to the problems created by the very great demands being made at the present day on the Archbishop of Canterbury.

Apart from the scholarly way in which these issues are treated, it has been fascinating to be introduced to some individual characters who have played small parts in the development of the whole story: was the Etfrid legend written by a nun, and if so, were her particular linguistic choices evidence of early 10th century feminism? Was it really William of Winchester, a renegade monk of Reading Abbey, who had been sent as a form of punishment to the small monastic house at Leominster, who wrote some of the earliest surviving polyphonic music? It is also fascinating to read about the difficult relationship which existed between the British Church and the later English Church, with the British clergy styling themselves *Cathari*, 'the pure ones', in distinction from the parvenu English Christians – and reaction on the part of the English to that characterisation, which was to condemn the British Church as degenerate and unfaithful in its missionary task.

These papers are about the very early history of the Church in Herefordshire, yet there are surprising similarities with some of the debates which engage Christian people today. We are deeply indebted to those who have contributed to this volume and those who organised the conference.

✝ John Hereford

The Bishop's House
The Palace
Hereford

Preface

In June 2000 a conference was organised by Leominster Historical Society on behalf of the Day-School Co-ordinating Committee of local history societies of Herefordshire. As it was 'millennium year' it was felt that an appropriate subject would be the Early Church in Herefordshire. This book contains papers given at the conference, with some additional material.

Our chosen subject is not an easy one. This is caused partly by geography. Herefordshire, 'the land beyond the Severn', has been open to a multiplicity of influences, British, Roman, Welsh, Irish via Northumbria, Anglo-Saxon, Norman . . . . The history of Christianity in the first millennium is difficult also because of the fragmentary nature of the written sources and the paucity of above ground archaeological evidence.

The last time this subject was on the agenda of a local conference was in 1990, when the British Archaeological Association met in Hereford. Seventeen of the papers from that conference, including one entitled 'Early Churches in Herefordshire: Documentary and Structural Evidence' by David Parsons, and also contributions by two of the speakers who have written for this volume, Joe Hillaby and John Blair, were published in 1995 as *Medieval Art, Architecture and Archaeology at Hereford*, edited by David Whitehead. Many of the questions under discussion in the papers presented then have been re-examined in the present book, and it is interesting to see how far matters have moved on in the intervening ten years.

One big change has of course been the restoration of Herefordshire as an independent county, which has brought with it the establishment of the County Archaeological Service under the leadership of Keith Ray. His interest in early churches gives us cause to hope that the future research agenda which John Blair looks forward to at the conclusion of his paper may be taken up with some enthusiasm.

At the end of his lecture, Joe Hillaby spoke in honour of Norman Reeves, who was retiring as President of Leominster Historical Society at the age of 95.

Several additional chapters have been added to the papers given at the conference. Throughout the day an exhibition was open in the Priory Church, with displays by many churches and history societies. One such exhibition featured a medieval wall painting still visible in a former chapel of the Priory Church, and a painting by a local artist, Arthur Davis, based on the medieval artwork, with a historical commentary by Ann Malpas. This has been rewritten and added to the papers given on the day, as has also a new translation by Hugh Pawsey of the Etfrid and Merwald story, a legend central to thinking about the origins of the church in Leominster.

The conference ended with a form of Evening Prayer, for those who wished to attend, arranged by John Harper and based on First Vespers for the Solemn Feast of Pentecost as sung in medieval abbeys and priories.

1 The Anglo-Saxon Church in Herefordshire: Four Themes

JOHN BLAIR

The millennium conference held at Leominster in 2000, and this record of the proceedings, show how much local knowledge and enthusiasm are now being applied to understanding the early Church in Herefordshire. In such company, I can only be an ignorant outsider. My claim to inclusion here is simply that I have been working for some years on general aspects of the Anglo-Saxon local Church, and am currently finishing a book on the subject.[1] What I can perhaps offer are some wider perspectives that may contribute to making sense of local problems.

I shall therefore take a brief look, using Herefordshire examples, at four central themes in the local institutions and culture of the English Church between 600 and 1100. Most of the examples are referred to elsewhere in this book, often in greater detail and more depth. Here I shall try to set the scene, and to suggest some possibilities for future research.

The Seventh Century Church and its Formation: Leominster

In the early middle ages, Herefordshire was a region in which different religious traditions and systems of ecclesiastical organization met and mingled: not just the English and the Welsh, but also Irish influences from Northumbria and perhaps elsewhere. The phrase 'Celtic Church', redolent of modern romantic notions of Celtic quaintness, confuses more than it illuminates and should be abandoned.[2] The reality, a melting-pot of diverse and sometimes fiercely competing influences from British, English, Irish, Frankish (or Irish-Frankish) and Roman sources, was both more complicated and more interesting.

In Herefordshire, and especially in Ergyng, which was incorporated as the southern part of the shire and diocese, the sub-stratum of sixth and seventh century British churches is clearly visible. Probably because they developed earlier, and from a more local base, Welsh and Cornish religious sites tended to be individually smaller, but much thicker on the ground, than the minsters of early Christian England. A dense network of this kind can be glimpsed both from the *Book of Llandaff* and later traditions, which show that sites such as Garway, Llanwarne, Dewchurch, Moccas and St Weonards were originally British foundations, and from topographical evidence, which shows that the round churchyards typical of British religious culture extend well to the east of Offa's Dyke.[3]

How far English colonists of the early to mid seventh century absorbed Christianity from their near (but presumably often hostile) British neighbours is much debated. In Worcestershire and Gloucestershire, where signs of a British infrastructure are more elusive than in southern Herefordshire, a good case has been made that burial practices and perhaps elements of territorial organization were adopted from indigenous modes.[4] At least in Ergyng, the continuance of so many church sites shows that assimilation of the British system into the English one must have happened eventually on quite a large scale. This fact sets Herefordshire apart from the English regions where a minster-based system was created from scratch – a point to which I shall return more than once.

The Ionan Irish were the dominant Christian element in early seventh century Northumbria, and by extension in those regions of the midlands and the north west which were evangelized through Northumbria's political and diplomatic influence. So it could well be, as Joe Hillaby has argued, that the Ionan influences found in liturgical material from Leominster were mediated to the region by Eadfrith, a seventh century Northumbrian missionary to the Magonsaete and perhaps the first ruler of Leominster minster.[5] It should not be assumed, though, that Northumbria was the only possible source of Irish influence. Between the mid sixth and mid seventh centuries, Irish ecclesiastics were active in many parts of the British Isles and north west Europe. They could have moved northwards into Magonsaetan territory from western Wessex, or even eastwards from Wales: the tombstone of a late fifth century Irishman at Wroxeter, 'Cunorix macus maqui Coline', shows how far inland the earlier Irish settlements on the Welsh coast could have penetrated.[6] In about 670 the Mercian king gave the hillfort of Hanbury (Worcs.) to an abbot Colman – an Irishman to judge from his name – to found as a minster.[7] Colman could have belonged to the Northumbrian delegation, but it is perhaps no less likely that he was one of the many independent operators whom Bede's tidied-up, Northumbrian-centred narrative chooses to ignore.

Through the English kingdoms as a whole, the local Church which took shape during c 650-750 was based on relatively large and important religious centres, known generically as *monasteria* ('minsters'), which housed religious communities of various different kinds, and seem to have been the main providers of pastoral care to the laity.[8] Just to the east of our region, in Worcester diocese, the exceptional written sources reveal a landscape of early minsters which can be studied more completely than in any other part of England.[9] The sources for Hereford diocese are much poorer, but it is still startling how fewer are the known pre-850 minsters west of the Severn: Leominster and Acton Beauchamp (both to be discussed shortly), and Bromyard, known from a stray mid ninth century reference,[10] make up the total. I do not believe that this contrast is entirely a fiction of uneven evidence, even though that may accentuate it. There is a strong possibility that the survival of the more decentralised, Welsh layer of religious sites meant that the formation of an English-style minster system was correspondingly retarded. It is this overlap of cultural and institutional origins that makes the region so fascinating, and it should be at the top of any archaeological research agenda for church sites.

If minsters were few and far between, one was outstandingly important. All that I can add to Joe Hillaby's fundamental work on Leominster is the observation that, from a national perspective, the place looks highly exceptional. Leominster's area of parochial dependence was at least twelve miles across, one of the biggest mother parishes known in England (Fig 2, page 10); it had three Anglo-Saxon saints, which is most unusual for a non-cathedral site before the Benedictine Reform; and the area around the monastic centre was articulated by complex territorial divisions and satellite settlements.[11] Whatever the reason for Leominster's exceptional character (and one possibility is suggested below), it is an early medieval centre of not merely local but national significance, which deserves far more archaeological investigation than it has yet received.

Eighth Century 'Family Minsters': Acton Beauchamp

Before 700, English minsters were founded by kings and bishops; over the next two or three generations a host of minor laity jumped on the bandwaggon. The foundation of so-called 'family minsters', and the associated abuses, are known primarily from the famous diatribe on the corruption of the Northumbrian Church which Bede wrote in 734 to his old pupil Bishop Ecgberht of York:

> But others commit a worse crime, seeing that they are laymen neither experienced in the monastic life nor attracted to it. Under the pretext of founding minsters, they give money to kings and buy territories for themselves in which they can more freely

indulge their lust. Furthermore, they have these ascribed to themselves in hereditary right by royal edicts, and get these documents of their privileges witnessed in writing by bishops, abbots and great men of the world, as though they were really worthy of God. Having thus engrossed for themselves little estates or villages, they do whatever they like on them, free from both divine and human service: laymen in charge of monks. They do not even gather monks there, but whomsoever they can find wandering around after being thrown out of real minsters for disobedience, or whom they themselves can entice out of minsters; or indeed those of their own henchmen whom they can persuade to promise them a monk's obedience and receive the tonsure. They fill their little minsters which they have built with these unseemly gangs; and it is a most hideous and unheard-of spectacle that those same men now busy themselves with their wives and begetting children, now get out of bed and occupy themselves with zealous application in whatever needs doing within the monastic enclosures.[12]

As recent work has shown,[13] this should probably not be taken quite at face value. The underlying problems may have been more tenurial than religious: the attraction for upwardly mobile aristocrats of wrapping up their property in privileged forms of monastic land tenure. If the way of life in 'fraudulent' minsters did not match up to the standards of Bede's Jarrow, it is unlikely to have been as completely and cynically irreligious as he presents it. Whereas Jarrow reproduced European monasticism, and Christian European civilization generally, in an extremely pure form, the aristocratic minsters embodied the rich, sometimes bizarre mix of Mediterranean and Germanic culture and values which gave the Anglo-Saxon Church its distinctive character, and was in some ways its greatest strength. But for Bede's 'laymen in charge of monks', the Church could scarcely have established itself so successfully at grass-roots level throughout the English kingdoms.

Herefordshire provides one extremely good illustration of the kind of place that Bede had in mind. In about 727 the great King Æthelbald of Mercia gave three hides of land at Acton Beauchamp to his retainer (*comite meo*) Buca, 'so that it may perpetually be a dwelling of servants of God'.[14] We should probably picture Buca, like his colleague Cyneberht to whom Æthelbald gave Kidderminster on similar terms and who later occurs as its 'abbot',[15] as a time-expired veteran: perhaps genuinely interested in the spiritual possibilities of the new monastic culture, but probably keen too on its material possibilities in offering him a comfortable and tax-free retirement home.

So did the minster at Acton Beauchamp have no future beyond Buca's personal needs? One might draw that conclusion, for there is no evidence that the church had any special status later, and today it stands in humble isolation. Yet built into its post-Conquest fabric is part of an exceptionally lavish carved cross-shaft datable to c800, probably from the same hand as a cross-head in the bishop of Worcester's church at Cropthorne (Fig 1).[16] This must mean that Acton Beauchamp was still a religious community of some wealth and status in the time of, say, Buca's grandson. While 'there is nothing about the site that clearly signals a minster, the location of the church, on a low crest in the bend of a stream, is at least consistent with the sorts of places in which minsters were commonly built.[17] Precisely because the site has remained so undeveloped, it would be a good candidate for the research excavation of a typical small-scale minster that is now so badly needed.

Fig 1 Two pieces of ecclesiastical sculpture of c 800 from the same West Midlands workshop.
   Left: Cross-head at Cropthorne (Worcs.)
   Right: Cross-shaft at Acton Beauchamp (Herefs.)
   (After S J Plunkett, *Mercian and West Saxon Decorative Stone-Sculpture: Schools, Styles and Patterns of Influence* (Cambridge Ph D thesis, 1984); reproduced by permission of Steven J Plunkett

For Acton Beauchamp church see colour plate 3

Hagiography: St Æthelbald and the Origins of Hereford

While several early Welsh saints are associated with Herefordshire sites, cults of English saints are only known at the two major centres. It is unnecessary to enlarge on the three Leominster saints, Æthelmod, Eadfrith and Hæmme, since the liturgical sources (and especially the remarkable prayer-book now split between British Library, MSS Cotton Nero A ii and Galba A xiv) have been effectively analysed by Joe Hillaby.[18] Suffice it to say that the survival of these cults from the beginnings of the Anglo-Saxon Church in the region, not to mention the two litanies in the prayer-book (which list more obscure local saints than any others known from Anglo-Saxon England), demonstrate the remarkable richness and continuity of Leominster's ecclesiastical culture. Here I should like to dwell instead on Hereford and its cults. The sources are much later and less satisfactory than those for Leominster; but embedded in them may be some extremely important clues to the political and religious reorganization of the region in the later eighth century.

The existence of twin religious communities in Hereford – the cathedral under the patronage of St Æthelberht of East Anglia (d 794), the other under that of St Guthlac of Crowland (d 714) – is first recorded in a will of c1000, but excavation has shown that St Guthlac's at least was already an ecclesiastical site in the eighth century.[19] The Guthlac cult is usually ascribed to King Æthelbald of Mercia (716-57), the saint's most powerful and devoted follower. But it is odd that both of Hereford's saints were from eastern England; as we shall see shortly, later hagiography weaves Guthlac's hermitage at Crowland into the story of Æthelberht's martyrdom. Could Guthlac's cult in fact have come to Hereford in the wake of Æthelberht's, in the ninth or tenth century rather than in the early eighth? Future work should reckon with both possibilities, even though it is hard on the available evidence to choose between them.

Reliable historical evidence for the other cult is confined to the *Anglo-Saxon Chronicle* annal for 794, which reports laconically that 'in this year King Offa ordered King Æthelberht's head to be struck off'. Again it can hardly be coincidence, and must be a reflection of later political circumstances, that this cult of a rival king killed by the great Offa of Mercia should have become established deep in Mercian subject territory and in a place which Offa himself may have fortified. Whenever exactly it developed, it looks very much like a local reaction to perceived Mercian tyranny.

By c1100, the traditions which had grown up in Hereford around Æthelberht's cult had been formulated in a Latin *Life*.[20] The story has received little attention (presumably because it is so late and in places clearly unhistorical), and before proceeding further it is worth summarising its salient points. Æthelberht, the pious king of the East Angles, goes into Mercia to seek the hand of Offa's daughter Ælfthryth. He is lodged in the royal vill called Sutton (*Suttun*), where he has a vision prefiguring his martyrdom: his palace collapses, and he soars in the form of a golden-winged bird above a post which stands in the 'royal city' and which bleeds from its east side. Offa is persuaded by his wicked wife Coenthryth, and an east Anglian exile Winberht, that Æthelberht is plotting against him, and allows Winberht to cut off Æthelberht's head. Ælfthryth, horrified, makes a vow of virginity and declares her intention to become a hermit at Crowland. On Offa's orders the body is thrown into a marsh beside the River Lugg, from which place a blazing column of light rises to the heavens. Berhtferth, Offa's chamberlain, is told in a vision to raise Æthelberht's body, wash it, and take it in an ox-cart to the place called *Fernlage* by the Wye. He and his friend Ecgmund find the body and head and set off with them on the cart; at Lyde (*Luda*) the head rolls off, but a blind man stumbles over it, recovers his sight, and runs after the cart, catching up with it at Shelwick (*Sceldwica*). The martyr's body is buried; the spot is marked by a column of light, and King Milferth comes to venerate Æthelberht and build a minster over his grave. 'This place was once called *Fernlage* by the local inhabitants, but the name was afterwards changed, and with a mystical significance the place came to be called *Hereford*.'

This narrative contains some fascinating folkloric passages revealing its basis in oral legend, notably the golden bird and the bleeding post, which derive ultimately from the same European myth as the Grimm brothers' fairy tale 'The Juniper Tree'.[21] But it is on its local context that I shall focus here, for it constitutes in effect a foundation legend for Hereford. If the story is to be believed, Hereford only came into existence after Æthelberht's body was buried there in 794. This seems at first sight to be nonsense, but might it contain a grain of truth?

The key to the problem may be 'the royal vill called Sutton'. The route of the funeral cortege through Lyde and Shelwick shows that this was believed to be Sutton St Michael, on the bank of the Lugg four miles north of Hereford.[22] But then why was the place called Sutton, not Norton: the southern *tun*, not the northern one? 'Directional' place-names – Norton, Sutton, Weston, Easton – commonly occur in the appropriate positions in relation to major Anglo-Saxon centres. Figure 2 shows all the names of this type in an area of central Herefordshire. In some cases the identity of the 'parent' settlement is ambiguous, and more than one interpretation of the data is possible. It is nonetheless striking that Leominster lies between a Norton twelve miles up-river and a Sutton – Sutton St Michael – eight miles down-river, and also a Weston seven miles to its

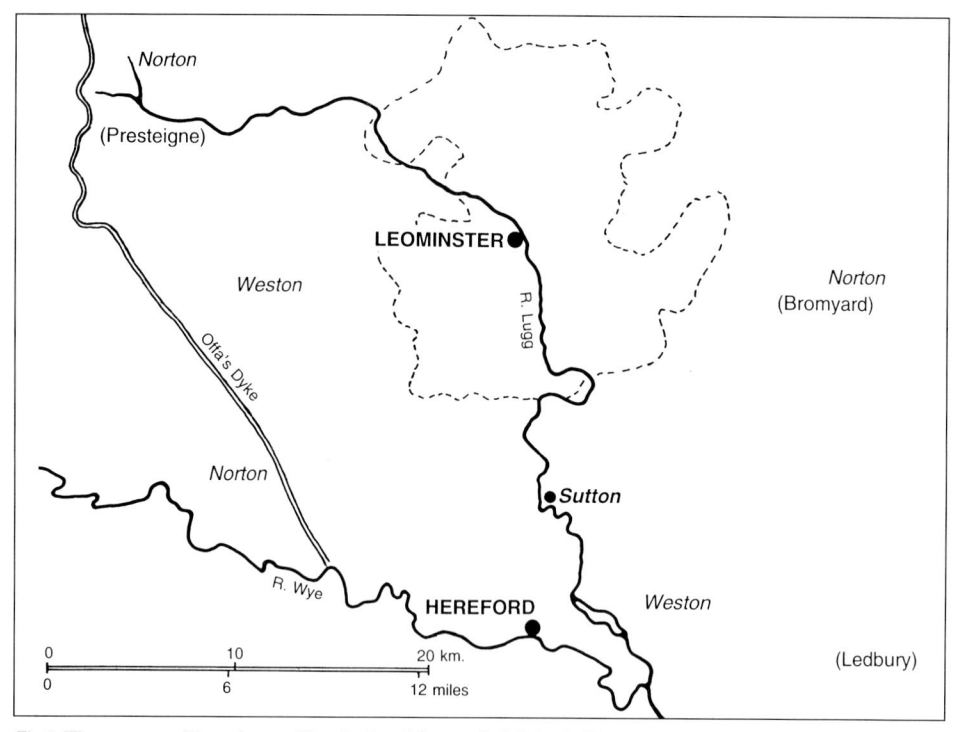

Fig 2 The context of Leominster, Hereford and Sutton St Michael. The map shows all directional place-names within its area. The known boundary of the residual mother-parish of Leominster is shown (after Kemp, 'Aspects of the Parochia of Leominster') in thin broken line. Names of potential 'parent' settlements of the directional place-names, other than Leominster and Hereford, are shown in brackets.

west. It is a tempting inference that Leominster's mother parish as recorded in the Norman period was only the rump of its previous still larger territory, within which the 'directional' place-names would have marked peripheral points. If this is right, the supposed site of Offa's palace was a dependency of Leominster despite being so much nearer to Hereford.

The excavations at St Guthlac's seem to prove that Hereford was an ecclesiastical site before the death of Æthelberht. Yet there are, as we have seen, signs that Leominster was in some respects more important. Furthermore, although there were bishops of the Magonsaete from 686, the first explicit reference to a bishop of Hereford only comes in 801, seven years after Æthelberht's death.[23] Excavations in Hereford have shown that the bank and ditch of the original fortified centre date from around the later eighth century, in other words probably from Offa's reign.[24] Could it be that Offa, around or shortly before the time he killed Æthelberht, reconstructed Hereford as a royal centre and re-located the Magonsaetan see there? Hazy memories of these events, interwoven with the emerging cult of the murdered East Anglian king, could lie behind the story that the body was moved from a dependency of Leominster to the site of the new see.

So where was the episcopal seat before Offa's time? A very late source locates it at *Lideburi* (Ledbury or Lydbury North), but in isolation this should perhaps not be taken too seriously. The obvious candidate on general grounds is of course Leominster. There is not a shred of direct evidence to support such a conjecture, but former episcopal status would offer one reason for its exceptional local importance.

The Foundation of Local Churches

Between about 950 and about 1100 the building of thousands of small churches, mainly by manorial lords, transformed the ecclesiastical face of England. It was in this period that local pastoral care shifted from a system based on minsters, and organized by their groups of priests, to the one which survived essentially unchanged into the twentieth century, based on parishes and parish churches.[25]

In the Domesday Book record (1086), Herefordshire seems rather poorly churched. Out of 311 itemised holdings, only 40, in other words 13 per cent, are stated to have churches and/or priests. This may be contrasted with (to take an extreme case) Kent, where the equivalent proportion is 43 per cent.[26] Furthermore, there is not a single small church in Herefordshire with standing remains that can conclusively be dated before the Norman Conquest, though there are a good many displaying the 'overlap' styles and technologies of the period c1050-1100.[27] The impression is that manorial church building had made little headway by the Conquest, though it may have speeded up rapidly thereafter. In context this is entirely unsurprising, since in late eleventh century England as a whole the incidence of churches decreased progressively from the east and south-east towards the west and north-west.

Herefordshire was therefore one of those areas where the critical shift to a system of local parishes came relatively late, and where the minsters might have been expected to remain powerful and prominent up to the late eleventh century. But in fact, with the obvious exceptions of Leominster and Hereford itself, no minster in the county makes more than a tenuous appearance in late Anglo-Saxon and Norman sources.[28] The most likely explanation for this rather odd combination of low-key minsters with retarded development of manorial churches brings us neatly back to our starting point: the mixed ecclesiastical culture of the region in earlier centuries, and especially the continuing influence of Welsh organization. It is not inconceivable that a high proportion of the small churches listed by Domesday are in fact early British ones. The decentralised pattern of small religious sites had always, especially in Ergyng, been more important than the more hierarchical English minster system overlain upon it. This view would stress the enduring rather than the changing aspects of local religious life during the period of Anglo-Saxon control of the region.

If few clear answers can currently be given, I hope at least that this brief review will suggest some items for a future research agenda. It is largely through excavation and landscape study that knowledge will grow, and although there are currently some encouraging signs, the archaeology of the early Church in Herefordshire is still largely unexplored territory. A major excavation in Leominster, Acton Beauchamp or Sutton St Michael, or more systematic monitoring of re-orderings and service trenches in a range of parish churches, could transform the picture rapidly. Comparative fieldwork studies at church sites, perhaps analyzed with the help of computerized GIS systems, would greatly broaden the evidence base without a spade being put in the ground. We have still hardly begun. If this conference is repeated in 2100 it should be possible to say a great deal more.

Notes and References

1 Blair, J, *The Church in Anglo-Saxon Society*, (Oxford, forthcoming)

2 Cf Davies, W, 'The Myth of the Celtic Church', in Edwards, N and Lane, A (eds) *The Early Church in Wales and the West*, (Oxford, 1992), 12-21

3 Davies, W, *An Early Welsh Microcosm*, (London, 1978), 134-5; Sims-Williams, P, *Religion and Literature in Western Britain 600-800*, (Cambridge, 1990), 44-7; Gelling, M, *The West Midlands in the Early Middle Ages*, (Leicester, 1992), 85-92, 114-19; Brook, D, 'The Early Christian Church East and West of Offa's Dyke', in Edwards, N and Lane, A, (1992), 77-89, see note 2; Barrow, J, *English Episcopal Acta: VII; Hereford 1079-1234*, (Oxford, 1993), xxvi-xxix

4 Bassett, S, 'Church and Diocese in the West Midlands: the Transition from British to Anglo-Saxon Control', in Blair, J, and Sharpe, R, (eds) *Pastoral Care Before the Parish*, (Leicester, 1992), 13-40

5 Hillaby, J, 'Early Christian and Pre-Conquest Leominster', *Transactions of the Woolhope Naturalists' Field Club*, 45, (1987), 557-685; Sims-Williams, P, (1990), 101, see note 3

6 Gelling, M, (1992), 25-7, see note 3

7 Sims-Williams, P, (1990), 105-9, see note 3

8 Blair, J, for an over-view, forthcoming, see note 1

9 Sims-Williams, P, (1990), see note 3

10 Sims-Williams, P, (1990), 169 see note 3

11 Hillaby, J, (1987), op cit see note 5; Kemp, B, 'Some Aspects of the *Parochia* of Leominster in the Twelfth Century', in Blair, J, (ed), *Minsters and Parish Churches: the Local Church in Transition 950-1200*, (Oxford, 1988), 83-95

12 Bede, *Epistola ad Ecgbertum*, cc 12-13 (ed Plummer, C, *Baedae Opera Historica*, i (Oxford, 1896), pp 415-17)

13 Especially Wormald, P, *Bede and the Conversion of England: the Charter Evidence*, (The Jarrow Lecture, 1984)

14 Birch, W de G, *Cartularium Saxonicum*, i (London, 1885), No 146; cf Sims-Williams, P, (1990), 150-1, see note 3

15 Wormald, P, (1984), 23, see note 13; Sims-Williams, P, 148-9, see note 3

16 Bailey, R, *England's Earliest Sculptors*, (Toronto, 1996), 109-110

17 Blair, J, 'Anglo-Saxon Minsters: a Topographical Review', in Blair J, and Sharpe, eds (1992), 226-66, at 227-31, see note 4

18 Hillaby, J, (1987), 563-72, 652-4, see note 5

19 Whitelock, D, (ed) *Anglo-Saxon Wills*, (Cambridge, 1930), 54; Shoesmith, R, *Hereford City Excavations*, i (Council for British Archaeology Research Report 36, London, 1980)

20 In Cambridge, Corpus Christi College, MS 308; edited by James, M, R, 'Two Lives of St Ethelbert, King and Martyr', *English Historical Review*, xxxii (1917), 214-44

21 This point is pursued by Blair, J, 'A Saint for Every Minster? Local Cults in Anglo-Saxon England', in Sharpe, R, and Thacker, A, (eds) *Local Saints and Local Churches*, (Oxford, forthcoming)

22 Excavations in 1999 during a Channel Four 'Time Team' programme indicated several potential early medieval settlement sites in and around Sutton St Michael: see Chapter by Keith Ray in this volume

23 Sims-Williams, P, (1990), 90-1, see note 3

24 Shoesmith, R, *Hereford City Excavations*, ii (Council for British Archaeology Research Report 46, London, 1982)

25 This process is explored by the essays in Blair, J, (ed), *Minsters and Parish Churches: the Local Church in Transition 950-1100*, (Oxford 1988)

26 Darby, H C, *Domesday England*, (Cambridge, 1977), 52-6, 346

27 The evidence is assembled by Parsons, D, 'Early Churches in Herefordshire: Documentary and Structural Evidence', in Whitehead, D (ed), *Medieval Art, Architecture and Archaeology at Hereford*, (London, 1995), 60-74. For criteria for the 'overlap' phase, which explain why even such ostensibly 'Anglo-Saxon' features as the doorway at Tedstone Delamere and the long-and-short quoin at Kilpeck cannot confidently be dated before 1066, see Gem, R, 'The English Parish Church in the Eleventh and Early Twelfth Centuries: a Great Rebuilding?', in Blair, J, (1988), 21-30, see note 25

28 The only other churches for which Domesday Book offers any hints of superior status, and then only very modestly, are Avenbury, Bromyard, Stoke Edith, Fownhope, Ledbury and Llanwarne; later evidence suggests a few others. See Barrow, J, (1993) xxx, see note 3

2 The Legend of St Etfrid of Leominster

HUGH PAWSEY

A missionary from a distant kingdom was making a dangerous journey on foot and alone. Late one evening a lion approached just as he was about to eat his own supper. The missionary broke off a piece of bread and gave it to the lion: and this act gave him the courage to face the local ruler and convert him from idolatry and paganism.

The translation which follows is from the British Library Manuscript: Harley 2253 f 132 where it is given the title *Incipit legenda de sancto Etfrido presbitero de Leominstria*.[1] Harley 2253 is the literary collection of Adam of Orleton who was a chaplain at Hereford c 1300. Of the 115 texts which he transcribed three are *Lives* of local saints: St Ethelbert (relics at Hereford, martyred by Offa 794), St Etfrid at Leominster and St Wistan (martyred at Wistanstow, a mile North of Craven Arms).[2] One might call them A49 saints.

The text of *Etfrid* in Adam of Orleton's collection is just a short excerpt from *Vita beatae ac Deo dilectae virginis Mildburgae*. Two manuscript copies of this full text survive.[3] The subject, St Milburga, daughter of Merwald and Domneva, was an abbess of Much Wenlock and the *Life* reached its present form between 963 and 1101.

The story of Etfrid and the lion has been used in many ways; from time to time over the centuries it has been revived in a fresh form to serve a new ideology. The translation is included with these papers because it is an account of the foundation of Leominster and because it is a primary source for the monastic vision of the post-Viking reconciled church. The legend itself is timeless.

At the simplest level our version is a good story. Etfrid receives his vocation in the form of a riddle. His destination truly is a riddle, for *Reodesmouht* [sic] is both the 'red mouth' of the lion (ie he knows he has arrived when he meets the lion) and at the same time the mundane 'reedy estuary' where the church was established.[4] The confrontation with the lion is followed by the interpretation of the King's hideous dream, the violent description of hell, the dramatic actions of the King to show repentance, and the happy ending.

The legend is also a little manual for missionaries. Etfrid receives his vocation in a vision and immediately takes advice about what he has heard. As to the lion, one should not assume that early Christians were more gullible about miracles, for the monastic schools had a rule of thumb: 'If it is impossible, it is an allegory'. Etfrid's next task is to meet the king, and he uses his wits. The hell-fire sermon and the description of heaven are appropriate[5] but not typical of the persuasion of Saxon Kings.[6] This is followed by five signs to discern genuine repentance, four acts of true commitment to Christianity and a general indication of the king's new obligations. The work ends with a doxology reconciling the threatening monster with the light of truth: the lion with the leam (gleam).[7]

The *Life* is written in rhymed couplets, which would have made the message easier to remember. And, whether the Latin was said or sung, the rhymes help to ensure that the inflection of the voice is correct. The chapters either side are in rhymed prose; but the Etfrid section is partly prose and partly verse and perhaps it is based on a lost original entirely in verse. The line divisions were not in the original text; they indicate where the Latin rhymes occur and they help to show how the text developed. Generally an extended line is associated with a tenth century topic, or a Ramsey turn of phrase.[8] Disruption of the rhyme scheme points to editorial revision.

Rhymed rhythmical prose was a fashion; it may help towards fixing the date of other royal legend texts.[9] A study of the form would have to begin with the anonymous *Christmas Sequence* and the *Alleluyatic Sequence* of Notker Balbulus (840-912).[10] J M Neale's translation gives an idea of how rhymed prose should sound:

> The strain upraise of joy and praise, Alleluya!
> To the glory of their King shall the ransomed people sing, Alleluya!
> And the choirs that dwell on high
> Shall re-echo through the sky, Alleluya!
> They, through the fields of paradise that roam,
> The blessed ones, repeat through that bright home, Alleluya!

Incipit legenda de sancto Etfrido presbitero de Leominstria

i   Erat Merwaldus rex Merciorum paganismo deditus
quando sanctus presbiter Etfridus,
vir doctrina clarus et vita magnificus
ad eum convertendum venit a Northimbrorum partibus,
celesti oraculo premonitus,
ut autem fertur divinum
ipse susceperat oraculum
ut in terra mercio loco Reodesmouht vocato pergeret,
ibique verbum dei predicans regem et eius gentem paganos ad christianismum converteret.
Segregatus itaque sacer Etfridus, tanquam alter amplius in opus predicatonis viam arripuit,
ignorans regem et locum quo pergere iussus fuit,
celitus ei via precipitur,
et celitus ad locum usque perducitur.
Demum ergo locum attigit
et sol occasum adiit,
nocte dies obducitur.
tecto carens novus hospes clyvo nocte tegitur,
ubi vero ne desolaretur
ambiguo proventu sue peregrinatonis
divinitus visitatur presagio regie conversionis.

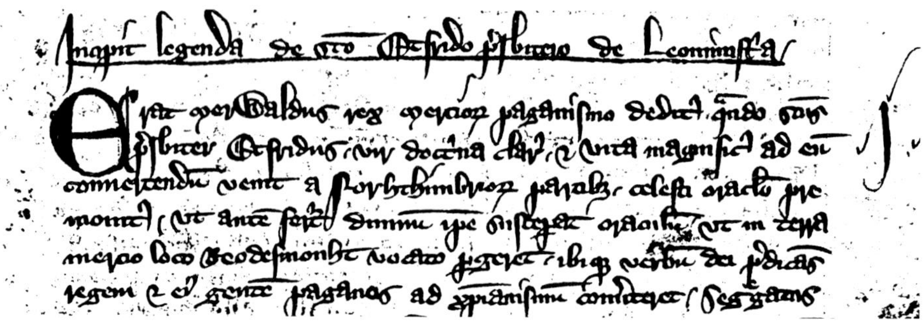

Fig 3 The legend of St Etfrid BL Harley MS 2253 f132r:
(Courtesy of the British Library)

Here begins the Legend of Saint Etfrid Priest of Leominster

i   Merwald king of Mercians was a devotee of paganism.
    At that time Saint Etfrid the presbyter, an outstanding teacher and greatly respected for his manner of life,
        was encouraged to come from the regions of the Northumbrians and
        convert the king by word of heaven.
        For this oracle, so we are told,
        got the man of God
        to cross the country to a place in Mercia called Reodes Mouth,
    and to convert the pagan King and his people to Christianity, preaching the word of God in that place.
    And that is how holy Etfrid received his vocation telling him where to go, although it was someone else, a man skilled in vision craft, who mapped out his exact path,
        though he had no personal knowledge of the king or of the place.
        Heaven's path was made clear to him,
        and under heaven he was led all the way there.
        So at last he reached his destination
        and the sun had just set;
        day was being swallowed up in darkness.
    Without shelter on a hillside there he was, a greenhorn stranger, surprised by nightfall.
        But at that moment, so as not to be let down
        by this unreassuring outcome to his expedition,
        he was given absolute certainty of the king's conversion.

ij   Cum enim assedisset cenulam, sub vesperta noctis,
prius deo debitis salutis laudibus et noctis[a]
adest leo inmanissimus,
iubis per collum crispantibus,
cui [viso][b] vir sanctus
ut deifer intrepidus
    nulla [timoris][c] cessit,
sed tanquam celesti misso,
fractum de pane suo
    porrexit.
Porrectum autem ipse iam non leo sed mansuecior agno, ritu blando suscepit,
    susceptum ante pedes porrigentis se pervolvens ut mansuecus commedit,
quid multa leo pastus disparvit,
vir autem sanctus in loco pernoctavit.
Sol redit ad superos, dies fulsit aurea,
de loco surgit vir praedictus advena,
cernit quaeque loci confinia.
Devenit ubi rex quaesitus manebat et eius familia
ad hospitandum sibi domus eligitur
et a quodam regis milite suscipitur.

[a]possibly a gloss intending *nocturnis*
[b]viso for ms *visio* [c]timoris for ms *timis*.

ii   For when he sat down to supper under the last glimmerings of nightfall
(first offering to God the proper psalms for his security that night),
a most threatening lion stood there,
the hairs of its mane in sinuous locks all round its neck.
But when he saw it the holy man,
God's unshakeable standard-bearer,
gave no sign of fear towards it,
but assuming it to be sent from heaven
held out to it
a hunk of bread.

And the beast itself, not a lion now but more tame than a lamb, took the offered bread with mild courtesy.

It ate its share at the good man's feet, tumbling about like a kitten;
and when it had eaten well the lion disappeared;
but the saint stayed all night in that spot.
The sun came up, a golden day blazed:
the man rose from his place, an explorer making his way;
he noted every landmark.

He came to where the king he had been searching for was in residence with his entourage;
and a household was picked to take Etfrid as a guest,
and he was looked after by a soldier in the king's service.

iij   Subsequenti autem nocte, rex vidit sompnium
quod mane facto suis prolatum solvere sibi poterat nemo [omnium][d]
Regi tandem suggerit memoratus miles de suscepto eius hospite
velut pincerna pharaoni de Iosep sompniorum conrectore,
'Domine mi rex', inquit, 'iubeat excellencia tua, tibi virum quemdam presentari
quem meum nocte transacta per [hospitem][e] sub tecto recepi,
cuius mores a nostris videntur aliene,
qui nisi fallor cultor est fidei christiane.
Diis nanque nostris detrahit et calumpniatur,
nobis eorum ob cultum, mortis eterne supplicium permittit et minatur,
qui fortassis, si domini mei regis sompnium audierit,
non falsus ut arbitror interpres eius erit'.
Rex ad militem, 'Accersiatur huc, inquit, ocius
talis hospes suus'

[d] 'omnium' for ms *suorum*   [e] 'hospitem' for ms *hospite*.

iii   Now, the following night the king had a dream.

And when morning came and he had described it word for word to his people, not one of them was able to unfold it for him.

In the end the soldier remembered the guest who was lodging with him, and suggested his name to the king

just as the cupbearer spoke to Pharaoh about Joseph as a master of dreams.[f]

'Lord my King', he said, 'let Your Excellency order to be presented to you one particular man

whom this night past I took in as a guest under my roof.

His culture seems alien to our ways,

and unless I am mistaken he is an adherent of the Christian faith;

for indeed he disparages and misrepresents our gods.

Because of our devotion to them he pronounces sentence of unending death upon us and threatens us.

Perhaps if he should hear the vision of my sovran king

he will be its interpreter and I think he will not lie'.

The King said to the soldier, 'Let him be summoned with due urgency,

if there is such a guest'.

---

[f] Genesis chapters, 40, 41, Joseph's promotion (prisoner to chief adviser)

iv   Accersito Christi legato coram rege,
rex sompnium ita cepit edicere.
'Nox preteritur, dum me sompno
datum in strato tenero,
      videbar michi videre
duos canes
teterrimos et inmanes
      me per iugulum arripere;
regione vero personam quemdam venerabili facie,
tonsa per auros, in coronam caesarie,
michi praesidio adesse,
et de canum dentibus, aurea cum clave quam in manu ferebat me potenter eruere.
Quo sic inhint, terreat me tanta canum inmanitas,
et eorum in me gaussabunda rapacitas
inde foveat tam festina ab eis erepcio,
et jocunda ereptoris mei visio.
Set qua nescio quod portenti habeat tam tetra bestia insolens et effera;
quid auspicii, tam grata persona, ereptrix mea, tam decens et clavigera;
utrubique mens mea redditur soli ritu'.[g]

[g] this line added to close the lection.

iv   When Christ's ambassador was summoned into the presence of His Majesty,

> the king began to tell his dream like this:
> 'Night wore on, with me asleep
> on my easy bed,
>> when I seemed to see
> two dogs,
> monstrous and terrifying,
>> grab me by the throat;
> but from sômewhere a certain person with a venerable appearance,
> with his hair tonsured from ear to ear, in the form of an imperial crown,
> came to my aid,
> and with a golden key which he carried in his hand, he plucked me mightily from the teeth of the dogs.
> As their mouths gaped open, such enormous size,
> such voracious greed to get me made me afraid;
> so you see, my lightning rescue from them,
> and the jolly appearance of my rescuer gave me the sense of being cherished.
> But whatever sort of threat such a stinking, ugly, vicious brute might hold,
> what significance so gracious and fine a person as my rescuer (the man with the keys) might promise,
> on both accounts my commitment is pledged to the worship of One only'.[h]

[h] this line, a gloss, muffles the questions, and spoils the drama of ch vi. Read: 'Whatever sort of threat is this?' 'Whatever can be the significance?'

v   Rex desierat loqui,
subinfert assecla Christi,
'Rex gratulare tue visione,
famulatur enim tue perpetue [salvationi].[i]
Quid ergo portentat sic canum in te guassancium
et te iugulare violencium,
    tam horrenda species.
Quid auspicetur clavigere persone,
liberatricis tue,
    tam iocunda facies,
rex accipe
et intellige.
Teterrimi canes
et inmanes
sunt sulliginosi plutonis satellites,
vite et salutis tue mortiferi hostes,
quorum tu faucibus in praedam et devoratonem daberis,
ubi devoratus semper devorandus eris,
ut sit usque moriens
et nunquam morte finiens,
perpetuis terroribus,
sulphureis fetoribus,
dencium stridoribus,
ignium ardoribus,
penis inmanibus,
et intollerabilibus,
cum impiis in tartaris medio crucieris,
    nisi funditus abnegaveris paganismum,
et ex toto te corde converteris,
    ad Christum dei vivi filium'.

[i] ms *perpetue saluti* perhaps 'salvatione' to rhyme.

v The King had no sooner stopped talking
than Christ's humble servant began:
'Take cheer from your vision, Majesty,
for it brings you closer to your eternal salvation.
And therefore, your Majesty, recognise
and understand
what the traumatic appearance
of the dogs signified when they lay in wait for your life
and wanted to catch you by the throat,
and what you are to make of the man with the keys,
the bringer of your liberty,
such a cheerful sight.
 The terrifying
and brutal dogs
are the soot-black henchmen[j] of the King of Hell,
they are mortal enemies of your life and salvation,
into whose jaws you will be given as a reward and a morsel,
where the devoured will always be ripe for devouring,
to be at the point of dying
but never achieving death,
in unremitting terror,
with sulphurous stench,
with the rasping of teeth,
with brutal
and unendurable punishments.
  With the wicked in the centre of hell you will be tortured,
    unless you completely turn away from paganism,
and are converted with all your heart,
    to Christ the son of the living God'.

[j] 'satellites' =thegn (Frankish 10th Century Latin)

vj   Reverendus ille claviger cuius potencia liberaris, sicut tibi videatur de beluis tam efferis et voracibus,

ianitor est principis regni celestis et in terra Christi salvatoris mundi vicarius.

> Clavis enim aurea,
> celestis est potentia,
> qua quicquid ipse ligat, ligatur
> quicquid liberat liberatur,
> cui tu domum edificabis in regno tuo,
> ad agendas laudes et gratias die noctuque regi superno,
> in quem in corde [credens],[k]
> quem ore confitens,
> cuius quoque baptismi vestem induens vitae.
> Gentilis demoniacos abdicaveris ritus,
> et idolatriae prophanos abiuraveris cultus,
> ut superni regni sedibus
> merearis fieri ijdoneus,
> cuius regni frequens et beata leticia,
> delectatus, que mortis est nescia,
> cuius tu felix et perhennis heros eris
> cum liberatus de canum dentibus fueris,
> per susceptonem sancte fidei,
> beati Petri liberatoris tui,
> qui confessione Christi filii dei vivi,
> claves meruit et principatum paradisi.

[k] 'credens' for ms c*cdens*

vi 'That reverend key-bearer by whose power you were being set free, as it appeared to you, from the utterly vicious and ravening monsters,

he is doorkeeper to the Prince of the Heavenly kingdom, and the representative on earth of Christ the saviour of the world;

for his golden key
is the heavenly power
by which is restrained whatever he restrains,
whatever he sets free is set free;[l]
and to him you will build in your kingdom a house
for giving praise and thanks by day and by night to the King above,
believing[m] in him in your heart,
confessing his name with your voice,
and also clothing yourself in the garment of his baptism of life.[n]
You will have given up your heathen cult of demons.
You will have abjured your pagan practice of idolatry,
so that among the thrones of his heavenly kingdom,
you may be ready to take your place,
able to come and go in his kingdom, endowed with a happy joy
which does not know death.
And you will be the lucky hero down the ages
when you have been set free from the fangs of the dogs of death
by taking the holy faith
of Saint Peter, your rescuer;
the very man who by his acclaim of Christ as son of the Living God,
was handed the keys and the chief place in paradise'.[o]

[l] Matthew 16:18   [m] ms vel cedens, aut credens
[n] a pious gloss   [o] Matthew 16:19

vij Diis et multimodis rudimentis fidei sacer heros regi christiani preconatur, Christo regem conformari preconando conatur, quibus diligenter auditis rex ait ad interpretem sue salutis,

    'Quicquid tua me christiana docuerit erudicio,
    mea paratur suscipere devota subjectio,
    quatenus evadere queam // tam horribilis belluae rictus.'[p]
    Preventus itaque rex superna clemencia;
        sua queque destruit et pessimidat ijdola,
    deponit regni insignia,
        septrum, purpuram et diadema;
    cinere conspersus cilicio induitur;
        dolet, ingemit
    et totus in penitencia compungitur,
    sancti pedis advolvitur,
        paganismum abiurat.
    Cultum dei perficetur,
    sacro fonte renascitur.
    Christicola sanctus efficitur
    prompte devocionis ad omnia,
    quibus eum cathezizat[q] suus evangelista

[p] The rhyme reflects: . . . us . . . queam/tam . . . us
[q] Greek; either from κατηχιζειν (catechise), or χαθαριζειν (cleanse), or ζιζανια (weed out).

vii   With the simple God-given principles of the faith and in many different ways our sacred hero made Christ thoroughly known to the king; and by his knowledge he managed to bring the king into Christ's pattern. When the king had assiduously listened to these matters, he said to the mediator of his salvation,

'Whatever your Christian understanding shall instruct,
my vowed obedience is ready to undertake,
so long as I escape the jaws of those repulsive monsters'.
  And that is how the king encountered the heavenly mercy.
    Every one of his idols he breaks and grinds in the dust;
he puts away the insignia of royalty,
    his sceptre, his crimson robe, his diadem.
Smeared with ash[r] he puts on a hair shirt;
    he is in anguish, he groans,
and he draws blood to gain forgiveness,
he throws himself at the feet of the saint,
    he abjures paganism;
he is made perfect in the worship of God,
he is reborn in the sacred font.
The convert, when he had received the chrism,
immediately offered public thanksgiving for everything
by which his evangelist made him whole.

[r] Micah chapter1;7,10.

viij   Anno domini
vi^(centi)lx

Iam vero lustra bissena · sexiens vicena · peregerat cursus, dominice incarnationis quando Merwaldus rex merciorum a sancto presbitero Etfrido, baptizatur. Ecce rex hactenus ut leo prefiguratus, leone superius memorato, iam non ferox ut leo set micior agno, erroris sui de luto se reum fatendo perdiit, et veritatis fidem, vitae panem, ab eius conviva, fidei scilicet et vite dogmatista percepit, ubi vero regis conversio per leonem ut dominum est, viro dei presagitur,

fundamen de domis regio liberatori regni celestis ianitori eligitur,

unde locus ipse postea vertitur

in leonis monasterium, domus autem fundata [sollerter],[s]

rebus et opibus regiis opulenter[t] dicatur;

cui beatus Edfridus[u] cuius doctrina, vere lucis gratia[v] primo refulsit, in plaga merciorum hesperia,

cuius ibi digne pro meritis est recolenda, celebris et felix memoria,

cui honor et gloria in seculorum secula amen.

[s] 'sollerter' for ms *soleratur* which makes no sense
[t] The Latin *opibus regiis opulenter* is a translation of the Anglo-Saxon Maer Wald
[u] Only here spelled 'Edfridus' elsewhere in this text 'Etfridus'
[v] The Latin *vere lucis gratia* is a translation of the Anglo-Saxon 'Et Friδ'

viii Now, six centuries and six decades[w] had run their course from the time of our Lord's incarnation when Merwald, King of Mercians, was baptized by St Etfrid the priest. See how the king, represented as the lion up to now, the lion mentioned earlier, is not now fierce as a lion, but meeker than a lamb. By making clear his condemnation of his own error and his belief in the truth, he escaped from the mire. He adopted the faith of truth, he received from a guest at his own table the bread[x] of life, that is to say the teachings of faith and of life. The place where the conversion of the king through the agency of a lion, as the Lord, was divinely foretold to the man of God,

that was chosen as the site for buildings dedicated to the royal deliverer, the gatekeeper of the kingdom of heaven.

Consequently that very place was afterwards converted

into the Monastery of the Lion. Furthermore the building is said to have been built skillfully

with materials supplied by the king; and it may be said, *richly with royal wealth.*[y]

And blessed Edfrid, whose gracious teachings of the True Light[z] shine in the western borders of the Mercian people,

and his popular and happy memory is rightly honoured there for his good deeds,

unto him be honour and glory, world without end, Amen.

---

[w] literally 'The passage of time had completed twice six lustrations and six times a score . . . ' but the interval of a lustration was not constant. A marginal note reads: 'In the year of the lord vi[hundred]lx' and I have accepted this computation

[x] at this time always a metaphor for teaching, not Eucharist.

[y] the Latin phrase gives the literal meaning of *Maer-warð's* name

[z] the literal meaning of *Et-frið's* name

Commentary on The Legend of St Etfrid

The Tenth Century Biographies

'In the tenth and eleventh centuries creative energy went to the invention of liturgical poetry and drama, to chronicles and the lives of the saints of the Order.'[11]

The *Lives*, almost all in Latin, must have been intended primarily for the monastery. Many address the problems of communal life, such as the abuse of rank,[12] or the acceptance of small miracles to avoid superstition.[13] Many were read in the choir or the refectory to celebrate Festivals. There might also be a verse *Life* for private study, a vernacular edition for pilgrims, and lyrics in strict metre for troubadours. In the cult of saints a full literature gained respect.

However, in several cases there was a precise and practical reason for writing a *Life*. At Durham, the monks presented the Norman lord imposed on them as their Bishop, with a *History* which contrasted his unprincipled behaviour with the founding principles of their religious house.[14] Goscelin's *Life of Mildrith* secured lands in East Kent for St Augustine's Abbey, Canterbury.[15] Osbert of Clare was preparing background material for the canonisation of Edgar when he wrote the *Life of St Edburga of Winchester*. Land was desperately important to the survival of the communities and it was not only secular powers which appropriated monastic land. Larger monasteries swallowed smaller ones and prince bishops also had canonries and grand schemes to support. Against closure, a strong tradition of miracles and an impressive *Life* carried some weight. In various ways the *Lives* promoted the institutions which caused them to be written and protected their interests.[16]

In the *Life of Milburga/Legend of Etfrid* the purpose, context, literary style and date are all bound up together.

The text must have been composed between 963 and 1101. In the chapter preceding the *Etfrid Legend*, Merwald's sisters 'shine at Peterborough' and since the relics were only transferred there in 963 this gives the earlier limit. In 1101 Milburga's relics were placed in a new shrine at Wenlock; an event of such importance would have been recorded in detail if it had taken place before the completion of the text.

David Rollason proposes 1080/81 as the most likely date for the text, when canons had been replaced by reformed monks at Wenlock. The restored foundation as a Cluniac monastery was indeed a most important event. The confidence and strength of the pan-European Cluniac Order can be seen in the scale of building and the craftsmanship at Wenlock, and that is precisely the problem. The author of the *Life of Milburga* is not particularly confident or triumphant, describing instead the responsibility of being among the *domesticis* of the shrine, amongst people who cannot even follow the services (*cultus*). Milburga's mother, Queen Domneva, fled 'Leominster as if from the snares of the hunter, a dove reaching safe haven on a roof top'.[17] Her nephew, it says, danced with joy to see her back in Kent. She is the Daystar recreated from Hesperus which has now set (and someone has added 'never again back to the West').[18] This is not the voice of someone about to spend vast sums on a major project in the area. So, what other event could have prompted the writing of the *Life*?

A second possibility is that the *Life of Milburga* was created out of fear after the closure of the nunnery at Leominster in 1046. The ease with which the Godwins seized Leominster's estates is shocking. Sweyn, Earl Godwin's eldest son and 'a complete maverick', abducted the abbess and compromised the Abbey.[19] The Earl, as the most powerful man in England, could not have failed to influence the disposition, and his daughter Queen Edith accepted ownership.[20] Fear may have inspired Milburga's *Testament* which prefaces the *Life* ; it resolves to 'set forth . . . and to confirm . . . all the landed estates . . . lest my successors be disturbed by the venomous attacks of envious men'.[21] But one might expect the references to Leominster to be either more cautious, or else more angry and vengeful; instead, they are just respectful acknowledgements of a local link with an ancient Christian centre (similar in tone to the reference to Leominster in Rhigyfarch's *Life of David*, written 1093).[22]

A third possibility places the *Life of Milburga / Legend of Etfrid* around the end of Edgar's reign, assigning it to the tenth century reform movement, which spread outwards from Winchester. The tide almost reached Wenlock which stands geographically at the limit of the reformed houses.[23]

Reform was needed because the Viking invasions from 786 onwards had in many areas destroyed the diocesan structure, as well as impoverishing the country. But also, Eric John adds, 'The Vikings have been blamed for what were serious shortcomings in English society. If we take the monasteries, the Vikings could and did steal valuable portable goods, they could and did burn down buildings, but the buildings stayed burnt because the inmates or their families had stolen the endowment that had supported the monastery.'[24]

It was Alfred who began the reform of the Church (and of civil and military Wessex); and his translation of Gregory's *Pastoral Care* spells out his 'personal awareness and fascination with cultural transmission and continuity'.[25]

In 964 with the accession of Edgar the reform began to be imposed without compromise, through Dunstan at Canterbury, Aethelwold at Winchester and Oswald at Worcester.[26] Parish clergy were forced to put away their wives and become celibate; at the cathedrals, canons were dispossessed and their place taken by monks; all houses of religious were obliged to sign up to the *concordia*, a standardisation of the Rule; and new laws and institutions were put in place to crack down on lawlessness. The book which is central to this phase of the reform is the *Passio Edmundi* by Abbo of Fleury who taught for two years at Ramsey Abbey while exiled from France.[27] It was 'designed to show would-be English hagiographers how spiritual biography could be used as a tool to further the aims of the ecclesiastical reformers . . . to provide an ideology and a sense of purpose to the entire programme of monastic and spiritual regeneration'.[28]

The influence of this book can be tracked by its distinctive Latin style. It effloresced with polysyllabic superlatives (to show familiarity with the manners of the Frankish court), it was sprinkled with Greek (in acknowledgement of Duns Scotus), and larded with metaphors from astronomy and mathematics (to show a Ramsey education). All of the early Ramsey characteristics are found in the *Life of Milburga*.[29]

However, it was not the style of writing that was important for spiritual regeneration. The *Life* exalts celibacy (in this case for a king and queen); the monastic life is adopted by the parents and their three daughters; and land is given to be held inalienably by the church. The cohesion of the country is expressed through the conversion by a Northumbrian missionary of a Mercian king with a Kentish wife. Both the style and the plot promote Edgar's reform.

There is a hint that the Etfrid legend was written up by a nun rather than a monk. See what you think. In the account of Merwald's dream, chapter iv, a *persona* comes to his aid, described as *eriptrix* (feminine gender); and in chapter v the person is *liberatricis* suae. Unlike an adjective, a noun in apposition does not have to agree in gender: a man writing *eriptrix, liberatrix,* instead of *eriptor, liberator,* when describing the person of St Peter would find it unexpected. Nuns, on the other hand would find them familiar forms and they often substituted a word while reading aloud, 'sisters' for 'brothers', 'daughters' for 'sons' when appropriate.[30] They kept a watch for cases where the grammar preferred the feminine. In any event Latin grammar ceased to be important for the nuns of Leominster or of Wenlock after the houses were closed down.

After Alfred's time, the implementation of the reform was the work of bishops; but the necessary transfers of land and closures of difficult or weak monasteries could only take place with the assistance of kings. Under Edgar,

957-975, the reform was imposed with millennial fervour and grim righteousness. Then Ethelred came to the throne with the support of the opposition. Those who had been dipossessed from church lands went to law.[31] And in 980 the Danish raids began. The *Life of Milburga* seems to belong to this period of reversal; it is written in a reformist style but clearly did not result in a reformation. The nuns died out. Canons were administering the Wenlock estates when the 1080 Cluniac reform took place.

The Setting of Merwald's Conversion by St Etfrid

The place and date seem to be simple, Leominster in the year 660; but society was seething with crosscurrents, and the legend was positioned in a time of political turmoil.

651 Half of Northumbria became a protectorate of Mercia, when Ethelwald of Deira ran to Penda for protection.[32]

654-6 Northumbria annexed Mercia after the death of Penda.[33]

657 Mercian independence was reasserted by Wlpher, son of Penda.

670 Wlpher began to consider the invasion of Northumberland after the death of Oswiu

674 Wlpher was killed in the invasion; Nothumbria regained control of Mercia.[34]

678 Aethelred brother of Wlpher defeated Ecgfrith at the Battle of Trent and regained Mercian independence.

Even the nationality of Leominster and Merwald are in question. Ekwall, the authority on place names derives Leominster from a Welsh word for 'flowing waters'. And Margaret Gelling is quoted as saying 'I am confident that *Merewaldus* is a latinisation of Old English *Merewalh* and that this means "famous Welshman" '.[35] Nevertheless, *leon* is Anglo-Saxon for a land grant, a gift; and *hleo* means 'refuge, shelter; protector, lord'; both of which are consistent with the foundation of a frontier town; while the Welsh *Llanllieni* is (? first) found in the translation of Rhigyfarch's *Life of St David* dated 1346.[36] Merwald also has Anglo-Saxon meanings to his name; *maer walð*, 'famous for wealth', when he is building a church; *maer ward* 'notable guardian' as father of four little saints; and more significantly, *mearu weald*, which would also be latinised as Merwaldus, means 'Marquis,[37] Margrave, Lord Marcher'. It is only in the Kentish Life of St Mildrith, where the bravery of Queen Domneva is being exaggerated, that her frontier husband is *Maer-weahl*, 'the famous Wealh': 'a foreigner, stranger, slave: Briton, Welshman: a shameless person' (J R Clark Hall, *Concise Anglo-Saxon Dictionary*).

Church allegiance is in doubt also. By 664 the decision was made and the Roman missionaries who had been sent by St Gregory were given authority throughout England, wherever the kings permitted them.[38] But before that there had been both Columban and Gregorian monks in the Northumbrian royal household.[39] In the *Etfrid Legend* St Peter's tonsure is confusingly described as *per auros*, from ear to ear in the Columban fashion and *caesarie*, like an imperial wreath in the Roman fashion, together in one phrase.

The dispute between the Columbans and the Gregorians was about Church Order. Between the British (Welsh) Church and the Gregorians these same rules about the tonsure and the date of Easter were also in dispute; and in addition the British feared that the political power of Augustine's bishops would eclipse the bishops of the native Church. Bede mentions a third conflict. The Gregorian missionaries were prepared to go to the Saxon kings and try to convert them.[40] And Augustine is quoted as threatening the British bishops, 'that if they refused to unite with their fellow-Christians, they would be attacked by their enemies the English; and if they refused to preach the Faith of Christ to them, they would eventually be punished by meeting death at their hands'.[41]

The Welsh view is expressed by Peter Berrisford Ellis: 'How do you convert a people who are attempting to annihilate you? The Saxons were out to dispossess and drive out the Celts. The Celts were, therefore, in no mood to argue the finer points of religious theology with them'.[42]

This is the lion which is at the heart of the Etfrid legend. The risk involved is put plainly on page one of Eric John's recent book: 'Many primitive peoples – including the Anglo-Saxons and their Irish contemporaries – leave the protection of the individual to the kindred group to which he or she belongs, backed by the blood feud or the threat of it. Unless we grasp this we cannot understand what the early missionaries from those parts were doing. By going on *peregrinatio* or pilgrimage they were putting themselves outside the normal forms of protection'.[43]

This is one of the few certainties in the Etfrid legend: it proclaims the Gregorian policy.

The History of the Etfrid Legend

A simple rhyming metric version of the legend, written in the seventh or eighth centuries before Latin became ornate, is a romantic hypothesis to which I cling.

The late tenth century *Legend of St Etfrid* was written to promote certain monastic values. It has links with a number of other Saint's *Lives*: St Mildrith, St

Werburg, and possibly St Edberg in one tradition.[44] The theme of the Etfrid pericope is still mission and the transformation of the lion through the gift of bread; obedience, benefactions and the supremacy of St Peter may be additions at this stage. By setting the legend in the context of Milburga's life, the cultivation of sanctity in the family is promoted.

About 1140, the West door of Leominster priory was completed, and the sculpture provides an insight into the theological understanding of legend at that time.[45] On the north doorpost is a small Samson. He also has come face to face with a lion in the course of a journey on foot to visit a pagan town. The position of the sculpture on the inauspicious north side, amongst the vipers, makes him an antitype. Instead of feeding the lion, Samson takes honey from its mouth. Instead of converting the pagans, he slays them. Instead of giving them baptismal gowns, he steals their shirts. Etfrid's uncomfortable puzzle, *Reodes Mouht*, contrasts with Samson's innocent riddle about sweetness and strength. Two vocations: two sorts of bravery. On the outside of the doorway, another man confronts a lion. Photographs do not make this clear; but anyone standing at the door finds 'the face of a man close to the palm of his hand from the one side, and the face of a lion close to the palm of their hand (*palmam*) from the other side'.[46] Their postures echo each other; a vine mimics the lion's tail; an arc of chevron moulding brackets them. The reference is to Ezekiel's temple of the age to come, which is to be not only the residence (literally) of God, but also the throne of the prince, the prior, (*princeps*) who administers justice within the door.[47] The Man/Lion sculptures are not in any way representations of Etfrid's encounter, but reflections on the eventual outcome of that meeting. Monastic reading, of scripture or legend, was expected to be an active search for the meaning and we are fortunate in having this insight into the twelfth century interpretation.

The inclusion of the legend in Adam of Orleton's literary collection turns Etfrid into a local hero. The message is not about converting bloodthirsty kings, but venerating ancient saints. In 1307 Papal Commissioners sat in Hereford Cathedral to examine witnesses in connection with the canonization of Thomas Cantilupe.[48] His relics were already bringing great wealth to the Cathedral. An interest in pilgrimage is a feature of the literary collection.

A version of the story which may have been written to celebrate the grant of Leominster's Charter by Mary in 1554 (though, in a more mature hand, the closing verses praise a benefaction of 1604) describes how Edfride appointed pastors pure, devout, zealous and righteous; and magistrates 'dekt with prudence, godlie foresighte and justice'.

> 'In dutie to God, Realme and Kinge
> so live and love God graunte you may:
> that strangers may with praises singe
> God is yor God, you him obay.
> That others seeing yor lampes burne
> to God through faith may daylie [turne].
> Then God who you preserves in health
> may maintaine it; & bless yor wealth'.

The distant past is made more distant by the use of deliberately old-fashioned language. What is important however is the Common Wealth. Edfride is a pastor who brings peace and prosperity to the town through the institution of clergy and magistrates.[49]

The interesting thing, I find, about the Etfrid legend in The Early English Text Society edition (their facsimile of Harley 2253) is that Etfrid's life and example is no longer the message. First of all, attention focuses on the manuscript. It is written in an early example of English handwriting soon after it became quite distinct from the professional book hand. Then, it is an antique, something which has survived Henry and Cromwell and more recent tyrants. And it is a literary collection in three languages which are not spoken in that form any more. And then one begins to explore the thinking which created the legend, and the people who adopted and transformed the legend. Neither Faith nor History, but insight is the quest.

I am continually aware of my complete dependence on the work of many authors, and especially N R Ker who edited the facsimile. Joe Hillaby, who first introduced me to the subject has been a help and inspiration.

Notes and References

1. Published in facsimile by The Early English Text Society *Original Series* 255, edited and with an introduction by N R Ker (1965)
2. Two lyrics are in Reeves, Norman, *The Town in the Marches*, Orphans Press (1972)
3. British Library Additional MS 34,633 from Beddgelaert; and Gotha Codex I, 81. Neither of these is the original Wenlock manuscript.
4. Or 'red estuary'; certainly the mouth of Ridgemoor Brook runs red in flood. I am grateful to Duncan James for this observation.
5. *Revelation*, 4, v4; 20, v4; cf 21, v8. Vergil *Aeneid* VI.
6. Bede, *Historia Ecclesiastica* eg II, 6; II, 10,12 (Edwin); III 22 (Sigbert)
7. from OE *leoma*; O Teutonic leuhmon-, leu-. *Shorter Oxford English Dictionary* (1933)
8. At Ramsey Abbey near Peterborough the literary style was ornate. See Lapidge, M, 'Hermeneutic Style in Tenth Century Anglo-Latin Literature', *Anglo-Saxon England.*, 4, (Cambridge 1975) 67-111
9. Ridyard, Susan, *Royal Saints of Anglo-Saxon England*, (C U P 1988) 269; 129 (Mistaken identity?) discusses the possibility of *Vita*

Edburgae coming from Mercia. It was reworked by Goscelin but has traces of rhyme; e g chapter 5

> 'Inter hec dum generose indolis regia proles adolesceret,
> et divine servututis exercitiis instaret,
> insignis pater virginis Wintoniam ingreditur, // ... sciscitatur.
> gratum // responsum;
> predicant // collaudant.
> execrabile // indignatione'.

10 Brittain, Frederick, *Penguin Book of Latin Verse* (1962) 158,162, gives these, as well as other sequences in other styles over several centuries, with unrhymed translations. The introduction is helpful. *English Hymnal*, OUP (1933) gives rhymed translations by J H Arnold, No 22, and J M Neale, No 494.

11 Smalley, Beryl, *The Study of the Bible in the Middle Ages* (Blackwell 1952) 45

12 The Abbess of Chelles pushed Merwald's daughter Mildrith into an oven. At Winchester nuns spied on Princess Edburga because she took solitary walks at night; they were temporarily blinded for their nasty mindedness. See Ridyard, Susan, (1988) see note 9, esp chapter 8

13 '(David's) disciple, Aidan, was reading a book to confirm a doctrine; the prior commanded him to fetch wood. During the journey such a downpour of rain came on suddenly that the ditches were filled with water ... He went to the place where he had left his book; and found it still open ... but uninjured by the rain'. *Rhigyfarch's Life of St David* ed James, J W (1967) ch 35.

14 Symeon *Libellus de exordio/ Hist.Regum.* The bishop is Ranulph Flambard (1099-1128)

15 Rollason, D, *Saints & Relics in Anglo-Saxon England* (Blackwell 1989) 213

16 These examples are all from the twelfth century. Bede's *Life of Cuthbert* is an eighth century example of a *Life* written in defence of a community's ethos and property

17 'sicut igitur columba / de laqueis avulsa
  turrim advolat amicam;
sic Domneva nobilis regina / carnis a nexu libera
  canciam adit nativam'.

18 'numquam ulterius iterum hesperus'. This line makes nonsense of the Daystar metaphor and it does not fit the rhyme scheme; but it is very expressive. All these quotations are from the *Life of St Milburga*, f 208v, BL Additional ms 34,633

19 John, Eric, *Reassessing Anglo-Saxon England* (Manchester U P 1996) 175.

20 *Domesday Survey*: 'Rex tenet LEOFMINSTRE. Regina Eddid tenuit, cum xvi membris.'

21 Rollason (1989) see note 15, is here quoting Finberg, H P R, *The Early Charters of the West Midlands* (Leicester 1972) ch 10

22 James, J W, (1967) see note 13, page 18. Text ch.xiii

23 Stenton, F, *Anglo-Saxon England* (Oxford, 1989) 450-4 and map

24 John (1996) see note 19, 67

25 Smyth, Alfred, *King Alfred the Great*, (OUP 1995) 525

26 From 952 Oswald studied at Fleury for six years; he was Bishop of Worcester from 961.

27 Frequent banishment toughened this group; exiles from England were also re-invigorated at Fleury.

28 Smyth (1995) see note 25, 276

29 By 1080, the texts preferred floral metaphors (St Edburga smells like a quince); liked quotations from Ovid and Plotinus; and vaunted the terrestrial power of relics.

30 Hillaby, J, 'Early Christian and Pre-Conquest Leominster' *TWNFC*, XLV (iii) (1987). In discussing the Leominster Saxon prayer book Hillaby argues from a substitution of this kind (*peccatrix // peccator*) that the book was at one time owned by a nun.

31 In many cases disputes were settled out of court, which suggests that real injustices were taking place.

32 In 651 Ethelwald, King of Deira was threatened by Oswiu, King of Bernicia. Stenton (1989) see note 23, 80-5

33 Oswiu of Bernicia killed Penda and annexed Mercia North of the Trent; and two years later when Peada was murdered Oswiu claimed all Mercia.

34 Ecgfrith was king of Northumbria. Bede see note 6, iv 21

35 Hillaby, J, (1987) see note 30, footnote 49, page 670

36 James, J W, (1967) see note 13, xl & schema following xliii. Buchedd Dewi is in any case a translation of a late text, possibly BL Vespasian A xiv dated c1190(ibid xxxiii)

37 Onions, ed (1933) see note 7, 'Orig., the title of a ruler of . . . 'marches' or frontier districts'.

38 Bede *H E* see note 6, iii 25

39 Paulinus (Bede *HE* see note 6, ii 9) and Aidan (Bede *HE* see note 6 iii 3-5)

40 Reluctantly, 'They began to consider returning home. For they were appalled at the idea of going to a barbarous, fierce and pagan nation, of whose very language they were ignorant'. Shirley-Price, Leo, trans, *Bede; A History of the English Church and People* (Penguin 1955) i 23.

41 Bede *HE* ii 2; Shirley-Price. (1955) see note 40. Bede's view that only the Gregorian missionaries were zealous and disciplined is partisan. He is likely to be correct in reporting mistrust between fiery rhetorical proselytizers and reserved conversational pastoralists, for this is recurrent in the history of Christianity.

42 Ellis, P B, *Celt and Saxon* (Constable 1993) 141.

43 John, Eric (1996) see note 19,1

44 Rollason, D, *The Mildrith Legend* (1972) and Ridyard (1988), see note 9, both discuss this group of related *Lives*.

45 The reasons for dating the sculptures 1123-30 (from written sources and on stylistic grounds) are spelled out in Selma Jónsdóttir's 'The Portal of Kilpeck Church: Its Place in English Romanesque Sculpture' *Art Bulletin* 32 (College Association of America, 1950) 171-180 & 28 figures. The date for their reassembly on the west tower c 1140 was first suggested by Sir Alfred Clapham working for the Royal Commission on Historical Monuments (1932-4). These arguments are assessed in Joe Hillaby's *The Sculptured Capitals of Leominster Priory* (Leominster 1993) where he discusses the sources for motifs in the sculptural repertoire, but I think he underestimates Cluniac theology and the noetic interplay of the icons. As to reassembly and a possible previous format he points out that the interior abaci (where our Samson had been carved) show 'all too evident signs of botching up' and the exterior abaci 'do not fit the spaces into which they have been placed'.

For the importance of recessed doorways in Romanesque sculpture of this period see Raspi Serra, J 'English Decorated Sculpture of the Early Twelfth Century and the Cosmo-Pavian Tradition' *Art Bulletin* 51 (1969) 352-62 & illustrations. Two threshold motifs (the watchman, chain/net, together with the shape of the stone blocks into which the capitals have been carved (more than three-quarters of the mass is built into the fabric of the wall) strongly suggest that in their previous position they were similarly configured round a door, although the mismatches of the abaci hint at a change of construction (ie a lintel and lunette, or a different form of springer or impost) where the pillar and the arch meet.

Arguing from 14/15th Century Gothic, some art historians (including Leland and Zarnecki) have seen the sculptures as whimsical. However the importance in Cluniac culture of poetry, music, limning, architecture and liturgical drama ought to imply that their Romanesque sculpture also was a purposeful and elaborate expression of spirituality.

46 Ezechielis xli 19 Faciem hominis iuxta palmam ex hac parte, et faciem leonis iuxta palmam ex alia parte: expressam per omnem domum in circuitu.

47 Ezekiel chapter 40, 41. Does the generous size of the window imply that the area at the base of the tower was dedicated to administration and arbitration?

48 Winnington-Ingram, A J, 'History and Architecture of Hereford Cathedral' in *Herefordshire its Natural History, Archaeology and History* (Woolhope Naturalist's Field Club Centenary Volume,1954, repr 1971)

49 The manuscript is held in the Hereford County Record Office, AG/25. I am grateful to Ann and Tony Malpas for bringing this to my attention and for other help generously given.

3 The Early Church in Herefordshire: Columban and Roman

JOE HILLABY

The diocese of Hereford originated in two stages. The first was the conversion, or reconversion, of the Magonsaetan, the folk who lived west of the Severn, by a Columban missionary from Northumbria, Edfrith, for whom Merewalh, their ruler, built a church dedicated to St Peter at Leominster. The second came a generation later when Merewalh's daughter, Mildburg, who had been brought up in Kent in the ways of the Roman church, returned to the land of her birth to become abbess of Wenlock. His son, Mildfrith, collaborating with his half-sister, established a tribal diocese on Roman lines with its bishop's seat at Hereford. For details of all but the foundation of the see we are dependent on a *Life* of St Mildburg of Much Wenlock, written about 1100. Almost 40 years ago, by a close examination of two of its sections, Mildburg's *Genealogy* and *Testament*, Finberg drew attention to the full import of this *Life*.[1]

The Columban Church at Leominster

Merewalh's lands extended from the Severn in the north to the Wye in the south. Its bounds are, for the most part, perpetuated by Hereford's diocese. Subsequent to his conversion, Merewalh, who already had two children, Merchelm and Mildfrith, married Eafe, a Kentish princess and great-granddaughter of King Aethelberht and Bertha. They had three daughters, Mildred, Mildburg and Mildgith, and a son, Merefin, who died young.[2] The couple then 'for the love of God and of mankind separated from their conjugal estate'. Eafe returned to Kent to become abbess of one of the earliest princess minsters, at Minster-in-Thanet. There she was succeeded by her eldest daughter, Mildred, whose relics were eventually translated to St Augustine's, Canterbury.[3] (Fig 4)

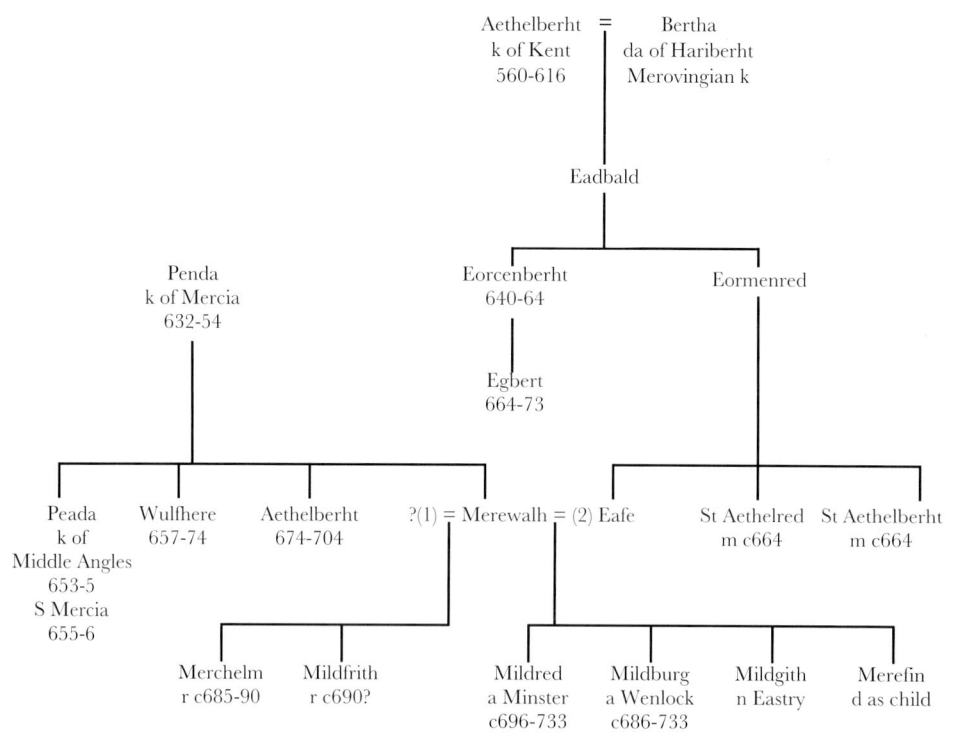

```
                              Aethelberht  =  Bertha
                              k of Kent        da of Hariberht
                              560-616          Merovingian k
                                       |
                                    Eadbald
                                       |
              ┌────────────────────────┼────────────────┐
           Penda                  Eorcenberht        Eormenred
         k of Mercia                640-64
           632-54                     |
                                    Egbert
                                    664-73
    ┌────────┬─────────┬────────────┐              ┌────────────┬────────────┐
  Peada   Wulfhere  Aethelberht  ?(1) = Merewalh = (2) Eafe   St Aethelred  St Aethelberht
  k of    657-74    674-704                                    m c664         m c664
 Middle Angles
   653-5
  S Mercia
   655-6
              ┌──────────┐        ┌──────────┬──────────┬──────────┐
           Merchelm   Mildfrith  Mildred   Mildburg   Mildgith   Merefin
           r c685-90  r c690?    a Minster a Wenlock  n Eastry   d as child
                                 c696-733  c686-733
```

a abbess; d died; da daughter; k king; m murdered; r regulus (sub-king)

Fig 4 Mercian and Kentish Royal Families

How much credence can be given to those parts of the *Life* which tell of Edfrith's conversion of Merewalh and the foundation of the minster on the banks of the Lugg? As recently as 1999 it was asserted that 'the long passage on the foundation of Leominster seems to be largely, perhaps entirely, imaginary and to be based on deductions from the name itself'.[4] Is it true, therefore, as Finberg gently put it, that 'in the face of determined scepticism it is impossible to prove the authenticity of this document'?[5] For Gelling, however, it represents 'the best historical record of events in the late seventh century in Western Mercia'.[6] Putting aside such obvious hagiographic devices as Edfrith's encounter with the lion and Merewalh's dream, the available external evidence supports the key elements of the conversion story. The Kentish royal legend, in the *Life* of St Mildred formulated 732-48, provides an early and independent witness to the marriage of Merewalh and Eafe, and a charter of Aethelbald of Mercia in 748 refers specifically to his blood relationship with Mildred. Above all the nature of Leominster's estates testifies that, as Mildburg's *Life* says, they were 'royally endowed'.[7]

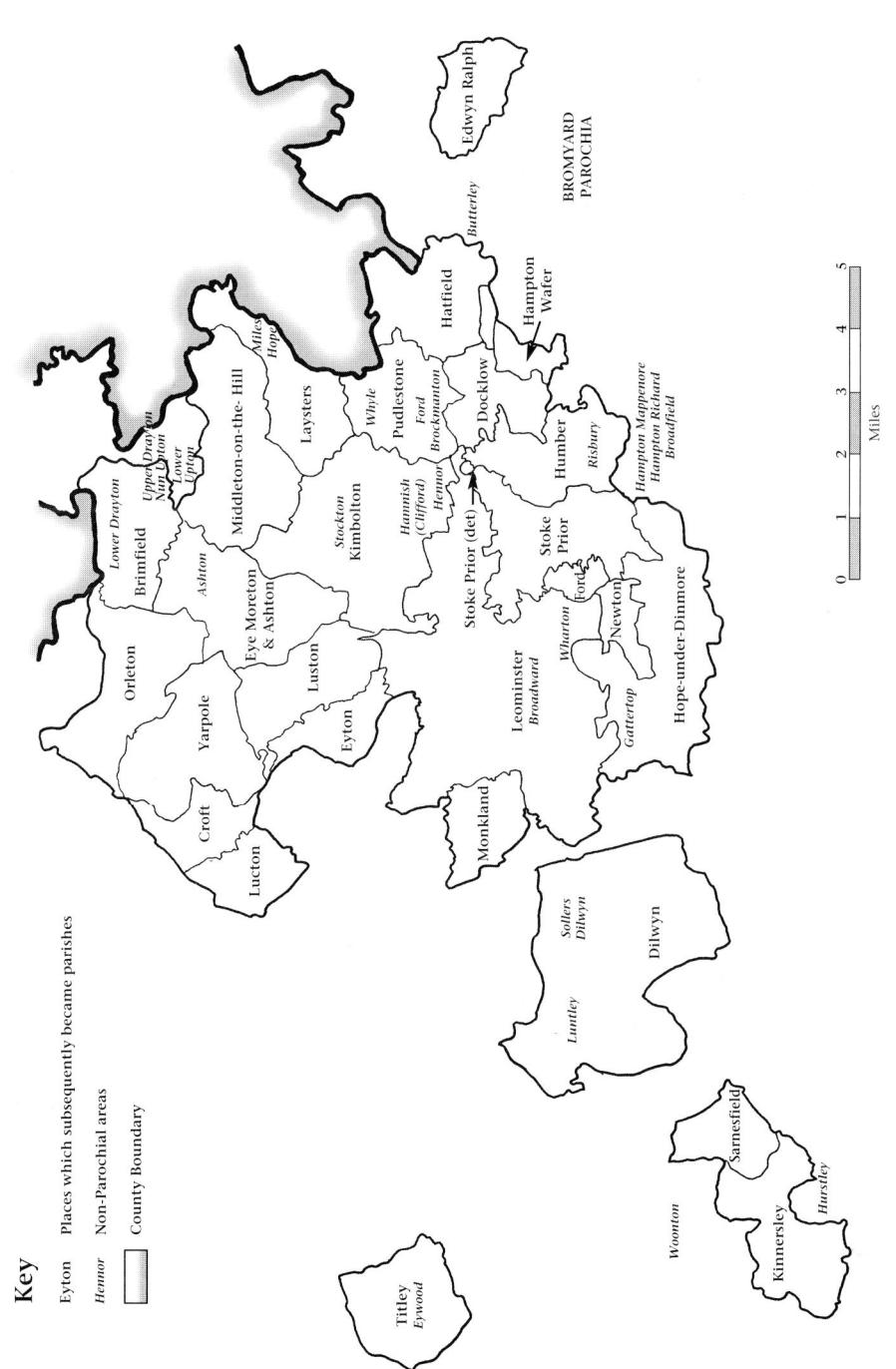

Fig 5 The Leominster Parochia as listed in the 1123 charter with places otherwise known as dependent

Royally Endowed

Discussing place-name evidence Gelling points out that Leominster stands in a large belt of territory where *ton* names, indicating farming communities, are frequent but *leah* names, indicating 'the presence of ancient woodland at a date when English speech was gaining ascendancy', are absent. Some, such as Aymestrey, Wapley, Titley, Almeley, Eardisley and Weobley, are found on the periphery. 'It is a reasonable hypothesis', she concludes, 'that Leominster, on a slight rise in the centre of the plain over which fifteen of its sixteen (Domesday) manors (members) were scattered, was a pre-English settlement of more than average size and importance'.[8]

The size and origins of the Leominster manor have provoked comments for many years. In 1960 for G R J Jones it was 'a magnificent example of a multiple estate . . . a pre-English entity taken over by (the) rulers of Mercia in the mid seventh century, perhaps (with) its origins before the Roman period', citing Ivington camp in particular, a judgment accepted by Hooke who refers to it as 'the centre of a vast and multiple estate'.[9] When comprehensive records become available in the fourteenth century they show Leominster administered in four *herneys*, based on burys at Luston, Ivington, Stockton and Stoke Prior. Close to each is a major multivallate hill-fort: Croft Ambrey (38 acres), Ivington (48), Risbury (28) and the Bache (10½).[10] Indeed more than a century ago F W Maitland, whose curiosity was aroused by what he called this 'gigantic manor', suggested that it 'very probably had a Welsh (British) basis'.[11] (Fig 5)

The manor to which Gelling, Jones and Maitland refer was the 80 hides of land, valued at £120, of 1086 but Domesday book makes it clear that many of its estates had been detached after the minster's dissolution in the reign of the Confessor. The details are summarised in the Table below.

Leominster: Domesday Entries

	hides	Value, 1086 £ s d
Members in 1086	80	120
Other lands: detached by 1086	20	13 16
included in 1066	35¼	36 6 11
included before 1066	21	35
Total	156¼	205 2 11
Lands held by Queen Edith, 1066 should possibly also be included	12	35

The size and compact character of the Leominster estates and their central position on the Lugg river system indicate that they were not merely a handsome but, more importantly, an early royal grant. They are firm evidence of the impact of Edfrith's mission on the ruler of the Magonsaetan and the consequent conversion, or more likely the revitalisation of the Christian faith, of his folk.

A Columban Mission: Edfrith

The second important statement in the *Life* is that Edfrith was a 'Northumbrian', that is a member of the church established by Aidan at Lindisfarne but whose roots lay in Columba's Iona and amongst the lands of the O'Neills at Derry and Durrow.[12]

After Penda's defeat at Winwaed in 656 by Oswy of Northumbria a Columban mission was sent to convert Mercia. Its first bishops, Diuma and Ceollach, were Irish; the third, Trumhere, was English but trained and ordained by the Irish; whilst St Chad, the first Roman bishop, had spent part of his youth in an Irish monastery. An Irishman, Maildubh, founded Malmesbury, one of the greatest Anglo Saxon monasteries. The second bishop of Worcester, Oftfor, was a Northumbrian, a monk of Whitby.[13] It should therefore hardly be a matter for surprise that it was a Northumbrian who evangelised the lands beyond the Severn. What further evidence is there of such a mission and what, if any, independent witness is there for the role of Edfrith?

Almost a century ago the great liturgist, Edmund Bishop, drew attention to an Anglo-Saxon prayer book. The fact that it was split into two parts prior to its acquisition by Sir Robert Cotton has caused considerable confusion. It remains BL Cotton MS Nero Aii, ff3-13, and Galba Axiv. As some of Galba's prayers are for nuns, most scholars followed Bishop in ascribing it to the nunminster at Winchester. However on the first leaves of Nero Aii is a kalendar of the saints' feasts observed in the house. As this ignores the festivals of all but four of its favoured saints it clearly did not belong to Winchester. Bishop pointed out that the kalendar was full of archaisms drawn from 'our earliest extant hagiographical records' and was 'of the old world indeed'. Prophetically he described it as coming from 'not merely the most remote but the most Celtic, backward, part of the country', a description fitting Herefordshire well but which Bishop took to be Devon before the time of Bishop Leofric.[14] These, apparently discordant, elements were held to confirm that Nero Aii, ff3-13, and Galba Axiv were distinct manuscripts. In fact palaeographic analysis by Ker and textual analysis by Muir have shown that they are part of one prayer book but both accepted it as a Winchester manuscript. This is not so; its home was Leominster.[15]

The evidence lies in the prayer book's reference to three Leominster saints: Edfrith, Hemma and Aethelmod. The feast of *S Eadfride* is found on 26th October in Nero Aii but in no other pre-1100 kalendar.[16] In the second of the Galba Axiv litanies is an invocation to *S Entferth*, not found in any other Anglo-Saxon litany. Immediately prior is *'Sancte Aethelmod'* and after *'Sancte Hemma'*. Both are also Leominster saints. Neither is found in any other litany or kalendar but in the Galba kalendar the former appears as *'S Aethelmodi C(onfessoris)'* on 9th January, the latter as *'Haemma, Abb(atis)'* on 25 May. In Galba Axiv there is also a two-line fragment of a prayer to *Hemma*. An entry in a Reading Abbey relic list of c1190 provides an explanation, for the mother house had seized 'A certain large bone and two ribs of *Sci hemme* first abbot of *leonis monasterii*'. Aethelmod's feast in January was still a principal feast of the priory in 1433.[17] In the Leominster relic list of 1286 he is 'king and martyr'; Leland makes a grander claim, that Leominster had 'the skulls of Merewald and Ethelmund, kings of the Marches'. Both claims are at variance with Aethelmod's status in the kalendar, as confessor. The earlier, ninth century, section of *The List of Saints' Resting Places* records that 'St Aethelred rests at Leominster near the river Lugg'. For the scribe to mistake, or adjust, the original 'mo' for 're' suggests that, even at that time, Aethelmod's reputation was not widespread.[18] That Nero Aii ff3-13 and Galba Axiv are two parts of a single prayer book of Leominster origin is thus incontrovertible.

Leominster continued to honour Edfrith's memory. In 1290 the borough's great autumn fair was held on the vigil and feast of St Edfrith and the four days following. Some 50 years later the *Legend of St Etfrid, Priest of Leominster* was compiled from Wenlock's copy of Mildburg's *Life*, probably for Bishop Adam de Orleton after his elevation to Worcester (see Chapter 2 in this volume). A century later, in 1433, Spofford's *Register* records that St Edfrith's was one of the principal festivals of the priory. Undated like the others, it was listed before that of Simon and Jude, of 28th October.[19] Edfrith survived both dissolution and reformation for his *Life* reappeared in the 16th century in a vernacular form as *Edfride the Monk: The account of his longe Journie into Mercia in 660, the Conversion of the Saxon Kinge Merewald, and the building of the Benedictine Minster at Leominster*. This was calculated to foster civic pride by stressing the town's antiquity.[20]

The prayer book contains even greater treasure. The Gaelic 'Elegy of St Columba', *Amra Choluimb Chille*, tells us: 'He went with two songs to Heaven'. Galba Axiv preserves the *only* British manuscript form of the *Altus Prosator*, 'The High Creator', one of two poems attributed to Columba. Of the seven other extant manuscripts three are Irish and four continental. Of the latter, two are of the ninth century, one a Bobbio manuscript at Bibliotheca Ambrosiana Milan, the other at the Medical School, Montpellier. A second, shorter poem, *Adiutor Laborantium*, 'Helper of those who Labour', is referred to in the prefaces to two Irish texts as composed by Columba on the same occasion, but no copy was known. Some scholars questioned its very existence. In the Leominster prayer book is a unique copy, revealed by its title and abecedary form.[21]

Columba continued to be venerated at Leominster, on 9th June, long after his feast had disappeared elsewhere in Anglo-Saxon England. 'Collumcylle' occurs in only one other pre-1100 kalendar and there has been erased. Moreover, from the prayers in Galba Axiv we still hear the voices of Leominster men and women across almost a millennium, expressing their most profound and innermost thoughts. Although the alliteration and end-rhyme indicate a type of prayer-writing characteristic of the Midlands c1000, the underlying nature of many prayers is drawn from early Celtic sources.[22]

The Influence of St David's and the Monastic *Vallum*

There is a stark contrast between our knowledge of the role of the early church in the lands to the south of the Wye and to the north. To the south the part played by the Welsh church is well documented. From chance survivals in the *Book of Llandaff* early churches have been identified at *Lann Cerniu* (Dore), *Mafurn* (Peterchurch?), *Lann Guorboe* (in Mawfield), *Lann Iunabui* (Bredwardine), *Lann Devi* (Dewchurch), *Mochros* (Moccas), *Lann Erbdil* (Madley), *Bolgros* (Bellamore/Preston-on-Wye?), *Lann Loudeu* (Llancloudy) and *Lann Guoroe* (Eaton Bishop?).[23]

North of the Wye the involvement of the 'British' or Welsh church has only been hinted at, by Gelling, Stanford and Sims-Williams.[24] Was this area in the orbit of St David's as the south had been in that of Llandaff? Certainly Leominster always had close contact with central Wales, an area it served with its fairs, throughout the post-Conquest period. As late as 1539 clients came from St David's, Pembroke, Carmarthen and Llanelli as well as Aberystwyth and the upper Severn. Half the beasts sold were lambs of which 58% were from Radnorshire.[25]

In his *Life* of c1090 Rhigyfarch claims that David founded twelve monasteries. Although late this probably included a traditional list of houses of the *familia* of St David such as Glascwm, Cregrina, Colva, *Croulan* (traditionally interpreted as Crowland in the Fens) and possibly *Llanllieni*, Leominster. The large and ancient manor of Glascwm remained with the church of St David's until disestablishment in 1920. It bestrode the principal route from the Roman road, linking Llandrindod and Carmarthen (and thus St David's), to the Arrow Valley. Two miles to the west along this route is Cregrina; two miles to the east is Colva.

Two miles to the south, at the entry to a parallel route over Glascwm hill, is Rhulen. All four churches, dedicated to David, are within stone-banked enclosures, rectangular at Colva but round at the others.[26]

St David's feast is recorded in the Leominster kalendar and only one other, Sherborne – where Asser, Bishop of St David's, was granted the see by Alfred in 900.[27] David's relics are not included in the Leominster list but a series of indulgences in its cartulary shows them to be accepted as at Leominster, 'even by Bishop Iorwerth of St David's'. Part of a rib and a bone were taken to Reading in the early 12th century and late in the century both houses had copies of his *Life*. David's remained one of the priory's principal feasts throughout the middle ages.[28] If the early Welsh church had had a presence north of the Wye, Edfrith's role at Leominster will have been not so much outright conversion as the rekindling of the waning flame of Christian faith.[29]

A curvilinear *vallum*, bank and ditch, is a characteristic of early Welsh church sites and can yet been seen at Glascwm, Rhulen and Cregrina and in west Shropshire and Cheshire.[30] By contrast the most distinctive feature of Leominster's topography is the rectangular bank which marks off the monastic precinct on the south and west. To the north the Kenwater and to the east the Lugg served a similar purpose. (Fig 6) In 1808, Jonathan Williams, the only Leominster historian who sought to explain this feature, believed it 'had strong indications of Roman art and construction'. Others have attributed it to the founding Reading monks in the early 1120s, but there is no such feature at Reading – or any other post-Conquest Benedictine house.

The whole concept of a very large free-standing near rectangular enclosure, as Charles Thomas says, is alien to western Britain but there is one exception.[31] Considerable evidence exists of a rectangular enclosure at Iona, and possibly at its daughter house of Lindisfarne. The Iona enclosure is similar in outline and size, some 1,200 feet by 1,000 feet, to that at Leominster.[32] Traces of another rectangular enclosure have been found at Glastonbury. These served not for defence, but to mark off the sacred from the profane, thus defining the holy area. The monastic *vallum* was not necessarily defined by bank and ditch. At Wimbourne it was a high stone wall and at Oundle a stout thorn hedge.[33]

Not only islands, such as Iona itself, but also insular sites on rivers and marshes were favoured for the seclusion they afforded. At Selsey Wilfrid's monastery was surrounded by the sea on all sides but for the western approach, about a sling's cast wide. Lindisfarne was accessible only at low tide. At Leominster both place-name and flood control data indicate that the minster occupied an island site similar to, if not so spectacular as, that of Glastonbury.

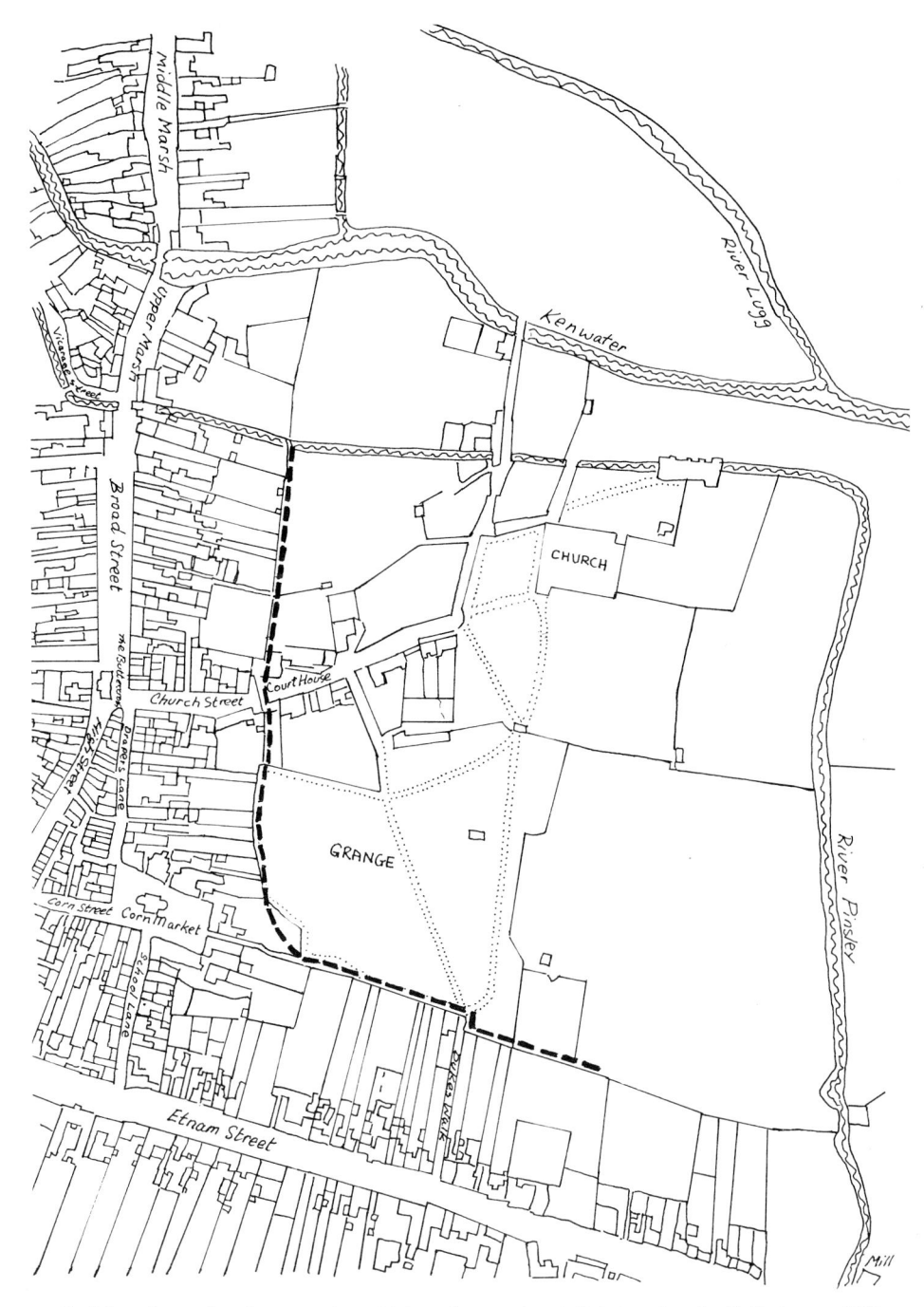

THE EARLY CHURCH IN HEREFORDSHIRE: COLUMBAN AND ROMAN

Fig 6 Leominster: the minster precinct with boundary, bank and ditch, based on the Gallier's map, 1825
– – – *Vallum monasterii*

Secluded on three sides by the marshlands adjoining the Lugg and Arrow and their tributaries, only to the west did a narrow neck of flood-free land along the Cholstrey ridge connect minster and the world beyond. To the end of the ninth century 'more', as in so many place-names about Leominster, was a 'low-lying marshy area'. Only with improvement did it become 'a low, flat level of former marshland, reclaimed and drained'. In terms of its precinct and monastic *vallum* Leominster is linked firmly, not to the Welsh, but through Lindisfarne and Iona to the Columban church.[34]

The Foundation of the Diocese

The early history of the see of Hereford was described by Christopher Brooke in 1967 as 'utterly obscure'. Since that date there has been much speculation and we have moved forward, a little.[35]

The traditional date for the foundation of the diocese, with Putta as the supposed first bishop, is 676. This is based on a misinterpretation of a passage in Bede's *Ecclesiastical History*.

> In 676 Aethelred, king of the Mercians . . . destroyed Rochester. When Putta found his (cathedral) church destroyed he went to Seaxwulf, bishop of the Mercians, who granted him a certain church and a small plot of land where he ended his life in peace, making no attempt to re-establish his bishopric. As I have said he was more at home in religious than worldly affairs and he served God only in his own church and went around whenever invited teaching church music.

Elsewhere Bede explains that Putta was 'especially skilled in liturgical chanting after the Roman manner and showed little interest in secular affairs, being content with a simple life'. These were not the qualities of a bishop founding a frontier diocese.[36]

For Plummer, writing more than a century ago, 'the whole tenor of Bede's narrative is against the idea that Putta discharged episcopal functions after the loss of Rochester. He lived as a simple priest to the end of his life. The "*agellus non grandis*" cannot refer to the extent of a diocese, but indicates the plot of land with which his church was endowed.' Sims-Williams' verdict, 'Putta, the first bishop in the episcopal list . . . cannot be identified with Bishop Putta of Rochester', has apparently not yet laid the ghost. If there is to be a Putta as the first bishop we must assume either, as Stenton suggested to solve this dilemma, that there was a second Putta or that Bede is inferior as a witness to the only early source naming Putta as founder of the diocese, a list of Hereford bishops of c 812.[37]

In support of Stenton, it has been noted that a 'Putta, bishop' is a witness in a 12th century copy of a charter granting land to Beorngyth, abbess of the double minster at Bath, in 681.[38] This does not prove the case. Once a bishop always a bishop. Putta of Rochester would have retained his title even in his new role. Further, given the few bishops serving at that time, to have two of the same name is, at the best, highly improbable.[39]

The Episcopal Lists

How does Bede's witness stand up against that of the episcopal lists which give Putta as the first bishop? With their companion royal genealogies they have been scrutinised by Sisam and Page. The latter points out that the archetype of the episcopal lists 'must have been a composite document made up of several earlier ones' and that the original Hereford list was compiled late in the reign of Offa. The earliest extant copy of the genealogies and lists is a fragment, folios 104-9, in BL MS Vespasian vi of c 812. This 'can be traced to Mercia in the last decades of the 8th century'. Seven bishops of the 'province of the Mercians' to c 691 are listed and then, in five subsequent columns, the bishops of the five *parochiae* (sees) into which that province was divided 'after Seaxwulf' (675-c691). This layout of the Mercian episcopal lists betrays their political intent. The Hereford list has disquieting features. The scribe was clearly on unfamiliar ground until Bishop Cuthbert (736-40). Only one of Putta's three successors is spelt correctly.[40]

How did Putta come to head the list of bishops of the folk west of Severn? Sisam indicates the hidden agenda. Both royal genealogies and episcopal lists were no mere fancy of some unknown 'person at Lichfield' but the policy of one with 'royal dignity as high as Charlemagne's'. Once he had consolidated his own power Offa's overriding concern was to secure the succession of Ecgfrith, his son. From the earliest time Mercia had been bedevilled by the claims of rival clans to the throne. To gain the crown Offa himself had deposed his predecessor, Beornred, within a twelvemonth of the latter's accession.[41] He then went on to murder not only Aethelberht, the young East Anglian king, in 794 but also, as Alcuin reports, all who could endanger Ecgfrith's succession.[42] In the same way two other Mercian princes were slain: Kenelm c 821 and Wistan in 849. As with Aethelberht at Hereford, popular cults sprang up – of Kenelm at Winchcombe and Wistan at Repton. Seeking protection for his son through the sacral nature of kingship Offa took the unprecedented step of consecrating Ecgfrith as king during his own lifetime. For this he needed, in place of the politically unreliable Kentish archbishop of Canterbury, his own malleable Mercian archbishop.

In his letter of justification to Pope Hadrian I, Offa emphasised the wide extent of his lands. The episcopal lists were a carefully constructed political document that sought to endow his claim for a third, Lichfield, archdiocese with specious legality. They were designed to demonstrate that in Seaxwulf's time the Mercian see had been so extensive that it had been divided into five dioceses, in 679. To complete these five diocesan lists of 'Names of the bishops after Seaxwulf' the scribe had to find a credible bishop of Hereford by 679. The answer was Putta. Had not Bede said Putta had received a church from Seaxwulf in 676? Offa's campaign was successful. In the words of the *Anglo-Saxon Chronicle*, 'there was a contentious synod at Chelsea (in 787) and Archbishop Jaenberht gave up part of his jurisdiction as metropolitan and Hygeberht (Bishop of Lichfield) was appointed . . . (as archbishop); and Ecgfrith was consecrated king'. Needless to say, some three years after Offa's death his archbishop was deposed.[43]

Bishop Cuthbert's Mausolea

Evidence in direct conflict with the episcopal list is found in a book of epigrams collected c 750 by Milred, fifth bishop of Worcester. For our knowledge of this book, apart from a few folios of a mid tenth century copy, the Urbana fragment, we have to rely on notes made by William of Malmesbury in the early 12th and John Leland in the mid 16th century. Both include transcripts of two epigrams of Cuthbert, Bishop of the Magonsaetan 736-40 and Archbishop of Canterbury 740-60.[44]

The first, an epitaph, is critical. It tells us that, to honour his predecessors in the see of Hereford, Cuthbert had erected a '*tumba*' by which was meant a porticus, in Salic law 'a little building erected over the tombs of the dead'.[45] Within he had placed six tombs. Three were those of his predecessors: Tyrhthil, Torthere and Walhstod; the others were of Mildfrith, ruler of the folk, his wife, Cuenberg, and a certain Osfrith, son of Oshelm. Tyrhtil, Torhthere and Walhstod are all documented elsewhere. Tyrhtil witnessed two charters, one in 693 and another by 709 which granted 50 hides in Fulham to Bishop Wealdhere of London. He was succeeded by Torhthere who was present at the Council of Clovesho in 716 and who witnessed in 718 the foundation of the minster at Acton Beauchamp. In 731 Bede described Walhstod (727x31-36) as 'bishop of the folk who live in the west, beyond the Severn'.[46]

In the porticus Mildfrith and Cuenberg were no doubt either side of the altar with the tombs of Cuthbert's predecessors and the layman Osfrith, son of Oshelm, to the west. Given Cuthbert's later career it would be surprising if he had not left a place for his own sarcophagus. To accommodate seven tombs we should anticipate, on the basis of the dimensions of the St Gregory porticus at Canterbury, that the Hereford burial chapel would be some 50 by 12 feet.[47]

The second of Cuthbert's epigrams shows that Walhstod was his predecessor and that the embellishment of the episcopal church was well advanced by 736. Walhstod had commenced work on an elaborate *vexillum*, a banner or standard. This, it has been said, was a cross-cloth, probably decorated with a cross in gold and silver thread, like that described by Bede over St Oswald's tomb. In this case it would have been 'the earliest evidence of luxurious liturgical embroidery made in Anglo-Saxon England'.[48] However, in discussing the origins of the stone cross in Britain, Cramp points out that 'the specific reference to the *signum* on the Jarrow inscription (No. 16), or the term *sigbecn* – sign of Victory – to describe the cross in the Bewcastle, Cumberland, inscription, clearly indicates that the Northumbrians interpreted the cross as the *vexillum regis*'.[49] Thus, given the Northumbrian origins of the church beyond the Severn, it is possible that Walhstod's *vexillum* was also a stone cross. His death brought the work to an end but Cuthbert, as his epigram proclaims, quickly completed it.

In early witness lists a bishop was identified, if at all, by the folk he served, as Bede in 731 described Walhstod as bishop of the folk who lived west of the Severn. The first reference to a 'bishop of the church of Hereford' is to Wulfheard in 799 but an agreement of 803 refers to the minsters at Cheltenham and Beckford as belonging to 'the church of Hereford in ancient days'. This takes it back to the mid 8th century.[50] On the other hand a puzzling, solitary, reference, some 500 years after the event, has raised doubts as to whether Hereford was the first site of the see. In this Bishop Gilbert Foliot drew the attention of Robert de Melun, his successor, to the respect due to the church of *Lidebiri*, 'for the sake of the episcopal see which it held long since . . . and for the holy bishops whose bodies lie there'. This the editors of Foliot's letters held to be the centre of the district of Lydas, referred to in Mildburg's Testament. Sims-Williams doubts that this was Ledbury, on etymological grounds. Barrow excludes Lydbury North, the alternative, as it was no longer under the jurisdiction of the bishops of Hereford, for Foliot's predecessor, Robert de Bethune, had given it to the Victorine canons newly established at Shobdon.[51] Coplestone-Crow, however, identifies *Lydas* as the district, taking its name from Lyde brook, between Lugg and Wye. Hereford grew up at the centre of its southern limits. Foliot may well have been misled by the reference to *Lydas* in the *Life* of St Aethelbert popular in his time. This is significant to the debate because, if a place other than Hereford had been the seat of the first bishop, it might explain Putta's non-appearance in the Hereford mausoleum. It is reassuring to find Keynes, in the recently published *Hereford Cathedral: A History*, at ease in describing Cuthbert as 'bishop of Hereford 736-40'.[52]

Cuthbert's inspiration for his burial chapel was no doubt the church of SS Peter and Paul at Canterbury, the foundations of which are still visible in the midst of the ruins of the post-Conquest St Augustine's abbey. Conforming to classical precedent, it had been built outside the city walls by Aethelberht in 613. In order that 'the bodies of Augustine, and of all the bishops of Canterbury, and of the kings of Kent might be buried there', it had two porticus.[53] In the southern Aethelberht and Bertha, his queen, were buried on either side of the altar of St Martin with Bertha's Frankish chaplain, Liuthard, to the west. In the northern porticus were St Augustine and five of his successors: Augustine to the south and Laurence to the north of St Gregory's altar; the others to the west.[54] (Fig 7)

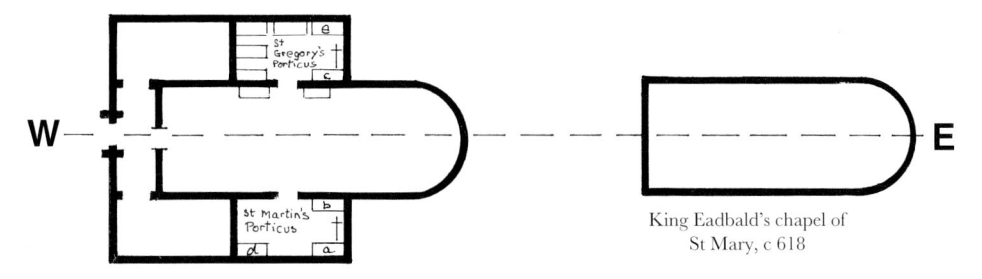

Fig 7 Canterbury: King Ethelbert's church of St Peter and St Paul, *c.* 613 showing the Tombs of a King Ethelbert, b Queen Bertha, c Augustine (d 604x9), d Liuthard and e Lawrence (d 619)

At Canterbury the Roman custom of carving epitaphs on the tombs of the eminent dead, adopted by the Frankish church, was quickly followed. The epitaph on the tomb of Augustine, 'who with God's help and supported by miracles guided king Aethelberht and his people from the worship of idols to the Faith of Christ' is recorded by Bede. That of Aethelberht Weever translates as:

'King Aethelberht lieth here, closed in the polyander

For building churches, sure he goes to Christ without meander'.

The epitaphs of Behrtwald (693-731?), the ninth, and Tatwine (731-4), the tenth archbishop of Canterbury, are recorded by Milred.[55]

A porticus was built so that interment could be as close as possible to the altar, and thus to the relics, without violating the prohibition of burial within the church itself. As there was inadequate space in the south porticus of SS Peter and Paul, King Eadbald built c 620 the much larger burial chapel of St Mary to serve the needs of the Kentish royal family. It was placed axially, some 40 feet east of the earlier church. When the north porticus of SS Peter and Paul was full, the edict of the Council of Nantes in 658, that 'no bodies whatsoever are to be buried in church but in the atrium or in a porticus or outside', was ignored. Archbishop Theodore (d 690) and Behrtwald (d 731) were buried *within* the church, by the wall adjoining the north porticus. Tatwine and Nothelm (d 739) are said to have been buried there also. Where is not known.

In making provision for his predecessors at Hereford and for his successors at Canterbury, Cuthbert was seeking a burial place of appropriate dignity for himself. At Canterbury, holding that interment with Augustine and his predecessors would be in conflict with the Nantes edict, Cuthbert, a man not easily diverted from his objectives, decided on a dramatic alternative.[56] By his own Christ Church cathedral, within the city walls, he built the church of St John the Baptist as a burial place for himself and his successors, an action branded as 'foul, snake-like and fratricidal' by the enraged monks of St Augustine's. Following Eadbald's example he chose an axial arrangement but, to secure the closest proximity to the relics, it was 'almost touching' the cathedral. It served also as baptistry and court of justice. Of its shape there is no record but if round or polygonal with a central baptismal basin, such as had been popular amongst the Franks, it would have been extraordinarily inconvenient as a court room.[57] (Fig 8a) At Hereford also Cuthbert may have followed Eadbald's example, placing his porticus axially to the east of the cathedral. In all probability, as later at Christ Church, it was much closer than the 40 feet adopted by Eadbald. (Fig 8b)

Archbishop Cuthbert's chapel of St John the Baptist, 740 x 758

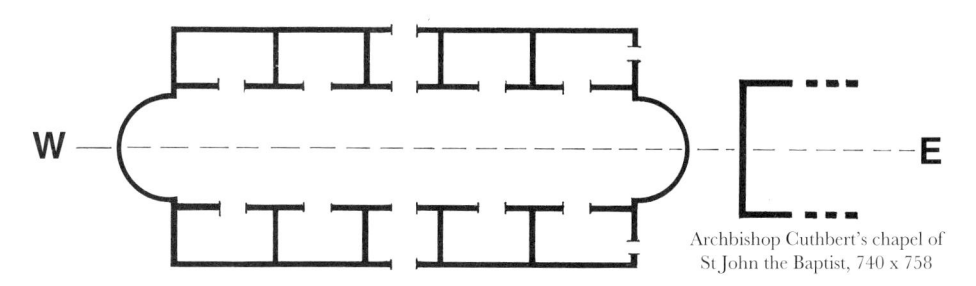

Fig 8a Christ Church, Canterbury: the Cathedral, a tentative reconstruction after H M Taylor (1969)

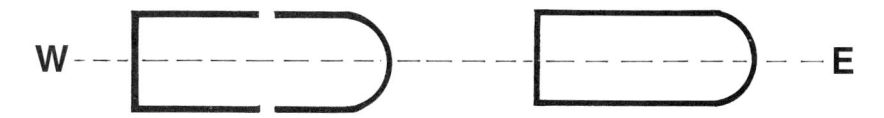

Fig 8b Hereford: the first Cathedral with Bishop Cuthbert's burial chamber, a hypothetical reconstruction dependent on analogy

In Hereford, as at Canterbury and Winchester, burial chapels were designed to express the prestige and authority of the local dynasty, its bishop and its folk. In such circumstances a certain descriptive hyperbole can be expected. Cuthbert's epitaph was no exception. Not only was the porticus 'of overshadowing marble' but the six there entombed were 'renowned wide through the world'. Even if Putta had been the founder of the tribal diocese but with a seat at *Lidebiri*, not at Hereford, his exclusion from such a memorial chapel would have been extraordinary. Given Cuthbert's character and interests, it would have been inconceivable for he had a powerful precedent.[58] In 670 Bishop Haeddi and King Cenwalh had translated Birinus, their missionary and first bishop, more than 50 miles from Dorchester to Winchester, now the seat of a reunited West Saxon diocese. There he was buried in the company of Cynegils, first Christian king of Wessex, his successors and their bishops.[59]

Putta's apparent exclusion from the Hereford mausoleum has been justified on the grounds that Cuthbert did '*not* translate the bodies of his predecessors at Canterbury'. This is quite wrong. He did not translate them because he could not. Much as he may have wished to, he lacked the authority and, more important, the power to launch a piratical attack on his cathedral's rival, the abbey of St Augustine. Thus he kept his intention a close secret and left explicit instructions that 'no one should be informed of either his sickness or death and that the bells should not be tolled for him until the time when his corpse was laid in the grave', thus forestalling Iambert and the monks of St Augustine's who 'arrived with haste' but 'returned home exceedingly disconcerted'. At Hereford he faced no such challenge.[60]

The Coming of Roman Ways

The late seventh century was an era of rapid change. In 666 the Northumbrians accepted Roman ways at the synod of Whitby. Three years later they were firmly established in Mercia with the reconsecration of Chad by Theodore of Tarsus, the newly arrived archbishop of Canterbury. At the synod of Hertford in 672 Theodore's proposals to create new smaller dioceses met stout resistance. That a synod at Rome decreed in 679 that there should be twelve bishops does not imply the foundation by that time of a see west of the Severn. As has been pointed out, 'the wily old archbishop bided his time' and, as will be seen, 'took his opportunities when they came'.[61] As neither Merewalh nor his eldest son, Merchelm, were included in Cuthbert's epitaph they, it seems, remained faithful to Edfrith and the Columban church – but the lands west of the Severn could not cut themselves off for long. In all probability a diocese had been established for the Magonsaetan at Hereford before the death of Archbishop Theodore in 690. There is no indication whatsoever that Leominster was the original site of the see although, as the minster estates so strikingly show, it was undoubtedly an earlier ecclesiastical centre of considerable importance.[62]

Mildburg may well have represented the advance guard of the new order. She had been well groomed for this task, having been educated in Kent by her mother, the companion of 'the holy Theodore and the blessed Hadrian'. We can therefore anticipate Mildburg's full commitment to the Theodoran views on diocesan re-organisation. Theodore himself and Bishop Seaxwulf of Lichfield played a critical part in establishing Mildburg at Wenlock. Both signed the charter, c 680, by which she was granted 144 hides of land, of which 97 were at Wenlock. This, her own princess minster, was thus a political stronghold for Rome on the northern confines of her father's realm. Mildburg was still abbess in Walhstod's time, 727x31-36.

What were the implications of the coming of the Roman order for Leominster? One can but speculate. The reference to Hemma as 'first abbot' suggests that after Edfrith's death his house was reorganised as a monastery on Roman lines. However the Frankish double monastery was now at the height of its popularity in England and possibly, with Mildburg's shadow cast over Leominster, it also came under an abbess's authority shortly after. Certainly in 1046 it was ruled by an abbess, Eadgifu.[63]

Throughout the middle ages Mildfrith, Merewalh's second son, was regarded as the founder of Hereford cathedral. Its muniments were lost in 1055, when the Welsh slew the canons and burned their minster 'to the ground', having despoiled it of its relics, vestments and of its treasures. Yet the oral tradition would have lived on. The anonymous early 12th century *Passion* of St Aethelberht is thus the first documentary evidence of foundation. It tells us that 'a certain Milfrith', a king from the remote parts of the land (near Leominster?), built the cathedral. This it links with the martyrdom of 794. Although some 100 years separated foundation and Aethelberht's death, the conflation of the two key events in the cathedral's history is hardly surprising for the *Passion* could only be 'based . . . on vernacular traditions current in Hereford . . . in Anglo-Saxon times'.[64] Under each of the nine windows of the dodecagonal chapter house of the 1360s were five niches. Mildfrith was painted in the first on the left as one entered; St Aethelberht followed.[65]

Territorial arrangements link the interests of Mildburg and her half-brother, Mildfrith. In the north the diocesan bounds included Wenlock's estates north of the Severn: Madley, Little Wenlock and detached estates at Beckbury and Badger.⁶⁶ In the south thirty hides of the lands of Mildburg's minster lay within the district called *Lydas* (Lyde). Coplestone-Crow is of the view that when the diocese was established this estate 'may have been taken from Wenlock and assigned to the bishop instead'.⁶⁷

Mildfrith's decision to place the bishop's seat at the former Roman site by the banks of the Wye, at the southernmost limit of his realm, is probably explained by dynastic interests. The name, Hereford, 'army ford', underlines its strategic character. The seventh century had witnessed a consolidation of Welsh kingship and territory in lands to the south. This peaked in the reigns of Morgan ap Athrwys, c 665-710, and his son, Ithel ap Morgan, c 710-45, kings of Glywysing. Felix in his *Life of Guthlac* refers to the Welsh 'troubling the English with attacks, pillaging and devastation' in Coenred of Mercia's brief reign (704-9).⁶⁸

By 1066 the church of Hereford held almost twice as many hides of land as Leominster. However Leominster's estates were highly compact and central, apart from Farlow in Shropshire and Marcle in the east. They were at the heart of the southern territory of the Magonsaetan when the Lugg, not the Wye, formed its backbone. The only compact holding of the cathedral was on the eastern periphery of its diocese, extending from Bromyard and Whitbourne through Stanford Bishop and Bishops Frome to Cradley, Bosbury, Coddington, Colwall, Eastnor, Ledbury and Donnington. A group of four manors, Preston-on Wye, Tyberton, Madley and Eaton Bishop, lay southwest across the Wye, in the area formerly under the jurisdiction of Llandaff. Three others, Walford, Ross and Upton Bishop, abutted the Forest of Dean. There was a concentration of manors around Hereford but the remainder, Wormsley, Canon Pyon, Ullingswick, Woolhope, Holme Lacy, Brockhampton and How Caple, were widely scattered. Such dispersal hardly betokens a single early grant, as at Leominster.⁶⁹

The lack of local pagan burials, and by implication of pagan Anglo-Saxons, indicates either that there were no Anglo-Saxons here by the late sixth century or that they had been converted prior to arrival.⁷⁰ In this case was there a British church at Hereford? Does St Guthlac's predate the foundation of the see? The documentary evidence has been submitted to close and detailed scrutiny by Pearn. She is of the view that the history of the 'temporal possession of college and priory, far from revealing the sort of structure that one might expect from an ancient minster with a wide *parochia*, suggests that, in so far as it is recoverable, its organisation was that of a late minster, essentially a secular foundation with a good temporal endowment but modest ecclesiastical rights'. Its high status, apparently achieved by the end of the tenth century, indicates a royal connection. Pearn concludes 'if the dedication to Guthlac is original, then this, with the archaeological evidence, suggests foundation in the ninth or early tenth century as most likely'.[71]

Mercia was in turmoil between the Viking raids on London in 839 and 851 and 877 when, with the Danes occupying Gloucester, it was divided along the line of Watling Street, the eastern half being incorporated in the Danelaw. The short period of the Mercian revival of 883-918, under the leadership of Aethelred and his wife, Alfred's daughter Aethelflaed, Lord and Lady of the Mercians, witnessed the creation of a series of strongholds, *burhs*. They sought to enhance their prestige by the foundation of a series of colleges of secular canons to which they translated relics from eastern Mercia: of St Werburgh from Hanbury, Staffs, to Chester; of St Oswald from Bardney, Lincs, to a site near the Kingsholm Palace at Gloucester; and possibly of St Alkmund from Derby to Shrewsbury. At Hereford St Guthlac's was the dominant feature of the *burh's* eastward extension in 'the late ninth or early tenth century'. This fits in well with St Guthlac's subsequent status, for the next period of church construction was the great monastic revival of the mid tenth century.[72]

Minster and Parochia: Leominster, Bromyard and Ledbury

Leominster

With the foundation of the diocese Leominster shared fully in the heritage of the Roman church. The cathedral muniments having been destroyed in 1055, Leominster's records provide unique documentary evidence of the cultural influences at work on the spiritual life of the diocese in the pre-Conquest period.

Although written in the early 11th century the Nero Aii kalendar includes entries from the earliest years of the Roman church in this country. They are, as Bishop said, 'of the old world indeed'. Some represent well-known cults introduced in the late seventh and early eighth century, including those of saints from Nicaea, Nicomedia and Cappadocia in Asia Minor, from Syria and especially from the Campagna and Sicily, all in vogue in Rome in the days of Gregory the Great and his immediate successors. St Euplius of Catania figures in his letters. These cults were derived from the earliest Roman service books, brought to Britain, as Bede explains, by Benedict Biscop, Theodore and others. These books had been preserved to his own day (731) and copies made by 'others elsewhere'.[73]

Additionally the kalendar has some 50 unique entries, cults which cannot be found in any other Anglo-Saxon source. Most are from the Hieronymian martyrology, a vast list of feast days attributed, erroneously, to St Jerome.[74] Had there been any major break in the life of the community these cults would have been lost. The kalendar thus proves not only Leominster's great antiquity but also its continuity during the Viking attacks. Further they indicate Leominster's cultural isolation for these early saints, whose fame had long since passed into oblivion, were culled from kalendars elsewhere, such as Winchester, Canterbury and Worcester. Even the tenth-century monastic reform movement which, we know from other evidence in the prayer book, had a considerable impact on Leominster, did not lead to their excision.

Analysis, not only of the kalendar, but also of the two litanies and the prayers in Nero Aii and Galba Axiv, and the 1286 relic list, identifies subsequent cultural layers: from the Irish as well as the Welsh church; of the Breton cults espoused by that avid relic collector, King Athelstan; and of the tenth-century reform movement.[75] The last came, no doubt through the agency of St Oswald, from his great monasteries at Ramsey and Worcester.[76] The combination of Mildburg's *Life* and the prayer book thus provides a remarkable picture of the spiritual life of Leominster in the four centuries before the Norman Conquest.

For Bede the duty of a bishop was to travel amongst 'the many hamlets and steadings lying amongst inaccessible mountains and bosky valleys to perform some ministerial act or bestow some heavenly grace'.[77] This the bishops sought to achieve by sending small groups of priests, members of their community or *familia*, to outstations such as Bromyard and Ledbury. These, confusingly, are also termed minsters, but their primary role was pastoral care, the cure of souls, within their *parochia*.

Leominster, however, had had a dual role, as a monastery and as such a priestminster. When the monastery was dissolved about 1046 the priestminster remained. After the foundation of the priory, as the charter of 1123 proves, this responsibility for the cure of souls continued. A lease of c1160 refers to a messuage in the vill that was 'Ailwin the canon's'. Some 30 years later a priest and three chaplains were serving the wide *parochia*. The vicar had received twelve sheaves from each virgate, part of the payment to a mother church, but the Abbot of Reading ensured that these successors to the minster priests never achieved the autonomy of the portionists found at Bromyard and Ledbury.[78]

In granting Leominster as a cell to Reading Abbey Henry I had invested the abbey with both its temporalities ('woods, fields, pastures, meadows and water with mills and fisheries') and spiritualities ('churches, chapels, cemeteries, offering and tithes'). In order to secure the latter, a charter of Bishop Richard de Capella in 1123 defined the bounds of Leominster's *parochia*.[79] Ancient and trustworthy men named 39 places, of which all but one, *Ach*, can be identified, but 'abstained from giving evidence about many others which of old were part of the *parochia* as they were too antiquated'. It is probable that previously a much closer relationship existed between lordship and *parochia*.

Bromyard and Ledbury

By the mid ninth century the division of the diocese into *parochiae*, similar to if smaller than that of Leominster, was already well advanced. Throughout the middle ages Bromyard and Ledbury remained the largest and most valuable of the episcopal manors in the county. Situated at either end of the group of bishop's manors which ranged along the diocese's eastern boundary, they were ideal places for two such early minsters. At Bromyard evidence is provided by a remarkable survival, a charter of Bishop Cuthwulf (836x39-857x66) found in a solicitor's office at Fakenham about 1870. By this, Cuthwulf, with permission of King Berhtwulf, gave Ealdorman Aelfstan four *manentes*, hides, of land in the *villa* by the river called *From* for three lives after which they were to be returned entire to the minster (*monasterium*) which is called Bromyard (*Bromgeard*). The carving of St Peter and the carved cross in relief on a sunken circular background above the south door of Bromyard parish church, for Taylor, 'seem to be pre-Conquest but not *in situ*'.[80] (Fig 9) At Ledbury there is no Anglo-Saxon charter. The case for a minster is based on post-Conquest evidence and the close parallels between the two portionary churches of Bromyard and Ledbury.

Fig 9 Bromyard Parish Church: the re-set stone carving of St Peter above the south porch

Domesday shows both churches were well endowed. At Bromyard two priests had one hide and a chaplain one hide and three virgates. At Ledbury two and a half of the manor's five hides belonged to one priest.[81] On evidence from the Leominster *parochia* the division into the parishes we know was, in Herefordshire, a predominantly 12th century phenomenon.[82] After this break-up of the districts they served as mother churches, Bromyard and Ledbury still retained large, if vestigial, parishes. At Bromyard it was some 9,600 acres and at Ledbury 8,200.[83]

By the 13th century most of the greater minsters were being transformed into collegiate churches. In the diocese of Hereford this process was never completed. Here the Anglo-Saxon minsterpriests became portionists. Ledbury had two portionists by 1201 when, the see being vacant, the king appointed William, Archdeacon of Hereford, to the portion in Ledbury church which Henry Bannister had held.[84] They were sinecure rectors, each with his own portion or estate, the Upper and Lower Courts. The bishop's palace lay close by. Their only responsibility was the presentation, and payment, of a vicar. It was he who was accountable for the cure of souls. In 1401 there was an abortive attempt to establish a college. John Prophete, Dean of Hereford, and his fellow portionist, Robert Prees, obtained a royal licence to appropriate their portions to found a college with a warden and eight chantry priests. This move foundered when Prophete's interests, as Keeper of the Privy Seal, moved elsewhere. At Bromyard the Courts of three portionists – Astley, Over or Upper and Middle – were within the minster precinct, as was the bishop's palace, abandoned in 1356. When Duncumb was writing in the early 19th century the portionists still had 'houses contiguous to the church'. After the first portion became vacant in 1849 it was sold by the ecclesiastical commissioners; the other two followed not long after.[85]

The first recorded attempt to establish the responsibilities of these portionists was made by Thomas Cantilupe when the portionists of Ledbury and Bromyard, the relatives of his predecessor, Peter de Aquablanca, were cited to answer charges of non-residence and plurality in 1277. The question was settled only in 1311 when Bishop Swinfield, who had also presented a relative to one of the Ledbury portions, sought counsel's opinion. He was advised that the Ledbury and Bromyard portions did not carry the care of souls or limit the right to hold other benefices. They were sinecures and could be held in plurality. The consequence was that the bishops of Hereford came under increasing pressure from king and pope to present their candidates.[86] In 1384 an episcopal inquisition defined the character of the churches of Bromyard and Ledbury more precisely, if in negative terms. They were not colleges or corporations sole, for the portionists had no common seal, no common chest, no common bell and no common chapter house for transacting their business; nor did they have any dean or provost etc. This status was confirmed in 1574.[87]

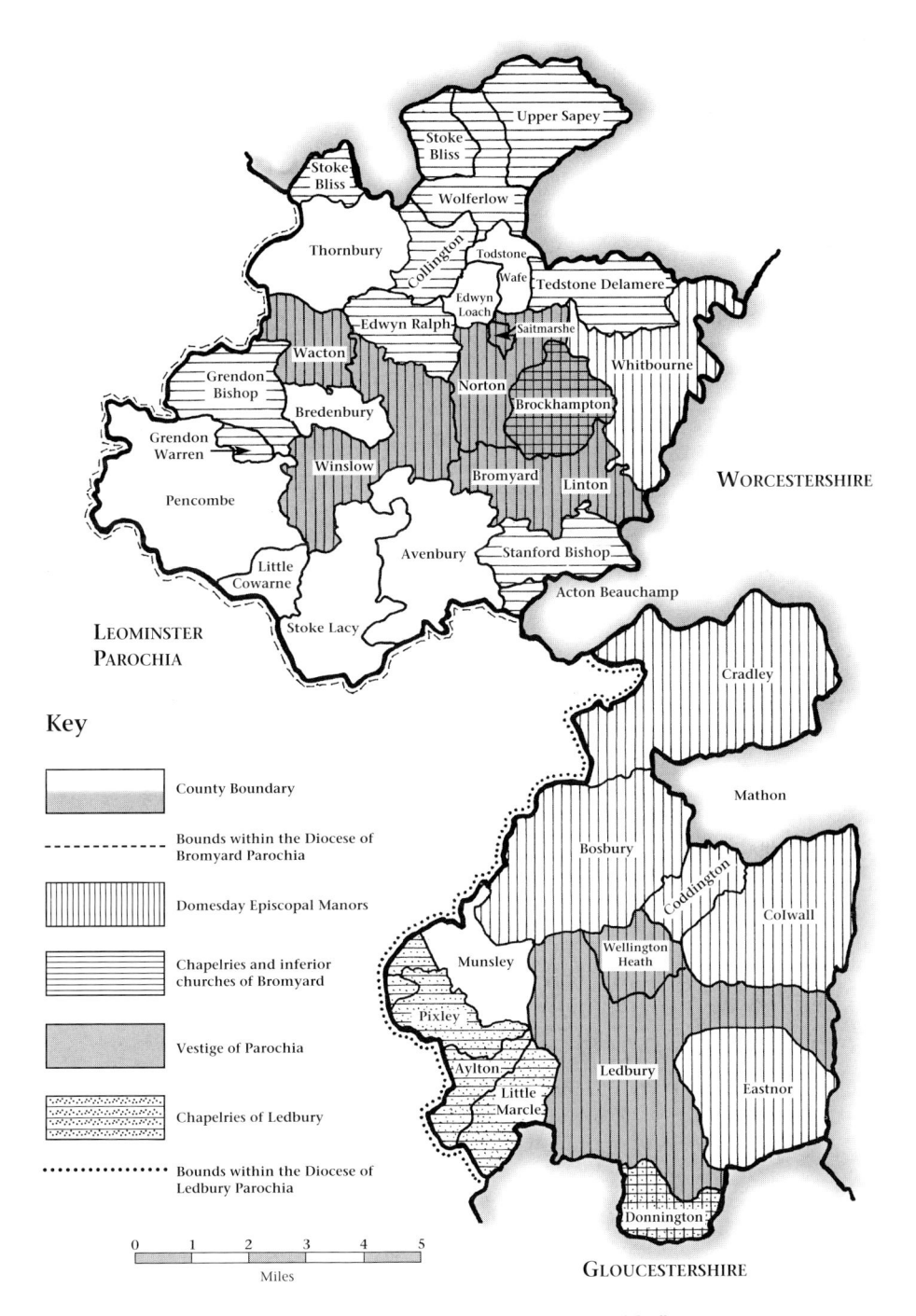

Fig 10 The Episcopal Parochiae of Bromyard and Ledbury

A comparison of the two minsters is revealing. For Pevsner, Ledbury is the premier church of Herefordshire. The late 11th or early 12th century church had a long north, and presumably south, aisle arcade of which four of the circular bases, some 5 feet in diameter, are still visible. Reconstruction c 1200 created a church some 190 feet in length. At Bromyard there was a considerable church, with two aisles and a crossing tower, by the late 12th century. Even with the early 14th century extension to the chancel it was no more than 150 feet long.

The size of Bromyard's *parochia* is first hinted at in 1276, when John of Monmouth was presented to the church of Wolferlow 'with the consent of the canons of Bromyard', and three years later, when 'the guardians of the portionists' sought the same right to presentation at Stoke Lacy.[88] Its full extent becomes evident in 1574, when the crown attempted to prove that Bromyard was a collegiate church and thus subject to the terms of the act of 1547, assigning all 'chantries, chapels, colleges' etc to the crown. In evidence it was shown that it was not a college but a portionary church. 'The stalls yet in the choir not only for the Prebends there but also for the XV other priests [sic] of XV inferior Churches thereabouts which come continually once upon a year upon Whitsun Monday to help say service in the Collegiate Church confessing the same to be the mother church. The Dean or first portionary there calling the said parishes by their names and they that come not to be amerced 6s 8d (half a mark) apiece and dividing one half to himself and the residue to the other two prebends there.'[89]

A terrier of July 1589 identifies some of these 'inferior churches' in terms of ancient dues accustomed to be paid to the vicar of Bromyard yearly at Easter: the parsons of Stoke Lacy 6d, Tedstone Delamere 2s 6d, Upper Sapey 6d, Collington 6d, Edwyn Ralph 6d, the vicars of Stoke Bliss 3s 4d, Wolferlow 2s and out of the lands of the Hide in Stanford Bishop 4d. In addition, burial fees were due to Bromyard from the parish of Collington, the chapelries of Tedstone Wafre, Grendon Bishop, Grendon Warren, Stanford Bishop and Brockhampton, and hamlet of Wacton. The *parochia* thus stretched from the county boundary in the northeast as far as Stoke Lacy in the southwest. All the indications are that it was virtually coterminous with the Domesday hundred of *Plegeliet*, Plegelgate, and thus included the parishes of Thornbury, Whitbourne, Avenbury and Little Cowarne, and the extra-parochial area of Saltmarsh. Edwyn Ralph apparently became detached from Leominster *parochia* after 1086 from whose minster it had always been very remote and Edvin Loach, part of the county of Worcester until 1832, was nevertheless within the diocese of Hereford. Brockhampton, Grendon and Stanford Bishop were chapelries in the middle ages and with Wacton only became parishes later.[90] (Fig 10)

Acton Beauchamp and Avenbury

Two other minsters in the Bromyard *parochia* pose interesting questions, particularly about that district's relationship with the neighbouring diocese of Worcester and its bishops. At Acton Beauchamp there is evidence of a minster more than a century earlier than for the mother church. The 12th-century text of a charter of 718, generally accepted as authentic, states that Aethelbald, King of Mercia (716-57), granted land to *Buca*, his *comes*, in return for payment, three *manentes* of land at Acton 'to be a perpetual abode for the servants of God'. The second of the two episcopal witnesses was Torhthere, Hereford's third bishop.[91]

A cross shaft re-used as a lintel in the south doorway of the tower provides further evidence of the early history of this minster. Only one face can be seen, of which part has been cut away to provide a segmental head. Nevertheless the carving of two beasts and a bird in plant scrolls is still well preserved (Fig 14). For Cramp this is 'incredibly' like the decoration on the back of the cross head at Cropthorne, Worcestershire. (Figs 11 & 12) She believes both may have come from the same workshop. Detached animal heads on scrolls, she adds, are found in England and the continent c 800, in particular in the Cuthbert gospels, and represent the earliest examples of the West Midland style found in manuscripts, metalwork and sculpture throughout the ninth century. On both crosses the birds are characterised by down-turned beaks, threatening claws and strongly differentiated primary and secondary wing feathers.[92] The birds, for Zarnecki 'doves', on the capitals of the 12th century west portal at Leominster, whilst boldly carved in the round, share these characteristics. Almost 150 such birds can be seen in the works of the Herefordshire School of Romanesque Sculpture, with fifteen on one shaft at Shobdon. One is thus bound to ask whether it was the birds on a work of the early ninth century school which provided the stimulus for such an outstanding feature of the Herefordshire work. (Fig 15)

What Bryant calls the 'thrush type' bird with a vine scroll on face B of the Gloucester cross shaft 30/31 is a more accomplished work than those at Cropthorne or Acton Beauchamp (Fig 13). Nevertheless it shares all three characteristics. Another Gloucester cross shaft, 33, recalls the hatching at Acton Beauchamp and Cropthorne. For Bryant 'early contacts with Nothumbria may offer a major potential source'. Cramp, who refers to the birds as 'parrot-like', draws attention to the firm links between the Gloucester shafts and the great northern cross at Bewcastle. The 50-hide manor of Cropthorne was in the hands of the church of Worcester well before 1066 as it formed the basis of one of the three hundreds of Oswaldslow. However a charter of Beorhtwulf of Mercia (840-52) indicates that in his reign it was still a royal manor.[93]

Anglo-Saxon Romanesque birds

The end of a long tradition: The Leominster Priory birds capital with some of its antecedents.

Figs 11 & 12 Cropthorne Worcestershire: arms of cross shaft, c 800

Fig 13 St Oswald's, Gloucester: cross shaft 31, face B, c 800 ?

THE EARLY CHURCH IN HEREFORDSHIRE: COLUMBAN AND ROMAN 67

Fig 14 Acton Beachamp: cross shaft of c 800 re-used as lintel for south door of tower

Fig 15 Leominster Priory: bird capital of west portal c 1135

Acton Beauchamp later had close associations with Worcestershire. It belonged to Evesham abbey in 1066 but for the monks of Worcester it was 'an old possession seized violently' by the powerful and acquisitive Abbot Aethelwig. The latter then granted it to the sheriff, Urse d'Abitot, who no doubt secured its inclusion in his county, eventually settling it on his daughter, the ancestress of the Beauchamps, who became hereditary sheriffs of the county. Only in 1897 was Acton reintegrated into Herefordshire.[94]

Complexities, however, do not end there. A further charter, of 972, purports to be a grant of privileges and restoration of lands to Pershore Abbey. Although generally accepted as a later fabrication, a 12th-century text does provide a detailed description of the bounds of Acton Beauchamp which reveals a firm knowledge of its terrain.[95] This underlines Acton's strategic position on a principal route linking Herefordshire with the outside world. In one place the bounds follow a '*saltera weg*', salt way. This came no doubt from Worcester. Its subsequent route has been traced by Houghton. Following Stoke Lane ridge road to Ullingswick, it passes along another ridge road and a parish boundary to the important royal manor of Marden and thence across the Lugg to Wellington. A deviation went to Burley Gate and Tupsley with a further branch leading from Stoke Lacy to Moreton Jeffries.[96] All these places, Domesday shows, had rights in salt pans at Droitwich. The major route may well have led ultimately to Leominster which had similar rights. Equally interesting, a further section of the Acton Beauchamp parish boundary ran by a feature described as *Scotta paeth*. In Bede's time and for more than two centuries after *Scotti* referred to the Irish. Thus for Bede, Columba and his Irish monks were, *Scotti*, and Iona a Scottish island, and for two centuries after, *Scottia* referred to Ireland alone.[97]

Avenbury, the second minster, had two priests as late as 1086. Both the size and form of the parish confirm its special status. Prior to boundary revision in the 1880s, with its chapelry of Bredenbury, it covered almost 4,000 acres. It was by far the largest parish in the district, apart from that of the mother church of Bromyard which was more than twice that size.

A brief note made by the great Warwickshire antiquary, Sir William Dugdale, refers to an Avenbury charter, now lost, which he saw in the cathedral at Worcester. This recorded its grant, to an unspecified recipient, by Waerferth, Bishop of Worcester 873-915, who translated Gregory the Great's *Dialogues* into English for Alfred the Great.[98] In 868 Mercia had felt the brunt of the Viking attack. The Danes were bought off but returned in 873, establishing their winter quarters at Repton Minster. Four years later Mercia was divided, the eastern half being incorporated into the Danelaw. Waerferth's grant of Avenbury may well have been made to raise money to meet Viking tribute demands.[99] Unlike Bromyard, which occupied a spur above the river, Avenbury's minster lay low in a great meander of the Frome. By 1066 Avenbury did not form a coherent parish. It was cut in two by the small manor of Keephill. The major part, stretching from Little Frome to Hopton Sollers, was on the south. To the north lay five detached parts, the Noakes with Sawbury, Wiggall, Ovendine and the Stake, with Avenbury chapelry.[100] If, as seems likely, Avenbury and Acton Beauchamp represent early attempts by Worcester to establish a minster on the banks of the Frome, they were soon eclipsed by Hereford's foundation, Bromyard, as mother church. Ironically Avenbury, one of Herefordshire's oldest churches, was, after 1931 allowed to fall into ruins.[101]

Ledbury

Ledbury's *parochia* included all the Domesday hundred of Wigmundstree excluding only the detached part of Much Marcle. By the 13th century, when parish churches had been established, the bishop presented both to the mother and all five of these later churches, Cradley, Bosbury, Coddington, Colwall and Eastnor. Elsewhere he determined the terms on which such parochial altars were dedicated. There was little conflict of interests, as there was in the Leominster *parochia*. Donnington was an exception. Domesday refers to a bishop's clerk there already in 1086 but by 1316 the abbot and convent of Wigmore had become patrons, probably through the gift of Bishop Robert de Bethune who c 1143 sheltered with the canons of Shobdon, the original foundation, to whom he had already granted the church of Lydbury North. Before he would dedicate the principal and two side altars at Donnington in 1231, Bishop Hugh Foliot insisted on an annual pension of 2s for the Ledbury portionists, one of them his brother Thomas, Cathedral Chancellor. It was still a chapelry in the 14th and 15th centuries.[102] (Fig 10, page 63)

The *parochia* extended west of the Roman road, now the A4172, to include Donnington, Little Marcle, Aylton, Pixley and Court-y-Park, all in the Domesday hundred of Radlow. All four were chapelries as Ledbury retained burial rights. References to 'rectors' in the bishops' registers arose when there were institutions to the livings. At Park and Aylton, as at Donnington and, one assumes, Pixley, this was 'with the consent of the Ledbury portionists'. The status of all but Little Marcle is confirmed in 1535 by the *Valor Ecclesiasticus*, although Park had already become a free chapel. Two years later a union of Aylton and Pixley was mooted, but did not take place until 1754. In 1655 Aylton chapelry was described as having 'no Burial place, nor register, neither was it subject to the Archdeacon's

Visitation'. The proprietors of the Upper and Lower Courts, Ledbury, each gathered one third of the tithe of sheaf corn. Pixley's register opens in 1745 and Aylton and Little Marcle's in 1748.[103]

Nationally there has been considerable interest in the contraction of the spiritual role of the minster churches. However in the case of Herefordshire the primary interest is now in the way they provided the earliest nuclei for economic activity. It is no accident that of the county's five market towns Leominster, Bromyard and Ledbury grew up around mother churches of ancient foundations. There is evidence to suggest that Ross should be included in this group. Kington alone was a successful castle town. It was natural that attendance at the mother church on the great festivals of the Christian calendar, Epiphany, Easter, Pentecost and the Nativity, as well as the patronal festival and Sundays should be combined with marketing. By the 1130s small boroughs had been established at these four sites. These rapidly developed into what they still remain, the principal market towns of the shire.[103]

Notes and References

Abbreviations
ASE   Anglo-Saxon England
EHD   English Historical Documents I ed D Whitelock (1955)
HD&CA   Hereford Dean and Chapter Archives by charter number, otherwise by page
HE   Bede Historia Ecclesiastica
Reg   Hereford Bishops' Registers, 1275-1535, Cantilupe Soc (1907-1921)
RS   Rolls Series
S   Anglo-Saxon Charters: An Annotated List and Bibliography ed PH Sawyer (1968), by charter number
TWNFC   Transactions of the Woolhope Naturalists, Field Club

1   BL Add MS 34,633 ff206r-9r, 210r-211r; Finberg, HPR, *Early Charters of the West Midlands* (2nd ed 1972) 197-224

2   The most recent discussion of the form of *Merewalh's* name is in Gelling, M, *The West Midlands in the Early Middle Ages* (1992) 81. For the family relationships see Hillaby, J, 'Early Christian and Pre-Conquest Leominster' *TWNFC XLV*, iii, (1987) 572-83; Sims-Williams, P, *Religion and Literature in Western England, 600-800* (1990) 47-51

3   For a fuller discussion see Hillaby (1987) see note 2, 557-685; idem, 'Leominster and Hereford: the Origins of the Diocese' in *Medieval Art and Archaeology at Hereford* Brit Archaeol Ass Conf Trans XV (1995) 1-14

4   Hare, M in *The Golden Minster* ed Heighway, C & Bryant, R (1999) 34

5   Finberg (1972) see note 1, 215

6   Gelling, M, 'The Early History of Western Mercia' in *Origins of the Anglo-Saxon Kingdoms* ed Bassett, S (1989) 192

7   Rollason, D W, *The Mildrith Legend: A Study in Early Medieval Hagiography in England* (1982) 15-16 but see also Hollis, S, 'The Minster-in-Thanet foundation story' *ASE 27* (1998) 41-62 who concludes 'the legend is unlikely to have arisen much later than the abbacy of Eadburga'. S91, BL MS Add 34,633, f208r

8   Gelling (1992) see note 2, 19, 6-7, 182

9   Jones, G R J, 'The Pattern of Settlement on the Welsh Border' *Agr Hist R 8* (1960) 66-81. Also see idem, 'Multiple Estates and Early Development' in *English Medieval Settlements* ed Sawyer, P H (1979) 9-34; idem, 'Early Historic Settlement in Border Territory: A Case-Study of Archenfield and its Environs in Herefordshire' in *Recherche de Géographie* ed Christians, C & Claude, J (Liège 1979) 117-32; Hooke, D, 'Early Units of Government in Herefordshire and Shropshire' in *Anglo-Saxon Studies in Archaeology and History* 5 (1992) 56

10 Hillaby (1987) see note 2, 594-600

11 Maitland, F W, *Domesday Book and Beyond* (1960 ed) 145-6

12 Herbert, M, *Iona, Kells and Derry: The History and Historiography of the Monastic Familia of Columba* (Dublin, 1996) 29-35

13 *HE* III, 24; IV,3,23; V, 18

14 Bishop, E, 'About an Old Prayer Book' *Liturgica Historica* (1918) 387; Gasquet, F N & Bishop, E *The Bosworth Psalter* (1908) 152, 156

15 Ker, N R, ed, *A Catalogue of Manuscripts containing Anglo-Saxon* (repr 1990) 200; Muir B J, ed, *A Pre-Conquest Prayer-Book*, Henry Bradshaw Soc, 105 (1998) xiv-xvi; Hillaby (1987) see note 2, 628-30; but Lapidge, M, 'Some Latin Poems as Evidence for the Reign of Athelstan,' *ASE* (1981) 84-9

16 Muir (1988) see note 15,12; Wormald, F, ed, *English Kalendars before AD 1100* I, HBS 72 (1934). Edfrith's feast apparently coincided with the traditional date of king Alfred's death. This prompted the interesting speculation that 'at least one (monastic) community happily commemorated "Saint Alfred" even though there had been no canonisation and though the cult did not spread', Perham, M, *The Communion of Saints*, Alcuin Club 62 (1980) 28

17 Muir (1988) see note 15, 126, 190, 3,7; Lapidge, M, ed, *Anglo-Saxon Litanies of the Saints* HBS 106 (1991) 303, 310; BL Egerton MS 3031 ff6v-8r; Bethell, D, 'The Making of a Twelfth Century Relic Collection' in *Popular Belief and Practice* ed Cumming, G J, & Baker, D, Studies in Church History 9 (1972) 61-72

18 *Reg Swinfield* 124-5; Toulmin-Smith, L, ed, *The Itinerary of John Leland* (1964) II, 74; Rollason, D, 'Lists of Saints' Resting Places' in *ASE 7* (1978) 68-90; Hillaby (1987) see note 2, 630-3, 652-4

19 *Charter Rolls* (1903-27) II, 356; BL Harley MS 2253 f132r-133r; *Facsimile of BM Harley MS 2253* ed Ker, NR, Early English Text Soc, 255 (1965) xxi-xxiii; *Reg Spofford* 162-3

20 Hillaby (1987) see note 2, 558-9 notes 6-8

21 Muir, B, 'Two Latin Hymns by Colum Cille (St Columba)' *R du Moyen Age*, 39 (1983) 205-9; Kenney, J F, *Sources for the Early History of Ireland: Ecclesiastical* (repr 1979) 264; Bernard, J H & Atkinson, R, ed, *The Irish Liber Hymnorum* 2, Henry Bradshaw Society 14 (1898) 23-6, 140-69. For translation and commentary see O'Clancy, T, & Márkus, G *Iona: The Earliest Poetry of a Celtic Monastery* (1995) 39-68

22 Winchester Cathedral Kalendar BL Cotton MS Vitellius Exviii f4v. For the prayers and litanies Hillaby (1987) see note 2, 635-54

23 Davies, W, *The Landaff Charters* (1979). Coplestone-Crow, B, *Herefordshire Place-Names* BAR British Series 214 (1989) provides amendments to the attributions

24 Gelling, M, *Signposts to the Past* (1978) 159; Stanford, S C, *The Archaeology of the Welsh Marches* (first ed 1980) 176-7; Sims-Williams (1990) see note 2, 78-9

25 Bathurst, J & Cole, E J L, 'Leominster Fair, 1556' *TWNFC* 42(i) (1976) 72-88

26 James, J W, ed, *Rhigyfarch's Life of David* (1967) 33. For Sims-Williams, 'Continental Influence at Bath Monastery in the seventh century' *ASE* 4 (1975) 1 'the assertion . . . by Rhigyfarch' is 'obviously invention'; idem (1990) see note 2, 59, 77. Also see Hillaby (1987) see note 2, 600-5.

27 It was added to the Glastonbury kalendar only in the 11th century and to Canterbury's CCCC 422 kalendar in the 15th century. Wormald, see note 16, 46, 172

28 Bethell, see note 17, 61-72

29 Hillaby (1987) see note 2, 600-5 esp note 194 & note 196

30 Hillaby (1987) see note 2, 607, plans 1 & 2

31 Thomas, C, *The Early Christian Archeology of North Britain* (1971) 32

32 For Iona see McCormick, F, 'Iona: The Archaeology of the Early Monastery' in *Studies of the Cult of St Columba* ed Bourke, C, (Dublin, 1997) 46-51; idem, 'Excavations at Iona, 1988' *Ulster J of Archaeol* 56 (1993) 78-108; Barber, J W, 'Excavations in Iona, 1979' *Proc Soc Antiq Scot* 111 (1981) 282-380; RCAHM (Scotland) Argyll: *An Inventory of the Ancient Monuments* 4, Iona (1982); O'Sullivan, D, 'The plan of the early Christian monastery on Lindisfarne' in *St Cuthbert, His Cult and His Communities to AD1200*, ed Bonner, G. et al (repr 1995) 125-42, fig 11

33 Radford, C A R, 'Glastonbury Abbey before 1184; Interim report on Excavations 1980-4' in *Medieval Art and Architecture at Wells and Glastonbury* Brit Archaeol Ass Conf Trans 4 (1981) 113-14; Ellis, P J, 'Excavations at Silver Street, Glastonbury' *Proc Somerset Archaeol Nat Hist Soc* 126 (1982) 17-24; Rodwell, W, 'Churches in the Landscape: Aspects of Topography and Planning' in *Studies in Late Anglo-Saxon Settlement* ed Faull, M, (1984) 18-21; 'Life of St Lioba' in *The Anglo-Saxon Missionaries in Germany* trans C H Talbot (1954) 207; *Life of Bishop Wilfrid by Eddius Stephanus* ed Colgrave, B (1927) 67

34 Hillaby (1987) see note 2, 594-5, 610-13 map 4; Morris, R, *Churches in the Landscape* (1989) 110-11; Gelling, M, *Place-Names in the Landscape* (1984) 53-7

35 *The Letters and Charters of Gilbert Foliot*, ed Morey, A & Brooke, C N L, (1967) 300

36 *HE* IV,2 & 12. For the debate on Putta and the foundation of the diocese see Hillaby, J, 'The origins of the Diocese of Hereford' *TWNFC* XLII(i) (1976) 16-52; Sims-Williams (1990) see note 2, 88-91, 97-8, 143, 341-5; Hillaby (1995) see note 3, 1-14

37 *Venerabilis Baedae: Historiam Ecclesiasticam . . .* ed Plummer, C (1896) II, 222; *HE* IV, 2, 5, 12; Sims-Williams, see note 2, 97-8; Keynes, S, 'Diocese and Cathedral before 1066' in *Hereford Cathedral: A History* ed Aylmer, G & Tiller, J (2000) 5-6; Stenton, F M, 'Pre-Conquest Herefordshire' in RCHME *Herefordshire* III (1934) iv

38 S1167; *EHD*, I, no 57; Sims-Williams (1975) see note 26, 1-10

39 Attention has also been drawn to the local place-names Putley and Putson as probably indicative of Bishop Putta. Coplestone-Crow, see note 23, gives Putley as 'probably hawk-clearing' and Putson as 'probably Putt's estate' but Putta was a common Anglo-Saxon name.

40 Sisam, K, 'Anglo-Saxon Royal Genealogies' *Proc Brit Ac* XXXIX (1953) 287-348 esp 289 & 329-30; Page, R,I, 'Anglo-Saxon Episcopal Lists', Parts I-III *Nottingham Med Studies* IX (1965) 71-95 esp 73-5 & 85, and X (1966) 2-24 esp 5-6

41 Sisam, see note 40, 329-30; Keynes (2000) see note 37, 6. William of Malmesbury, *de gestis regum Angorum* ed Stubbs, W, RS 90(i) (1987) 79 attributes the assassination of king Aethelbald (716-57) to Beornred but this may be an attempt by Offa to justify his own actions

42 Sisam, see note 40, 330 note 1 quoting Alcuin; Rollason, D W, 'The Cult of Murdered Royal Saints in Anglo-Saxon England' *ASE* 11 (1983) 1-22; idem *Saints and Relics in Anglo-Saxon England* (1989) 105-29; Hillaby, J, 'King Burgred: the Severn Stoke Coin Hoard and the Demise of the Mercian Kingdom' *Trans Worcs Archaeol Soc* 3S, 17 (2000) 137

43 *Anglo-Saxon Chronicle sa* 785

44 William of Malmesbury *Gesta Pontificum* ed Hamilton, N E S A, RS 52 (1870) 299; Leland, J, *Collectanea* ed Hearne, T (2nd ed 1774) III, 116-17; Lapidge, M, 'Some Remnants of Bede's Lost *Liber Epigrammatum*', *Eng Hist Rev* 90 (October, 1975) 798-820; Sims-Williams, P, 'Milred of Worcester's Collection of Latin Epigrams and its Continental Counterparts' ASE 10 (1982) 21-38

45 Cange, C duF du *Glossarium mediae et infirmae Latinitatis* (Paris, 1840-50) 5, 345

46 S53; S1248; S1785; *Councils and Ecclesiastical Documents* ed Haddan, A W & Stubbs, W, III (1871) 300; S85; *HE* V,23

47 Hope, W St J, 'Recent Discoveries in the Abbey Church of St Augustine at Canterbury' *Archaeologia* 66 (1914/15) 377-400 esp fig 7

48 Lapidge (1975) see note 44, 812-3; Budny, M, & Tweddle, D, 'The Maaseik Embroideries' *ASE* 13 (1984) 89-90; Sims Williams (1990) see note 2, 339-41

49 Cramp, R, *Corpus of Anglo-Saxon Stone Sculpture I(i) County Durham and Northumberland* (1984) 5, 112-13

50 Haddan & Stubbs, see note 46, III, 528-9; S1431. See also Sims-Williams (1990) see note 2, 138-9

51 Morey & Brooke, see note 35, 300, no 227 & note 1; Sims-Williams (1975) see note 26, 1-10; idem (1990) see note 2, 88,91-2; Brooke, C N L, 'The Diocese of Hereford, 676-1200' *TWNFC* 48(i) (1994) 27; also *English Episcopal Acta: Hereford 1079-1234* ed Barrow, J (1993) xxviii quoting *Monasticon Anglicanum* VI, 345

52 Coplestone-Crow, see note 23, 11, 12 map 4; James, M R, 'Two Lives of St Ethelbert' *Eng Hist R* XXXII (1917) 243; Brooks, E C, *The Life of St Ethelbert, King and Martyr 779AD-794AD* (1996) translates both *Lives*; Keynes (2000) see note 37, 8; see also p 56

53 *HE* I, 33

54 *HE* I, 33; II,3; Hope, see note 47, 377-400 esp fig 7; Sparks, M, *St Augustine's Abbey, Canterbury* English Heritage Guide Books (2nd ed 1990) 19 has a plan showing the sites of the tombs and the relationship of St Mary and SS Peter and Paul

55 *HE* II, 3; Weever, J, *Ancient Funerall Monuments of Great Britain, Ireland and the Islands Adjacent* (1st ed, 1631); Potts, R U, 'The tombs of the kings and archbishops in St Austin's abbey' *Archaeol Cantiana* 2S 38 (1926) 105

56 Doubts have been expressed as to whether Cuthbert the bishop and Cuthbert the archbishop were one and the same man. Sims-Williams, P, 'Cutswith, Seventh-Century Abbess of Inkberrow, near Worcester and the Wurzburg Manuscript of Jerome on *Ecclesiastes*' *ASE* 5 (1976) 16, note 5; Brooks, N *The Early History of the Church of Canterbury* (1984) 80 but Sims-Williams in 1990, see note 2, 339, now believes 'further poetic material tends to tip the balance in favour'

57 Brooks, N, see note 56, 37-51, 80-83, note 54; Taylor, H M, 'The Anglo-Saxon Cathedral Church at Canterbury' *Archaeol J* 126 (1969) 102, 126; Milburn, R *Early Christian Art and Architecture* (1988) 203-14

58 See note 42

59 *HE* III, 7

60 Sims-Williams (1990) see note 2, 342, note 60; Hillaby (1976) see note 36, 30 quoting Gervase of Canterbury *History of the Archbishops of Canterbury* trans Stevenson, J, *Church Historians of England* Vi (1858) 296. For theft of relics, by such piratical attacks, as those of St Benedict from Monte Cassino by the monks of Fleury, St Benoît-sur-Loire, c700 see Geary, P J, *Furta Sacra* (1990)

61 Sims-Williams (1990) see note 2, 87-8; Mayr-Harting, H *The Coming of Christianity to Anglo-Saxon England* (1972) 131

62 Barrow, see note 51, xxvi-xxvii, note 10

63 BL Add MS 34633 f208v; Finberg (1972) see note 1, 138 (no 404), 201-11, 220-4. For Hemma see p 46. Anglo-Saxon Chronicle 'C' sa 1046; *Florence of Worcester's Chronicle* sa 1049; Thorn, F & C, *Domesday Book: Herefordshire* (1983) 1:14

64 James, M R, see note 52, 218-20, 244; Wright, C E, *The Cultivation of Saga in Anglo-Saxon England* (1939) 96-105

65 BL Harley MS 4040 f1-20; Duncomb, J, *Collections towards the History and Antiquities of the County of Hereford* 1 (1804) 583-4 provides a more detailed account than Price, J *Historical Account of the City of Hereford* (1796, repr 1971) 135-6. For the chapter house and Stukeley's drawing of 1721 see N Drinkwater, 'Hereford Cathedral: The Chapter House' *Archaeol J* 112 (1955) 61-75

66 Gelling see note 2, 97-8, fig 40; Bassett, S, 'Church and Diocese in the West Midlands; the transition from British to Anglo-Saxon control' in *Pastoral Care before*

the Parish, ed Blair, J & Sharpe, S R (1992) 35-7

67 Coplestone-Crow see note 23 11, map 4

68 Davies, W, *Wales in the Early Middle Ages* (1982) 93-102; idem *An Early Welsh Microcosm: Studies in the Llandaff Charters* (1978) 80, 88, 93-5 and idem (1979) see note 23, 76 but Sims-Williams (1990) see note 2, takes a different view of the evidence of the Llandaff charters; Finberg, H P R *Lucerna* (1964) 69-73; *Felix's Life of St Guthlac* ed Colgrave, B (1956) 1-2, 108-10, 185-6

69 Thorn, see note 63, 2:1-58; 32 of the church of Hereford's 300 hides were omitted by its men

70 Pretty, K, 'The Welsh Border and the Severn and Avon Valleys in the 5th and 6th Centuries AD: An Archaeological Survey', unpub Cambridge Ph D thesis (1975); idem, 'Defining the Magonsaete' in *The Origins of the Anglo-Saxon Kingdoms* ed Bassett, S (1989) 174-5

71 Shoesmith, R, *Hereford City Excavations I: Castle Green* CBA Research Report 36 (1980) 1-5, 52; Pearn A M, 'The Origin and Development of Urban Churches and Parishes: A Comparative Study of Hereford, Shrewsbury and Chester', unpub Camb Ph D thesis (1989) 125-6. On p124 the one early burial is considered 'not sufficient evidence on which to base the chronology of ecclesiastical provision in Hereford'. Robert Foliot's notification in the St Guthlac's cartulary (Oxford Balliol College MS 271 f112v), in which St Guthlac's is described as a mother church with deaneries, prebends, dignities and parishes, is spurious; Barrow, see note 51, 107-9

72 Thacker, A T, 'Chester and Gloucester: Early Ecclesiastical Organisation in Two Mercian Burhs' *Northern Hist* 18 (1982) 199-211; idem 'Anglo-Saxon Cheshire' in *VCH Cheshire* I (1987) 237-85; Heighway, see note 4, 3-12, 33-6; Bassett, S, 'Anglo-Saxon Shrewsbury and its Churches' in *Midland Hist* 16 (1991) 9-11, 18-19; Shoesmith, see note 71, II, 72-80

73 Bede *Historia Abbatum* ed Plummer, C (1896) 368-70

74 Quentin, H *Les martyrologes historiques du moyen âge* (Paris 1908)

75 *Reg Swinfield* 124-5; Hillaby (1987) see note 2, 625-8

76 Hillaby, J, 'St Oswald, the Revival of Monasticism and the Veneration of the Saints in the Late Anglo-Saxon and Norman Diocese of Worcester' *Trans Worcs Archaeol Soc* 3S 16 (1998) 96-109

77 *Epistle to bishop Egbert* c 7 & 8 in *EHD* I, 735-45

78 BL Cotton MS Domitian A iii f115r (not printed by Kemp) & ff56v-64r in *Reading Abbey Cartularies* I ed Kemp, B R Camden Soc 4S 31 (1986) 289-93

79 BL MSS Egerton 3031 ff54v-55r & Cotton Vespasian Exxv f59v; Kemp (1986) see note 78, I, 287-8; idem, 'Some Aspects of the Parochia of Leominster in the 12th Century' in *Minsters and Parish Churches: The Local Church in Transition, 950-1200* ed Blair, J, CBA Monograph 17 (1988) 83-95

80 Greaves, C S & Warner, J Lee, 'Charter of Cuthwulf, Bishop of Hereford (AD 840)' *Archaeol J* 30 (1873) 174-80; for photograph and translation of Cuthwulf's charter Hillaby J & Pearson E, *Bromyard: A Local History* (1970) plate I and Williams, P, *Bromyard: Minster, Manor amd Town* (1987) plate I; Taylor, H M & J, *Anglo-Saxon Architecture* II (1965) 716

81 The Hazle was assessed separately at one hide

82 For the Leominster evidence see Kemp (1988) see note 78, 83-95. The overall process is described in Blair, J 'From Minster to Parish Church' in Blair (1988) see note 79 and idem, 'Secular Minster Churches in Domesday Book' in *Domesday Book: A Reassessment* ed P H Sawyer (1985) 104-42 especially map p108 and idem, 'Minster Churches in the Landscape' in *Anglo-Saxon Settlements* ed Hooke, D (1988) 35-58

83 For area see *Census Tables* (1841, 1851)

84 Winnington-Ingram, A J, 'The Constitution of the Church of Ledbury' *TWNFC* (1942), 70

85 For the Bromyard portionists and their portions see Williams, P (1987) see note 80, 19-25, maps 2 & 3; *Reg Cantilupe* lxix, 135, 141, 184, 188, 192, 208, 247, 248; *Reg Trillek* 40-1; *Reg Gilbert* 60-1; *Register of Renn Dickson Hampden* (1848-68) 5 Aug 1856

86 *Reg Cantilupe* 125-6; *Reg Swinfield* 464-7

87 *Reg Gilbert* 60-1; HD & CA 2342

88 *Reg Cantilupe* 107-8, 208

89 HD & CA 2342

90 Williams, P, (1987) see note 80, 19-27; *Reg Trefnant* 180; *Reg Orleton* 385; *Reg Trillek* 379; *Liber Regis* ed Bacon, J (1786) 356-60. The parishes of Collington Magna and Parva were united in 1352, 'so much has the plague reduced the people and impoverished the land', *Reg Trillek* 174-6. The parish of Little Cowarne was annexed to Ullingswick in 1478, *Reg Mylling* 39 and Hopkinson, J, *Little Cowarne* (1983) 26-8. Before the end of the 19th century all five chapelries with Wacton had become parishes.

91 BL Cotton Vespasian Bxxiv f39v; S85; Finberg (1972) see note 1, no 406. S83 which purports to be a grant by Aethelbald of Acton to Evesham in 716 is clearly spurious.

92 Kendrick, T D, *Anglo-Saxon Art to AD 900* (1938) 105; Cramp, R, 'Schools of Mercian Sculpture' in *Mercian Studies* ed Dornier, A (1977) 225-30; Twiddle D, in *The Making of England: Anglo-Saxon Art and Culture, AD 600-900* ed Webster, L & Backhouse, J (1991) 244-5

93 Bryant, R, 'The Cross Shafts' in *The Golden Minster: The Anglo-Saxon Minster and later Medieval Priory of St Oswald at Gloucester* ed Heighway, C, & Bryant, R, CBA Research Report 117 (1999) 154-64; Cramp (1977) see note 93, 225, fig 61a; Cramp (1984) see notes 50, 28, 40; Gelling, M, *Early Charters of the Thames Valley* (1979) no 264; S731; Bassett, S, 'The Administrative Landscape of the Diocese of Worcester in the Tenth Century' in *St Oswald of Worcester* ed Brooks, N & Cubitt, E (1966) 169-72

94 *The Evesham Chronicle* ed Macray, W N, RS 29 (1863) 95, 97; *Heming: Cartulary of Worcester* ed Hearne, T (1723) 249-51; S1479; Thorn, F & C *Domesday Book: Worcestershire* (1982) 11.1; VCH *Worcestershire* I (1901) 253, 308 n2

95 S786. The earliest form, without the bounds, is BL Cotton MS Augustus ii, 6 of the second half of the tenth century. Copy in Bond, E A, *Facsimiles of Ancient Charters in the British Museum* (1873) III pl 30. It is BL Cotton Tiberius A xiii f163v-64, of the second half of the 11th century, which gives the bounds of Acton. On the authenticity Keynes, S, *The Diplomas of King Aethelred 'the Unready' 978-1016* (1890) 98-102 but also see Hillaby (1998) note 76, 92 and in *Bishop Aethelwold: His Career and Influence* ed Yorke, B (1988) Wormald, P 'Comments on the Comparable Abingdon and other Charters' 38, 40, 53-4

96 Houghton, F T S, 'Salt Ways', *Birmingham Archaeol Soc Trans* 54 (1929-30) 1-10, 15, plate IV

97 Grundy, G B, 'Saxon Charters of Worcestershire, I' *Birmingham Archaeol Soc Trans* 52 (1927) 8; C W M Pratt's reconsideration of the charter bounds was published in *TWNFC* 49 (i) in January this year; Hughes, K, 'Evidence for Contacts between the Churches of the Irish and English from the Synod of Whitby to the Viking Age' in *England before the Conquest* ed Clemoes P & Hughes, K (1971) 49-67; idem 'Some Aspects of Irish Influence on Early English Private Prayer' *Studia Celtica* 5 (1970) 48-61; Campbell, J, 'The Debt of the Early English Church to Ireland' in *Ireland and Christendom* ed Ní Chatháin, P & Richter, M (Stuttgart 1987) 332-46

98 Bodleian Dugdale MS 12 p505; S1838

99 For the events of 873-4 Hillaby (2000) see note 42, 125-48

100 The first impression of one-inch Ordnance Survey (1831) and Bryant, A, *Map of the County of Hereford* (1823-35) give parochial bounds prior to the amalgamation of Bredenbury with Wacton as a single parish and the subsequent incorporation of the five detached parts of Avenbury into that

parish by an order under the Divided Parishes Act in March 1884. For the manorial history and Bredenbury chapel, Weale, J, *A History of Bredenbury and its Landed Estates* (1997) and Williams, P, *Avenbury and the Ruined Church of St Mary* (2000) especially maps 1,8 & 9

101 See 'The Church of St Mary's: Final Days' in Williams (2000) see note 99, 267-82 with illustrations recording the church from 1840-50 to 1931 and subsequently in various stages of decay

102 *Reg Swinfield* 544; Dickinson, J C & Ricketts, P T, 'The Anglo-Norman Chronicle of Wigmore Abbey' *TWNFC* 39(iii) (1969) 422-6. The chronicle points out that prior to the building of Shobdon church, Oliver de Merlimond freed the wooden chapel of St Juliana from the jurisdiction of Aymestrey by a similar pension of 2s. *Reg Bothe* 199; *Reg Thomas Charlton* 81; *Reg Lewis Charleton* 5; *Reg Myllyng* 189

103 *National Index of Parish Registers* 5, comp Steel, D J (1971) 75, 86, 88; *The Registers of Ledbury: Baptisms, Marriages and Burials 1556-76* Pt 1, transcribed Piper, G H, ed Mayo, C H, Parish Reg Soc (1899); *Parish Registers of Herefordshire* ed Harnden, J (1987). For 'rectors' *Reg Cantilupe* 152, 157, 302; *Reg Swinfield* 85; *Reg Orleton* 392; *Reg Trefnant* 180, 182, 189, 190. For institutions *Reg Cantilupe* 185; *Reg Lewis Charleton* 68; *Reg Thomas Charlton* 81. For free chapel *Reg Foxe* 376, 367. 'Aylton Church' *TWNFC* 36(i) (1958) 55. For the *parochia's* relationship to that of Stoke Lacy see King, J W, 'Two Herefordshire Minsters' *TWNFC* 48(ii) (1995) 283-7

104 Williams, P, 'Borough and Town' in Hillaby and Pearson, see note 80, 36-50; Hillaby, J, *Ledbury: A Medieval Borough* (1997) 1-52

4   Echoes from the Stones

JOHN HARPER

Just one surviving piece of medieval music may perhaps have been written at Leominster. It is a work of considerable international fame for its polyphonic complexity, a landmark in Western musical history, and one that is still fresh and accessible to modern listeners. David Wulstan's recent study[1] observes that 'Sumer is icumen in'/ 'Perspice Christicola' may be linked to Leominster Priory through its likely composer, William of Winchester, a monk of Reading Abbey, Leominster's mother-house. Leominster, a small priory of no more than twelve monks, was clearly a place to send the troublesome brothers of the mother-house. William of Winchester was rusticated from the community at Reading, and even in Leominster there is evidence that he continued to misbehave: charged with 'incontinency' in 1281, he failed to appear before the Bishop of Hereford, and was summarily excommunicated.

The English text of the Sumer Canon will not have been heard in church in the Middle Ages. But there is a possibility that the Latin text 'Perspice Christicola' for Easter, which appears below the English in the original manuscript, could have been sung in the Priory. Though not liturgical, an Easter procession or other occasion might have offered the opportunity for its use in church. Or it may simply have been sung in the monastery. At about this same time, the liturgical laxity among the monks was censured by the Archbishop of Canterbury, John Pecham, a Franciscan with a zeal for reform. (See colour plate 1)

Apart from 'Sumer is icumen in' there is scant evidence of the liturgical or musical practices of Leominster Priory between the Conquest and the Dissolution of the Monasteries. It is possible to posit the general nature of the daily services, plainsong and ceremonial from the extant manuscripts and archives of other Benedictine houses in Britain and on the Continent. But there are anomalies at Leominster which suggest that straightforward reconstruction of a Benedictine pattern is not appropriate. Our best evidence is the partially surviving medieval church, and this paper sets out a preliminary reading of the building from a liturgical and musical point of view. Is it possible to draw out 'echoes from the stones' which enable us to have a better idea of the use of the church before the Dissolution and the Reformation? Might others be able to take this tentative thesis further?[2]

Walking into the Priory Church at Leominster, one is immediately struck by its scale and its distinctiveness. Approaching from the town, its size and grandeur are immediately apparent, but nothing is exceptionally untoward. From the west it appears to be a medieval church with a substantial nave and two large aisles; only the north-west tower seems unusual in its position. On entering, one gains a different impression. The south aisle and nave have a spaciousness not unlike one of the 'hall' churches of the fifteenth century (eg St Margaret, King's Lynn or St Thomas, Salisbury). But the north aisle is far more substantial than the western facade suggests. The large Norman pillars at the lower floor level, and the whole scale of this aisle confirm that it is the nave of an earlier church.

The later history of Leominster church means that it is harder to read as a building than many others of similar scale and age. Apart from recent liturgical reordering, which has brought the nave altar to a central position between the people's chairs and the choir stalls, there is far more fundamental restructuring. Two principal phases of alteration have distorted the appearance and balance of the church as it was known between the mid fourteenth and the earlier sixteenth centuries.

The more recent phase of alteration was occasioned by the great fire of 1699 which had greatest effect in the nave and south aisle. The wall and the arcade between the nave and aisle were rebuilt in the earlier eighteenth century. However, that rebuilding was not the last. A far more ambitious programme of restoration took place between 1862 and 1884 under the guidance of the architect, George Gilbert Scott. Scott had a major impact on the present appearance of both the nave and the south aisle. The early eighteenth century arcade was taken down and replaced by the slender pillars and austere arches that now stand there. The eastern wall of the nave was pierced with a window which matches the great windows of the south aisle, and a more modest window added at the east end of the south aisle.

The earlier phase of alteration took place at the time of the dissolution of the Priory in 1539. The eastern transepts, presbytery and Lady Chapel were all taken down, and a substantial wall placed at the eastern end of the nave. Sitting in the present nave it is hard to reconstruct the architectural form of the earlier church which at that time was some 50 per cent larger. The church which already dominates the surrounding space, must have been so much more imposing at that time, standing aloof from the town in 30 acres of monastic precinct.

What are no longer visible in the church are the Saxon minster and the succeeding late Saxon monasteries which occupied the same site. And, on the face of it, the early minster and the subsequent monastic foundations, which were eventually dissolved in 1046, have little or no connection with the Benedictine monastery founded from Reading under the patronage of Henry I in 1123. The new twelfth century church was a thorough-going Norman building whose eastern apse, with three radial chapels, ambulatory around the choir, transepts (each with an apsidal chapel) and nave were typical of other monastic churches of the time (including not only Reading Abbey but also St Augustine's Canterbury, Battle Abbey and a number of churches in Norman France). The area for monastic worship is clearly delineated by the outline of the inner wall of the ambulatory and the western pulpitum, whose stairway is still visible in the north east corner of the later nave (Fig 16). West of the pulpitum, the nave and two narrow aisles afforded space for at least one parish altar and probably several others.

The pattern of worship must have been typical of many modest Benedictine houses which afforded space for parish worship within the monastic church. East of the pulpitum the small number of monks (perhaps reinforced by a few novices and boys in the monastic school) would have sung the daily office laid down by St Benedict (seven services in the day, and the night office of Matins), together with the liturgical accretions which were a typical part of Benedictine worship by this time, as well as at least two conventual masses. The monks would also have celebrated their own individual mass at the altars in the transepts and eastern chapels. In the nave or aisles the parish services would have followed the Use of the Diocese of Hereford, a local variant of the Western Latin Rite. This is principally distinguished from monastic liturgy by the forms of some of the services (eg Matins), the number and ordering of the psalms, and possibly by some variants of calendar. Only at the greatest feasts (eg Christmas, Holy Week, Easter and Pentecost) when the monks followed 'mores canonicorum' (ie the use of the secular canons) would the liturgies west and east of the pulpitum have coincided. Musically the focus would have been in the monastic choir, and the repertory that of Latin plainsong.

Less than a hundred years after the completion of the Norman church, the first phase of rebuilding was taking place. There are four matters of note here. First, the new building was not within the main monastic church. As a rule, where churches were enlarged or improved this began at the east end. The Benedictine monasteries of Worcester, Gloucester and Tewkesbury are examples of this process. At Worcester the rebuilding reached almost to the far west of the nave; at Gloucester and Tewkesbury the Norman nave remains. Here at Leominster it is

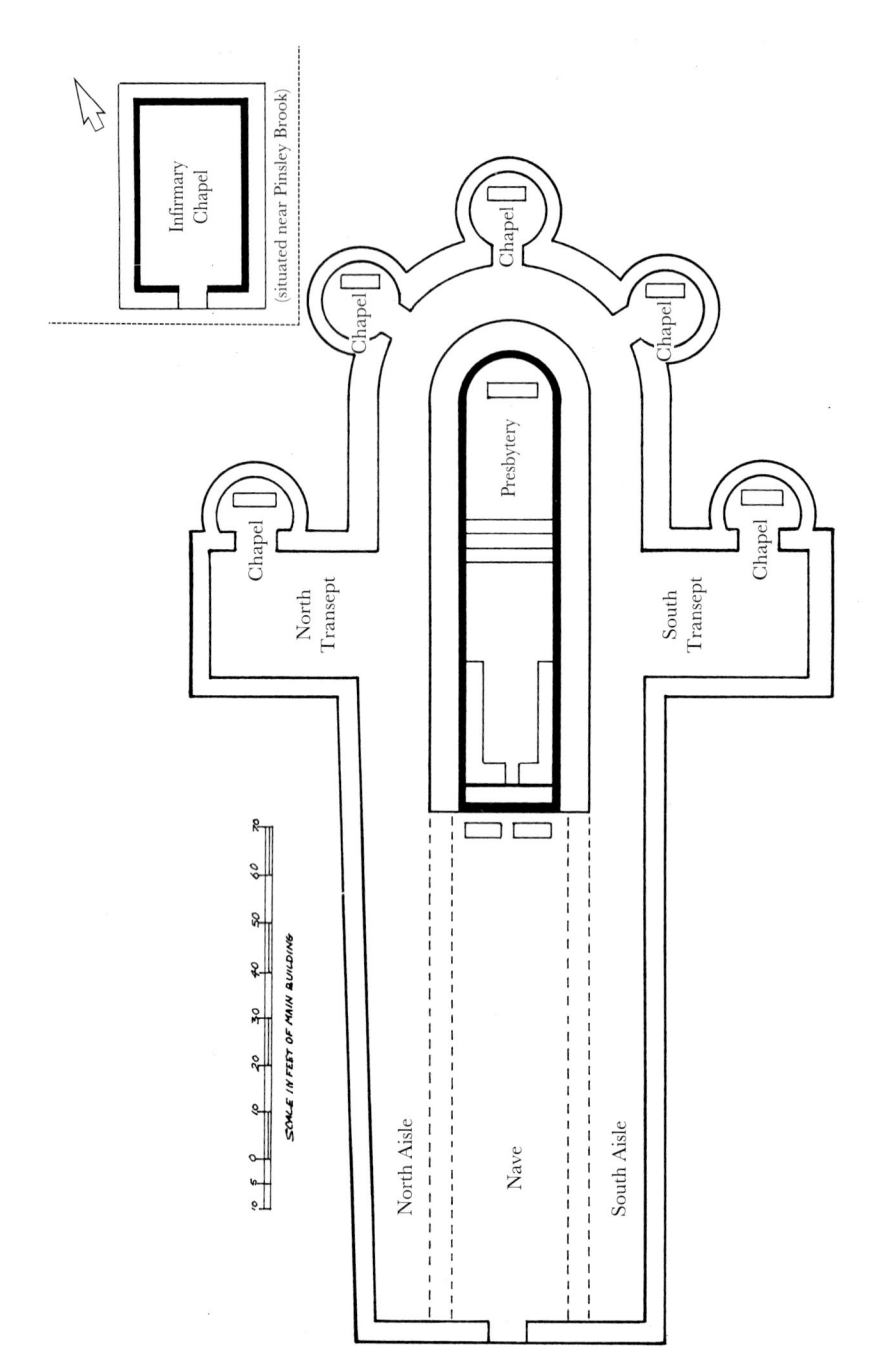

Fig 16 Diagrammatic plan of Leominster Priory Church, as it may have been c 1150, showing the location of the monastic choir, the principal space for worship. Other services would have taken place in the nave or aisles (for parish worship), the side chapels (private masses), and the infirmary chapel.

the south aisle of the original Norman nave which is rebuilt. The second feature is the scale of that rebuilding. The provision of a south aisle for parish worship can be found at a number of monasteries in Britain, including Dorchester and Minster (and both were also minsters before the Conquest), but in no other case is the scale of rebuilding quite so spectacular as at Leominster. The Norman south aisle has been transformed into a lofty thirteenth century nave, which outstrips the monastic nave in both height and volume. The third matter for note is the question of funding. Although the income from the monastic lands and holdings at Leominster was substantial (at the time of the *Valor Ecclesiasticus* it was almost £600 per annum net, not so much less than the cathedral at Hereford, and substantially more than a number of independent abbeys) much of that income was due to the mother house at Reading. The Priory at Leominster was left with less than 20 per cent of its income, a sum of little more than £100 per annum. Indeed, there were times when the monastery came close to bankruptcy and was in severe financial straits. If there were relatively modest funds to support the monastery, let alone such a substantial development, who provided the funds for such an ambitious development in the south aisle? In another town or city one might look to the townspeople or local lord for the source of benefaction. But at Leominster, the town was a monastic borough and both the rents and the management of the town were in the hands of the Priory.

The fourth point is the most speculative. Notwithstanding the question of funding, the scale of the new thirteenth century nave suggests that it was intended for something far more elaborate than parish services. A G Edouart, the vicar who oversaw the nineteenth century reconstruction and restoration, notes in his history of the church that before the fire of 1699 there had been carved stalls in this nave.[3] It is not clear whether they had been moved at the Reformation, or whether they had been made for that part of the church. If the latter, it suggests that a body of priests observed a pattern of communal observance of the daily mass and office there in the manner of a collegiate church.

If this perhaps explains the scale of the new thirteenth century nave, who might have staffed this 'collegiate' establishment? Later in the Middle Ages it is quite common to find that priests funded from chantries and other bequests were grouped together to form an informal 'college' of priests who celebrated the office and mass together in choir. Often these informal foundations attained a high standard of liturgy with elaborate music, and by the early sixteenth century there was an element of competition between one large parish church and another. At Leominster we know that there were three chaplains attached to the vicarage of Holy Cross. The vicar served in the *parochia*, but the chaplains served

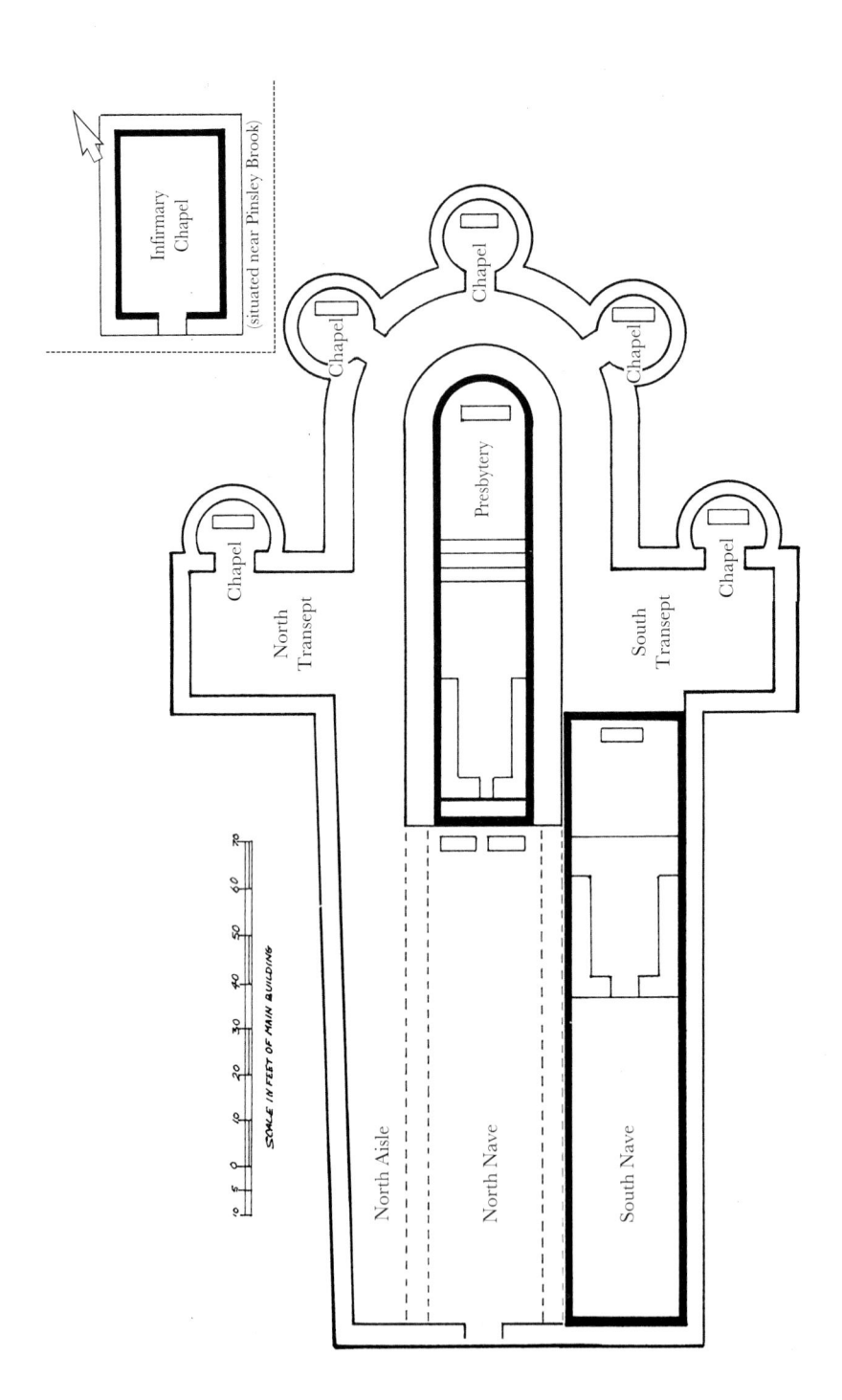

Fig 17 Diagrammatic plan of Leominster Priory Church, as it may have been c 1250, showing the new South Nave, an additional space for worship, perhaps conducted by secular priests.

in the Priory Church. A later reference from the fourteenth century also refers to the repairs of Holy Cross aisle in the church. These three chaplains may perhaps have formed the nucleus of a quasi-collegiate body. Might William of Winchester have written his canon to be sung by the secular priests, who may perhaps have been more skilled than his monastic colleagues? Certainly the chaplains in other foundations were often skilled in both chant and simple improvised polyphony.

In the later thirteenth century a series of visitations recorded in the correspondence of Archbishop John Pecham establish that all was not well at Leominster.[4] The parishioners complain that they are unable to enter their church, and the bishop complains that the monks are failing to observe the monastic services. The immediate outcome was the building of the chapel of St Thomas à Becket in the Forbury on the edge of the monastic precinct. Were the parishioners unable to use the church because of lack of access (certainly the building of a chapel at the entrance to the precinct may suggest this), or because the parish services were displaced by other liturgies in the great church? Did the small number of monks abandon their monastic services because they were joining with the secular chaplains in the new south nave to sing the secular office with them? Certainly their small numbers may have encouraged them so to do. At Hereford, the chaplains and the members of the Lady Chapel choir joined with the vicars choral at least on Sundays and feast days. At Durham, the sixteenth century Rites of Durham record that the organist of the Lady Chapel choir joined the monks to strengthen their singing. Further research will be necessary to establish whether the reading of the building accords with actual practice.

A century after the building of the second nave, a further phase of new building took place. This consisted of two distinct projects. For the first time the monastic church was deveoped. At the far east end of the apse, a rectangular Lady Chapel was built early in the fourteenth century, a building which accords in date, proportion and scale to the Lady Chapel built at Reading Abbey. The cult of the Virgin Mary grew during the later Middle Ages, and the provision of Lady Chapels in monastic, cathedral, collegiate and parish churches is typical of the time. The new Lady Chapel at Hereford had been built in the thirteenth century, but the foundation (which operated as a separate institution within the cathedral with its own warden and funding) was enlarged in the fourteenth century. At Worcester, a second Lady Chapel was established in the western part of the cathedral priory church.

In addition to the Lady Chapel there was further development in the south west of the church. Alongside the new nave was built a lofty south aisle with

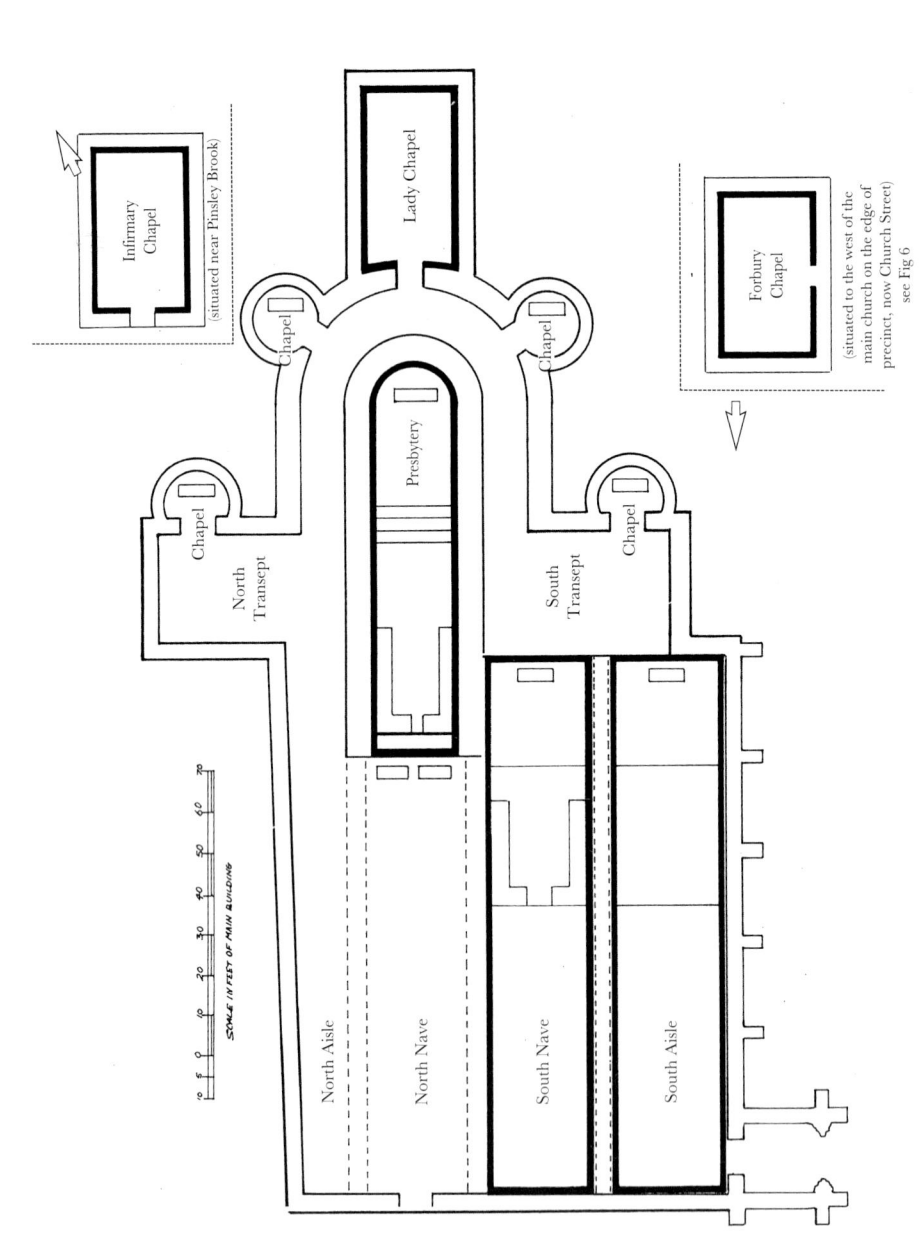

Fig 18 Diagrammatic plan of Leominster Priory Church, as it may have been c 1350, showing the new Lady Chapel (for the monastic community), South Aisle (perhaps staffed by secular priests), and Forbury Chapel (for the parish), all additional spaces for worship.

magnificent Decorated windows, large and ornate. The scale of the building, the quality of the windows, and the provision of carved stone sedilia in the sanctuary suggest that this was intended again for liturgy of some substance and elaboration. It does not suggest a church of convenience for the parish. We may ask whether this represented a 'secular' Lady Chapel for the chaplains and their patrons, or else a place of other devotions. Although the dedications of some of the altars in the church are known, it is not clear where some were sited, nor are all of them necessarily accounted for. At a time of increasing devotional fervour, such development is not untypical.

No further building work took place to enlarge the church at Leominster. However, the thirteenth century nave was provided with a spectacular new window in the fifteenth century, emphasising once again that this was the focal part of the church, and furthermore that light was important. (The eastern wall of both nave and south aisle abutted the south transept of the monastic church, and was therefore solid.)

The implication of the building is that by the mid fourteenth century there were at least five areas where liturgical celebration might take place: the monastic Lady Chapel, the monastic presbytery, the original monastic nave, the new nave, and the south aisle. To these may be added the extant parish Forbury Chapel and the monastic infirmary chapel which still survives in part in the range near the Pinsley Brook. In addition there were the small apse and transept chapels for 'private' masses and chantry observances, and other altars including 'St Antony's aisle' in the north aisle of the monastic nave. Our modern expectation is that one service takes place in a church at any one time. However, plurality of celebration was common in the medieval church, and we know that these services sometimes caused disturbance. At Hereford the chapter forbade the celebration of parish services west of the pulpitum at St John's altar because of the disturbance it caused during services in choir.

Leominster is a remarkable and unique church. The substantial development on the south side of the monastic nave suggests that there was considerable additional non-monastic worship. At other former minster churches there is some evidence that the development of the south aisle for parish use was a feature. Such an arrangement has already been observed at Dorchester and at Minster, both Benedictine monasteries. This raises the question of the continuing influence of the minster pattern in the later Middle Ages. John Blair has shown that at least one minster survived in an unreformed state at Bampton in Oxfordshire,[5] and that less overt influences persisted elsewhere in spite of the Norman dismantling of the old *parochia* with the establishment of the feudal parish model which followed Domesday.

Nowhere is the development of the non-monastic nave so marked as at Leominster. In many Benedictine centres the parish church was built at the edge of the precinct (as at Ely, at Reading, and in due course at Leominster). In large cities there were far more independent parish structure. In Norwich, for instance, the large church of St Peter Mancroft and numerous other medieval parish churches form a substantial group to vie with the cathedral priory. This suggests that there were very particular circumstances at Leominster which contributed to the development of a unique ecclesiastical configuration, where within a century the focus of the monastic church moved from the monastic choir to the new nave on the site of the monastic south aisle. While that may parallel arrangements at both Minster and Dorchester, it does not account for the scale of building, or for the further phase and elaboration of the south aisle in the fourteenth century. Given the complaints of the parish access that they were unable to have adequate access to the main church, it seems unlikely that parish use was its primary function.

Although no post-Conquest liturgical books are known to survive from Leominster, it is possible to reconstruct some of the liturgical and musical practices. The Benedictine liturgy followed a standard pattern with local variations. It is possible to go some way to reconstruct the pattern of monastic worship at Leominster from (for instance) the extant customary of Norwich, the Hyde Abbey breviary, and the antiphoner from Worcester, all of which are published. If there was a separate observance of the secular Use in the thirteenth century nave, then this would have followed the secular, diocesan Use of Hereford. The partial survivals of Hereford Use (constitutions, breviary, part of a gradual) provide some insight, and the books of Salisbury and York Use are not so extremely different as to prevent further reconstruction. In both the monastic Lady Chapel and in the fourteenth century south aisle there may have been sung services in honour of the Blessed Virgin Mary, services which elsewhere were staffed by a small and specialised choral group. The duties of such a group are described in a number of indentures of masters of the choristers of the early sixteenth century (eg Durham and Hereford), and also constitution of the refounded cathedral at Rochester after the dissolution of the monastery.

By the end of the Middle Ages we may look to the nearby churches of Ludlow and Old Radnor for further indication of liturgical practice, in addition to the cathedral at Hereford. In all of these churches we may be certain that some form of polyphonic elaboration was applied to the plainchant. By the sixteenth century, Ludlow, Old Radnor and Hereford Cathedral all had organs, and both Ludlow and Hereford had at least two. The location of the organs in

Plate 1 The Summer canon Sumer is icumen in, British Library Ms 478, f11b. By permission of the British Library. The English text is in black and the Latin sacred text is in red, set to the same melody. The cross indicates where the other parts of the round enter. The music on the two staves at the bottom (Pes: 'Sing cuccu') provides a repeating two-part accompaniment for the round. The other Latin text on the page gives performance instructions.

The Early Church in Herefordshire

Plate 2 Wheel of Life wall painting on the north wall of the nave,
St Mary's Church, Kempley, Gloucestershire.

Plate 3 Acton Beauchamp, St Giles, from the south. The Anglo-Saxon cross-shaft forms
the lintel over the doorway at the base of the tower.

Plate 4 Modern interpretation of the Wheel of Life painting (2.30m x 1.50m) in Leominster Priory Church by Arthur Davis

The Early Church in Herefordshire

Plate 5 Llanveynoe, St Beuno & St Peter, from the south east. The short-armed cross stands in the churchyard near the porch.

Plate 6 The Llanveynoe cross

Plate 7 Llangarron, St Deinst, view from the bridge over the Garren brook

Plate 8 Upton Bishop, St John the Baptist, from the south east. The sandstone frieze is set in the south wall of the chancel next to the hexagonal vestry.

Plate 9 The Upton Bishop sandstone frieze set between two other stone fragments

The Early Church in Herefordshire

the main choir and in the Lady Chapel at both Hereford and Ludlow (as elsewhere in cathedral, collegiate, monastic and larger parish churches) is typical. At Old Radnor the original sixteenth century organ case survives, as do the screens and return stalls. We have here some clues to the possible physical configuration of the nave choir in Leominster. Polyphony was sung in larger Benedictine monasteries: surviving manuscripts have provenances in Winchester (tenth century), Bury and Durham (fourteenth century), as well as the midland provenance of the 'Worcester fragments'. And, of course, David Wulstan has supported the case for the composition of the famous Reading Rota ('Sumer is icumen in'/'Perspice Christicola') at Leominster itself.

At the dissolution of the monasteries the parish must have been quite clear which area of the church was to be saved for subsequent parish use. The monastic transepts, presbytery and Lady Chapel have been demolished with thoroughness. Whereas at Pershore and Abbey Dore the parish chose to retain the eastern part of the monastic church for their use, and at Tewkesbury they retained the whole building, at Leominster they preserved the monastic nave, the new nave and the south aisle. Although one may regret the loss of the monastic presbytery and Lady Chapel, one may speculate that they were already less well cared for than the newer parts of the building, and that what survives is the part of the church which had greater importance in the later Middle Ages.

Notes and References

1. Wulstan, David, 'Sumer is icumen in' – a perpetual puzzle canon?, *Plainsong and Medieval Music*, 9/1 (2000), pp 1-18

2. This paper draws on the work of Joe Hillaby and John Blair who have also contributed to this volume, and I am grateful to them for materials and suggestions. However, this is a speculative personal esquisse, and does not therefore include scholarly citations which might give an air of certainty that could be misleading. Rather, it sets out to challenge others to seek out more of the liturgical history of Leominster Priory between the twelfth century and the Dissolution of the Monasteries.

3. Edouart, A G, *A Paper on the Priory Church of Leominster* (Leominster, 1892).

4. *Registrum Epistolarum Fratris Johannis Peckham Archiepiscopi Cantuariensis*, ed Martin, Charles Trice, (London, 1884, Rolls Series), 505-7

5. Blair, John, *The Medieval Clergy of Bampton* (Bampton Research Papers 4, Oxford, 1992)

88 THE EARLY CHURCH IN HEREFORDSHIRE

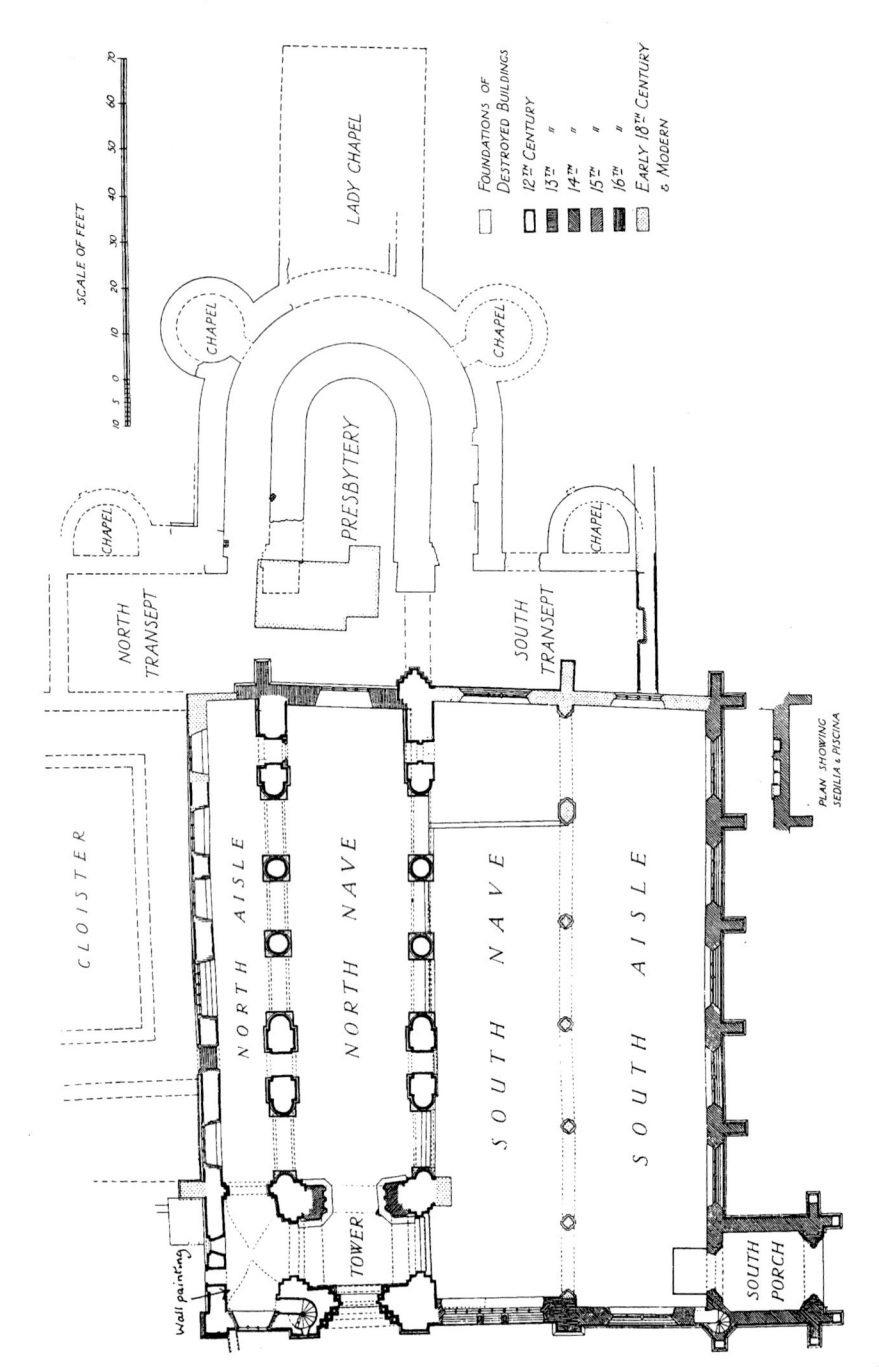

Fig 19 Plan of the Priory Church of S S Peter and Paul, Leominster
By permission of the National Documents and Records Centre, English Heritage

5 The Wheel of Life in Leominster Priory Church

ANN MALPAS

The Priory Church of St Peter and St Paul at Leominster stands on the north side of the market town. This large and impressive building is almost square in shape and comprises those parts of the church which were not pulled down when the Priory was dissolved in 1539. At that time the monastic parts of the church, ie the crossing, the transepts and the presbytery and associated chapels were all destroyed. The present day church consists of a Norman nave with a north aisle built in the twelfth century, a south nave which replaced the Norman south aisle in the early thirteenth century and a south aisle added in the fourteenth century. This accounts for the shape of the church as we see it today (Fig 19). It is in the westernmost bay of the north aisle of the north nave that the medieval wall painting is to be found.

In 1121, following the sudden death by drowning of his eldest son William, Henry I founded a new Benedictine abbey at Reading.[1] Among the endowments of the new abbey was the manor of Leominster and soon a dependent priory was established strictly under the control of the abbey.[2] This was a refounding of a religious institution at Leominster, there having been a Christian establishment there for some five hundred years previously.[3]

The building of the Priory Church began soon after 1123 and the work must have proceeded quickly as the eastern monastic parts of the church, that is the presbytery, transepts and crossing with the tower above, were consecrated by Bishop Robert de Bethune in 1130.[4] The completion of the parochial parts of the church – the nave, together with its side aisles to the north and south – followed soon after. It has been suggested that a later decision to incorporate a west tower necessitated a rebuild of the west front and this work is dated to the second half of the twelfth century.[5]

The Chapel in The North Aisle

The westernmost bay of the north aisle is now used as a choir vestry and is divided from the rest of the north aisle and from the bay under the tower by panelled screens, the upper parts being glazed and the lower parts made of wood.

The round headed arch leading from the vestry into the north aisle is dated to the twelfth century.[6] At some time in the past this arch was filled by a wall to make a separate chapel, possibly dedicated to St Anthony.[7] The groined vault of the bay is also of the twelfth century. In the west wall is a 13th century window of three lancet lights and in the north wall is a 12th century window of one round-headed light with reveals of two square orders. Further west in the north wall is a doorway with a segmental head also probably 12th century, and it is on this north wall that the large painting of the wheel of life is to be found.[8]

Wall Paintings

Today the interior of the Norman part of the church presents a somewhat grey and austere aspect. In medieval times all exposed stone surfaces were deemed unfinished and unworthy and were clothed with plaster or limewash and adorned with paintings.[9] The Gloucestershire churches of St Mary at Kempley and St James the Great at Stoke Orchard reveal how extensively churches were decorated with wall paintings.

The subject matter used in church wall painting has been described by E Clive Rouse under five main headings:

(1) purely decorative schemes including scrolls, tessellations, chevrons, roses stars etc occurring either by themselves or in association with figure subjects. The most common scheme was the masonry pattern or imitation stone joints with ornaments in the blocks themselves of scrolls, flowers and tendrils

(2) Bible stories

(3) single figures of saints, apostles, martyrs, etc

(4) scenes from the lives of the saints

(5) moralities concerned with warnings against particular sins or modes of life. This group includes such themes as the Last Judgement, the Weighing of Souls, warnings to swearers, sabbath breakers and others and the struggle between good and evil. The themes were variously represented, often using diagrammatic forms such as trees and wheels.[10]

In the north nave at Leominster, on pilasters of the south triforium of the sixth, seventh and eighth bays are the barely discernible remains of painted zigzag and diapered ornament dated to the late twelfth century.[11]

In the west bay of the north aisle, much more wall painting survives. On the north wall is the wheel of life painting and there is also decorative painting in other parts of the chapel. The large wheel of life painting is dated to the late thirteenth century, c1275.[12] It is difficult to see properly because of the light from the window in the west wall; also the bay is closed off from the nave by a screen. The painting may have suffered some damage during the Priory Church restoration works of 1863 and it is also possible that not all the whitewash has been cleaned off (Fig 20).

Fig 20 Existing wall painting of the Wheel of Life, Leominster Priory Church

Discovery of the Wall Painting

At the Reformation all church wall paintings were obliterated by covering the walls with coats of limewash. In 1852 A E Freeman visited the Priory Church at Leominster with the Cambrian Archaeological Association. He found that much of the Norman part of the church was in a poor state and the western bay of the north aisle was at that time used as a coal hole.[13] He did, however, note considerable traces of mural paintings on the west face of the wall dividing this bay from the north aisle.

In 1862 when the Revd Augustin Gaspard Edouart came to the living at Leominster the restoration of the church was put in hand under the direction of George Gilbert Scott. During the work the ceilings and walls were cleaned of the coats of plaster and whitewash covering them. When the restoration of the

Norman part of the church was complete the *Hereford Times* carried a long report on the completed work. The following extract describes the work at the west end of the north aisle:

> Whilst the work of restoration was being executed in the chapel, specimens of ancient fresco painting were found on the walls and ceiling. These have been carefully preserved, in the hope that the whole of the chapel may be some day restored to its original beauty. At the commencement of the work, and while the walls and stonework were being denuded of their thick coatings of whitewash, they were found to be generally covered with painting of this description, but from carelessness, or some other cause, it was nearly, if not quite all destroyed. Unfortunately there was no one to superintend the work in its earlier stages; but when it was found that these interesting features were being destroyed, Mr. Scott then applied to Mr. Chick, of Hereford, under whose able supervision the work was continued, and brought to a successful termination.
>
> *Hereford Times* 7th July 1866

The Wheel of Life

Descriptions of the Leominster wall painting have been made by The Royal Commission on Historical Monuments of England[14]; by Professor E W Tristram[15] and by G McN Rushforth, MA FSA in a paper presented to the Society of Antiquaries in 1914.[16] This paper was accompanied by a reproduction made by C J Praetorius of what could be discerned of the painting at that time (Fig 21). Detailed examination of the original wall painting is not easy but the features described in the above articles can mostly just about be discerned.

The wheel is portrayed as a large circle which is seven feet in diameter. Inside the wheel are ten smaller discs each 19 inches in diameter and each connected by a spoke to a central disc. The rim of the wheel contains lettering in Lombardic capitals much of which is fragmentary. In at least one place the lettering is placed in a horizontal band meeting the rim and continuing around the outside of the rim for a short way. There is also similar lettering curving around the outside of the central medallion. Several of the illustrations in the medallions are indistinct and others are fragmentary. The wheel is set against a background of imitation masonry, each stone being ornamented with a scroll ending in a flower or a bud. To the left of the lower part of the wheel is a seated figure – King David – wearing a crown and playing a harp. There also seem to be traces of a figure or figures above the top of the wheel. Further decorative painting is visible elsewhere in the bay.

Fig 21 Reproduction of the Wheel of Life painting by C J Praetorius 1914
By permission of the Society of Antiquaries of London

Another example of a wheel of life wall painting can be seen on the north wall of the nave of the church of St Mary at Kempley in Gloucestershire (Colour plate 2). This wheel also has ten spokes radiating from a central hub, each ending in a medallion and all enclosed in a rim. Little further detail can be made out. The wall on which the wheel is painted is dated to the early 12th century.[17]

There is an early 14th century manuscript version of a wheel of life in a Psalter which belonged to Robert De Lisle.[18] The general arrangement of the component parts of the illustration in the Psalter are much the same as those at Leominster but the inscriptions in the Psalter encircle the scenes instead of being placed on the corresponding part of the rim of the wheel as at Leominster. The Psalter version also lacks a rim to the wheel. The ten outer medallions contain illustrations of the ten stages of life and the central medallion shows a representation of the head of God also circumscribed by a Latin verse. The four corners of the design outside the wheel are occupied by four figures representing the four main ages of life. In the lower left corner a boy in a grey tunic is seated on the ground and points to a scroll on which the word *Infantia* is inscribed. In the upper left corner is a king pointing to a scroll with *Iuventus*, the prime of life. Opposite to him on the right is an old man *Senectus*; and below him is *Decrepitus* a man reclining with his head supported by his left hand.

The similarities between the Latin verses and illustrations in the Psalter and the fragmentary remains of those at Leominster are such as to allow the former to be used in a possible interpretation of the latter.[19] Arthur Davis has painted a modern interpretation of the Leominster Wheel using these sources (Colour plate 4) and incorporating images and verses from the Psalter where these are unreadable in the Leominster wall painting. In each part of the following discussion reference is first made to the complete version as portrayed in the Davis painting, and the Praetorius reproduction of 1914 is taken as the representation of what can be seen of the original painting.

The centre of the wheel portrays the Godhead: the centre of the ordered life of the universe

Cuncta simul cerno : totum racione guberno

I perceive all at once : I govern the whole by reason

The image in the medallion is that of the head of God or head of Christ with a nimbus or halo and this scene is taken from the Psalter. Praetorius describes the image as a bust with a nimbus and describes traces of long hair belonging to the head but further detail of the image was not discernible. The inscription is placed outside the medallion between the spokes. Praetorius could only make out the last part of the verse . . . tum racione guberno and noted that the last syllable was placed above the line of lettering possibly for reasons of symmetry if the verse began in the corresponding space on the left where no traces could be discerned.

Peripheral Medallions

The images are read in a clockwise direction beginning with the one at the bottom on the left hand side.

(1) Infancy: a woman with a child in a cradle

Mitis sum et humilis : lacte vivo puro

I am meek and humble : I live on pure milk

The Psalter shows a woman seated with a child on her knee, before a fire over which is a pot with the handle of a ladle protruding from it. This perhaps suggests that the pot contains something more than hot water. Praetorius and Rushforth suggest a woman with her child in bed and Tristram suggests a woman holding a baby. Praetorius shows only the end of the inscription as . . . *ivo puro*.

(2) Boyhood: a boy pointing to a pair of scales which he is holding
Numquam ero labilis : etatem mensuro
I shall never stumble : I measure my age

Curiously scenes two and three in the Psalter have been transposed but not the Latin verse. This is clear because the Latin lines are in rhyming couplets. No traces of the scenes were recorded by Praetorius and so the modern painting follows the order of the verses and uses the images from the Psalter. Praetorius shows only the first letters of the text *Num*. . . . the rest is missing.

The scales to which the boy is pointing are suggested to refer to both his occupation and his character. Rushforth suggests that as an apprentice, 'he has to weigh the quantities of his master's goods and at the same time, symbolically, he begins to estimate the value and contents of life.'[20] This is the beginning of the age of self-consciousness and the boy becomes aware that he is growing up and must make the most of each stage of life if he is not to make mistakes.

(3) Adolescence: A youth combing his hair before a mirror which he is holding.
Vita decens seculi : speculo probatur
A life worthy of the world is tested by the mirror

The scene and the inscription are taken from the Psalter. Praetorius shows the first word of the inscription as missing and the next as . . . *nitens*, a variant used in connexion with dress and personal appearance.[21] The rest of the text is as in the Psalter. This is the age of puberty; the age of taking an interest in one's personal appearance, and the mirror is used for assurance that the image is presentable.

(4) Manhood: a young man on a horse with a hawk on his wrist
Iam non visus specie : vita me letatur
Now real life not its outward appearance gives me joy

The image is taken from the Psalter as none is intelligible in Praetorius. The text is placed outside the rim of the wheel starting as a horizontal band and then following the outer rim of the wheel. As Rushforth points out, there is not sufficient room for all of the Latin texts to be placed around the circumference of the wheel. If at least two texts are treated as described then all of the texts can be placed close to the images to which they refer and this seems to be the solution adopted at Leominster. The text in the Psalter reads *Non ymago speculi sed vita letatur*. (Not the image in the mirror but life itself pleases me). At Leominster the inscription is different and Praetorius deciphers the following *Iam . . . sus specie: vita me letatur* which Rushforth suggests should read *Iam non visus specie vita me letatur* (No longer does mere appearance please me by its comeliness, but real life). An alternative reading could be *Iam decursus specie* . . . (Life which is a rejection of superficiality gives me joy).[22]

(5) The prime of life: a king seated on a throne holding a crown and sceptre
Rex sum regens seculum: mundus meus totus
I am king I rule this age : the whole world is mine

Praetorius shows an image resembling that in the Psalter. The inscription in the Psalter reads *Rex sum rego seculum; mundus meus totus*. Praetorius gives *Re . . . regens seculum mundus . . .* the rest of the verse was missing.

(6) An older man in a long robe with a hood and holding a staff
Sumo michi baculum : morti fere notus
I take up a staff : I am aware death is approaching

Praetorius shows no traces of the image and the inscription is placed in the rim of the wheel and not outside it as might be expected on grounds of symmetry from the position of inscription number four. He also shows the fragmentary remaining lettering as an *m* and . . . *culum*, giving the same inscription as in the Psalter. The image shows the man looking to the right, perhaps looking back over his life as he becomes conscious of the approach of old age. The word 'baculum' can be translated as a prophet's staff, or a walking stick or a schoolmaster's baton.[23]

(7) An aged man leaning on a stick with his hand raised and a child in front of him
Decrepitati deditus : mors erit michi esse
I am given over to decay : death will be my lot

In the Psalter the old man's hand rests on the shoulder of the child in front of him. Praetorius found no lettering discernible. This inscription was presumably placed outside the rim of the wheel, possibly a little lower than that of the Davis painting so as to lie near the scene.

(8) An old man on his sick bed attended by a doctor who holds up a vial
Infirmitati deditus : incipio deesse
Given over to infirmity : I begin to fail

Praetorius found little or nothing of this scene and only the end of the verse . . . *esse*.

(9) A coffin on a bier covered with a pall and a clerk behind reading the office of the dead.
Putavi quod viverem : vita me decepit
I thought that I would go on living : life has deceived me

Praetorius suggests there may be another figure in the scene but this is not the case in the Psalter. The inscription given by Praetorius is the same as in the Psalter and is well preserved. The second phrase could be translated as 'life is an illusion' or 'it was all a dream'.[24]

(10) A churchyard with three figures standing behind either a grave or a shrouded corpse about to be interred.

Versus sum in cinerem : vita me decepit
I am turned into ash : life has deceived me

Praetorius shows the possible outline of this scene, which differs from the Psalter, which shows a tomb with a cross on its cover. The inscription by Praetorius shows the first letters and, further on, the third word *cinerem*. The second part of the verse is inscribed in smaller letters and in the reverse direction below the rim of the wheel.

The Ages of Man and Wheels of Life

There has long been a fascination with describing the aging process from birth to death as a series of phases or stages through which an individual progresses. The span of life of any man could be divided into a number of ages and many different systems of age division were formulated throughout the centuries. Schemes have been put forward for three, four, five, six, seven, eight, ten and twelve divisions which could be related to some other division or classification.[25] Thus three ages could refer to youth, adulthood and old age; four could be correlated with the four seasons or virtues or temperaments; five with ages of the world or divisions of the day; seven with the planets; eight with hours of the day; ten divisions each lasting seven years, giving a lifespan of three score years and ten, or each lasting ten years, giving a lifespan of 100 years; and twelve, correlated with signs of the zodiac or twelve months of the year.

A seven age scheme forms part of the painted decoration of the vaulted hall at Longthorpe Tower near Peterborough, dated to c1330.[26] The seven images are distributed around an arch, thus showing a rise from infancy to prime, and subsequent decline to decrepitude. The sequence begins with a baby asleep in a cradle (infans), followed by a boy (puer) in a short tunic holding a ball and playing with a whip top. The next figure (adolescens) is incomplete but the fourth (probably once labelled iuvenis) is at the top of the arch and represents a falconer equipped with glove, lure and hood. A sword bearing figure comes next (probably vir) and then a fragmentary figure of a man with a money bag (probably senex) and lastly decrepitas shown as a hooded figure in a long robe walking on two crutches.

Among pictorial schemes for representing the ages of life, trees, wheels and steps all represent a rise to the prime of life and a decline to death.

The Wheel of Life is a variant of the Wheel of Fortune. In this representation a figure representing fortune stands behind a large wheel which she turns by holding the spokes, or she stands beside the wheel turning a crank. A crowned figure is usually placed at the top of the wheel and a prostrate figure at the bottom. On one side a figure ascends and on the other a figure descends. The personification of fortune controlling the wheel decides who is where and when.

The wheel of life is a closed system. An individual is allowed one revolution, rising to the top and then declining, to end where he started. The cycle begins with infancy, the age of learning to speak, progresses through boyhood, adolescence and manhood to the top of the wheel – the prime of life. At this age the individual is like a king and all things are possible. With the start of the descent, an older man takes up his staff and perhaps philosophically reviews his past life and passes on his wisdom to the young. He is aware that death is approaching. The last two verses seem to speak despairingly from beyond death. 'I thought that I would go on living'; 'I have been turned into ashes'.

The moral message of these schemes describing the ages of man is that life is short and transitory and worldly gain is of no value in the context of eternity. Man should look beyond the vanities of worldly life, bound by time and subject to rhythms of growth and decay, to a spiritual existence.

Notes and References

1. *Reading Abbey Cartularies* i, ed by B R Kemp, (Camden 4th series xxxi, 1986), 14
2. Kemp, B R, 'The Monastic Dean of Leominster', *Eng Hist Rev*, 83, (1968), 506
3. Hillaby, J, 'Early Christian and Pre-Conquest Leominster', *Transactions of the Woolhope Naturalists' Field Club*, xlv (3) (1987)
4. Hillaby, J & Boulton, R, *The Sculptured Capitals of Leominster Priory* (1993)
5. Hillaby, J & Boulton, R (1993), see note 4
6. Royal Commission on the Historical Monuments of England, *An Inventory of the Historical Monuments in Herefordshire, III North West* (London, 1934), 113
7. Townsend, G F, *The Town and Borough of Leominster*, (1862) p 229 note
8. RCHME (1934), see note 6, 113
9. Rouse, E C, *Medieval Wall Paintings*, Shire Publications, (1996), 9
10. Rouse, (1996), see note 9, 35-70; Tristram, E W, *English Medieval Wall Painting: the Thirteenth Century*, Oxford University Press (1950), 32-61
11. RCHME (1934), see note 6, 113
12. Tristram, E W, (1950), see note 10, 559
13. Freeman, E A, Leominster Priory Church, *Archaeologia Cambrensis*, 2nd series vol 4 (1853), 9
14. RCHME (1934), see note 6, 113
15. Tristram, E W, (1950), see note 10, 261-2, 558
16. Rushforth, G McN, The Wheel of the Ten Ages of Life in Leominster Church, *Proceedings of the Society of Antiquaries of London*, 2nd series, vol 26 (1914), 47-60.
17. Tristram, E W, (1950), see note 10, 555
18. DeLisle Psalter, London, British Library, ms Arundel 83, fol 126v. Reproduced in Rushforth, (1914), see note 16
19. Rushforth, G McN, (1914), see note 16, 9
20. Rushforth, G McN, (1914), see note 16, 49
21. Rushforth, G McN, (1914), see note 16, 53
22. Pawsey, H, personal communication
23. Pawsey, H, personal communication
24. Reeves, N, personal communication
25. Sears, E, *The Ages of Man: Medieval Interpretations of the Life Cycle*, Princeton University Press, (1986)
26. Sears, E, (1986), see note 25, 37-8

6 Archaeology and The Three Early Churches of Herefordshire

KEITH RAY

This chapter concerns itself entirely with the history and archaeology of Christianity in the first millennium AD in Herefordshire. The geographical location of the county outside the area of earliest English settlement had far-reaching consequences for the early development of Christian communities here. The chapter is ordered within a chronological framework. This inevitably means that the discussion concerns not simply one 'early Church', but successively three contrasting church traditions.[1] I shall refer to these, respectively, as the Romano-British, the British, and the Anglian (Anglo-Saxon) Church.

The three main sections of the chapter relate to each of these traditions in turn. For each of them the particular characteristics of the Church and the general nature of the archaeological evidence that might be expected to be present are considered, before the evidence actually available is reviewed. The discussion of each Church is concluded by an examination of a key material representation that throws vital light on the Herefordshire context. It should be noted at the outset how little archaeological work has been done in the county on any sites with possible early church connections. Therefore, much of what is discussed here arises from a recent and so far fairly superficial re-examination of clues that exist within or around existing Herefordshire churches. This evidence was often first noted during the Royal Commission on the Historic Monuments of England survey of the county in the 1930s.[2]

The Romano-British Church

The background

Direct historical evidence for the existence and writings of the earliest Christian church in Britain is limited to fifth century sources. Prominent among these works are those of Prosper of Aquitaine (writing about the visit of Bishop Germanus of Auxerre), St. Patrick's *Confessio* (which is more informative about Ireland), and lesser known and more fragmentary pieces such a homily *de Vita*

Christiana by an otherwise unknown bishop, Fastidius.[3] These literary sources attest to the presence of Christian communities in Britain in the third century AD. The names of three early Christian martyrs are known. Alban is the most famous, although Julius and Aaron at Caerleon were closer, geographically, to Herefordshire.[4] All three were soldiers claiming an allegiance superior to their oaths of loyalty to the Emperor. As such, they are not necessarily representative of the local or regional population.

It is not until the Council of Arles in 314 that an episcopal organisation of the Church in the western Roman Empire is evident. Three British bishops, plus a priest and a deacon, attended that Council. Further presence of British clergy at Church Councils in Europe is documented throughout the fourth century.[5] However, just as in the later decades of the fourth century Britain had become renowned as the cradle of would-be usurpers, it also became notorious as a seedbed for heresy. The most famous of the alleged heretics was Pelagius.[6] He taught that through prayer and good works, believers could accumulate sufficient merit to achieve salvation after death. This markedly contradicted the doctrines of his famous contemporary, the North African bishop, Augustine of Hippo.

Pelagius' teachings made a considerable impact throughout the Empire due to his travels and through his presence and preaching in Rome. It was probably in response to this influence that one at least of the two documented senior episcopal missions to Britain in the early fifth century took place. The first of these missions was that of Victricius, Bishop of Rouen, in 405, apparently at the invitation of the British Church. However, it has been pointed out that Pelagius's career can only have just got going by then.[7]

The second mission, of Germanus, Bishop of Auxerre, was more certainly focused against Pelagian beliefs. It occurred sometime around 429 AD, at a time when the Augustinian orthodoxy on Original Sin and Divine Grace had become firmly established, and ten years or so after the proclamation of heresy against Pelagius and his followers in 418.[8] However, it has been observed that Germanus' mission had little long-term impact within Britain.[9]

The archaeology of Romano-British Christianity

The unequivocal material evidence for Romano-British Christianity is more limited than previously thought. Until recently, it was said that the quantity available amounted to compelling evidence of the existence of definite communities otherwise only hinted at by the sparse documentary data.[10] Most often cited have been the chi-rho monograms incorporated into villa mosaics at sites such as Frampton and Hinton St. Mary in Dorset. Portrayals and symbols were also painted onto villa wall-plaster, as at Lullingstone in Kent, or inscribed onto stonework, as with the converted shrine at the villa at Chedworth near Cirencester. Further Christian symbols were also cast into metal tableware and ritual items, as in the Water Newton group.[11]

Frances Mawer has noted, however, that many of the inferentially Christian devices or formulae are questionable. She therefore undertook two studies, one of fixed representations, and the other of portable objects. So far, only the latter has been published.[12] She noted that many of the marks, devices and formulae recorded have been mis-read or misunderstood. Many others were just as likely to be pagan as Christian in character. Of the total of 260 artefacts claimed as pertaining to Christian communities, she regarded only 70 as being unequivocally so linked, and a further 60 possibly linked.[13] Some widely-quoted phenomena such as the 'paternoster' word-squares were entirely discounted because they are just as plausibly pagan.[14]

Mention of the sharing of symbols between pagan and Christian practice serves to introduce two important further aspects of Romano-British Christianity. These are its grounding in local traditional religious practice, and its parallel existence with other eastern mystery cults. This means that much of the material evidence is difficult to disentangle from pagan belief and ritual. We need to be cautious in viewing it with the benefit of the hindsight provided by fifteen hundred years of the supremacy of Christian belief.[15] Even after its adoption as the Roman state religion, Christianity remained a minority cult, one of many in the late Roman world. Several of these religions were, like Christianity, both gnostic and monotheistic. An example is the cult of Iao, or Abraxas, represented on the famous mosaic from the villa at Brading on the Isle of Wight.[16]

The more equivocal evidence for religious identity and practice includes supposed Christian cemeteries, as around towns such as Winchester, York and Dorchester in Dorset. At Poundbury west of Dorchester, and elsewhere, the careful use of gypsum to preserve the body has been taken to imply a literal reading of the concept of resurrection by an early Christian community.[17]

From the late nineteenth century archaeologists have identified churches from the basilical plan of late Roman structures, perhaps most famously at Silchester. Here, the identification was based on the presence of an apse facing west, aisles, and what has been interpreted as a baptistery outside the eastern (and not western) doorway.[18] The Christian interpretation of such structures has now been extended to a similar example at Wroxeter, the major Romano-British town of Viroconium east of Shrewsbury.[19]

As a result of Mawer's studies of finds, it can be concluded that the most definite indications of the presence of a Christian community are present when key figures, formulae and signs are found inscribed together on objects.[20] Apart from inscriptions that accord with a VIVAS IN DEO formula, the presence of signs such as the alpha and omega and chi-rho, and figural symbols such as the peacock, tree-of-life, and (sometimes) fish, are regarded as sure indicators. Some vessels such as bowls carry some of these devices together, but these are very rare. Spoons (especially long-handled ones) bearing such inscriptions and devices are slightly more common. However, the only unequivocally Christian artefacts with a wide distribution (though still few in number) are finger-rings and belt-fittings.

Markers of identity for British Christians

To understand the nature of the Romano-British Church in Herefordshire, it is worth considering briefly the society within which it existed. The pattern was of small country towns linked by major roads and surrounded by farms. The farms were connected to the main routes by a dense network of roads, and this pattern is as evident in eastern Herefordshire as it is in central Shropshire, in Worcestershire, southern Warwickshire and Gloucestershire (Fig 22).[21]

What form would traces of the earliest Christian activity take, and where in the landscape should we look for such traces to survive? The former is very much a question of how Christians could have marked their identity materially, while locating their presence requires a realisation that the Christianity of late Roman Britain was familial in scale and custom.

For the latter, much has been made of the idea that Romano-British Christianity was the preserve of the wealthier classes, since the most unambiguous architectural evidence has been retrieved from the grand villa sites such as Lullingstone in Kent and from Hinton St Mary and Frampton in Dorset, or on silverware.[22] However, this is to over-emphasise the class-distinctiveness and to fail to appreciate the kin-centredness of Romano-British society. The outward symbols of belief expressed in these locations or on these objects represent the collective actions of practising Christian communities. The principal patrons of these groups were no doubt wealthy, but the paraphernalia were shared.[23]

In fact, the material evidence for Christianity in Britain is distributed evenly between the towns, and farms with substantial buildings (in this sense, 'villas', but by no means all of which feature the mosaics, wall-paintings and underfloor heating systems of the wealthier sites). More surprisingly, several forts have also produced such finds, and especially those of the third century and later around the south-eastern coasts.[24] Herefordshire was very much within the civil

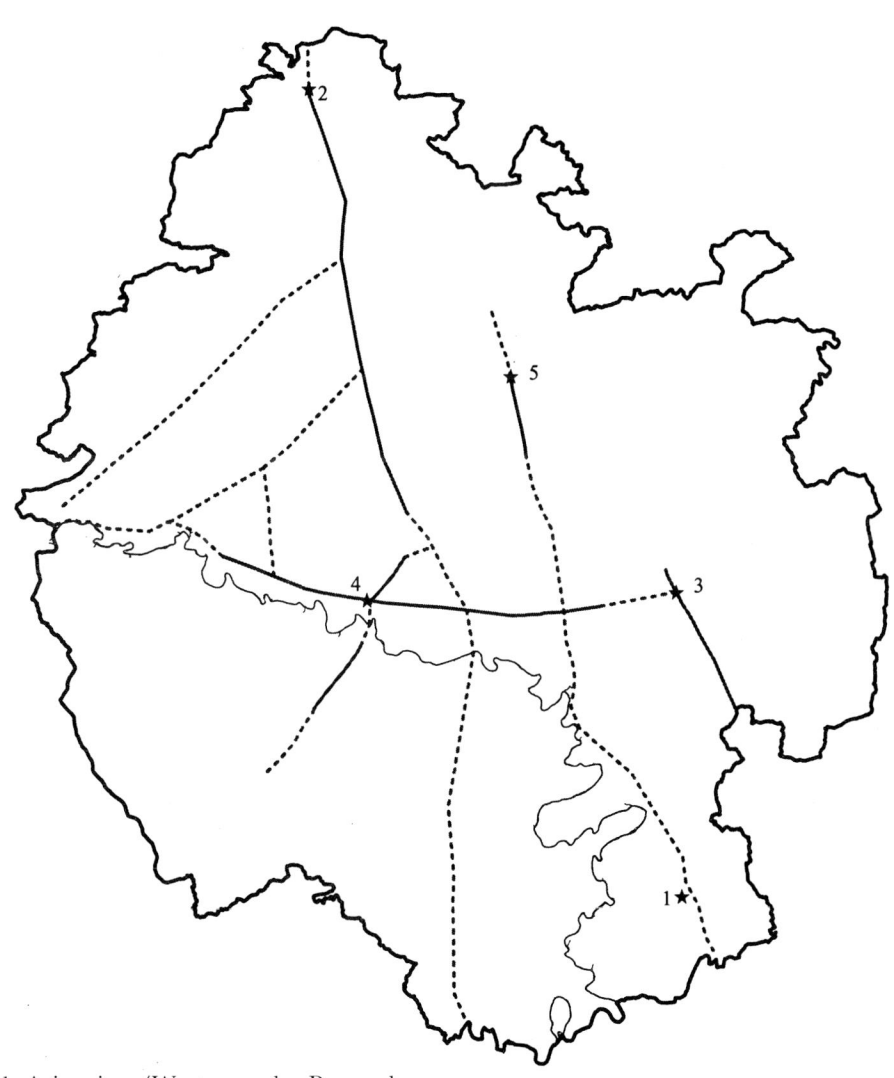

ARCHAEOLOGY AND THE THREE EARLY CHURCHES OF HEREFORDSHIRE 103

1. Ariconium/Weston-under-Penyard
2. Branogenium/Leintwardine
3. ?Epocessa/Stretton Grandison
4. Magnis/Kenchester
5. Blackwardine

© Crown copyright. All rights reserved. Herefordshire Council. LA09069L. 2001
© Copyright Herefordshire Archaeology

Fig 22 Roman roads and major Romano-British settlements in Herefordshire.
Possible routes are shown as dotted lines

province, and was apparently as intensively-settled as areas to its south and east. Across its eastern two-thirds its landscape encompassed, as so far understood, at least five substantial settlements and upwards of thirty farms with indications of the presence of major structures. Any of such sites could therefore have had Christian residents.

The picture provided by the province-wide distribution of small-finds suggests that rings were often a vehicle for marking personal Christian faith-allegiance. In contrast, belts (attested by metal buckles, buckle-plates, and strap-ends) may have been public insignia denoting rank within the Christian community. Meanwhile, inscribed bowls and possibly also spoons had a role in Christian ritual. Circular lead tanks, apparently an entirely British phenomenon, may also have been used in ritual, perhaps as basins for baptism. At least in later Roman Britain, more than half of discovered examples of these tanks appear to bear chi-rho symbols as decorative devices.[25]

Christian identity could also be marked in a funerary context, as with a bone plaque bearing a VIVAS IN DEO inscription found in a stone sarcophagus at York.[26] A coin of Magnentius pierced for attachment to a wall with the chi and rho on the reverse facing outwards was found inside Mausoleum 8 at the Poundbury cemetery in Dorchester. A chi-rho symbol was also claimed as present there, painted onto the wall-plaster found within the same mausoleum.[27]

Evidence for Romano-British Christianity in Herefordshire

Little material evidence for Christianity has so far been found in Herefordshire. Neither the architectural symbols, nor the collections of silver plate, nor the large organised cemeteries that exist elsewhere in southern Britain are currently known. This absence of evidence is to some extent more apparent than real and it is likely that, buried among the records, finds and even field monuments of later Roman Herefordshire that have already been recovered and recorded, there are clues that have been neglected. As will be noted below, the potential significance even of material that has long been published may have been missed.

However, the difficulties of locating such evidence should not be underestimated. Due both to the similarity of Christian to other beliefs, and the very simplicity of much of the ritual, the material evidence even for late Roman Christianity in Herefordshire is difficult to trace.

The largest collection of excavated or otherwise recovered material has come from the site or the vicinity of the walled town at Kenchester. It is therefore pertinent to search first among the finds from the excavations within the walls carried out in the early years of the twentieth century.[28] Among the excavated material the only objects that echo those identified by Mawer as having strong Christian connotations are silver or pewter long-handled spoons.[29] Such spoons have been found with chi-rho symbols marked upon them among groups of other plate, as at Water Newton in Huntingdonshire. They have also been decorated with inscriptions and with incised fishes, as with a group from Dorchester in Dorset. However, this does not mean that all spoons of this kind were implicated in Christian ritual. For instance, Martin Henig has noted an example from a temple at Thetford in Norfolk, that bears the inscription 'Dei Faunus Narius', '(Property) of the God Faunus Narius'.[30] Several examples of such spoons were found at Kenchester among the more easterly buildings examined by Jack. They may have had secular uses unconnected with religion, and may have belonged alternatively to a different cult, but a specifically Christian use cannot as yet be entirely discounted.

More intriguing is the discovery less than a quarter of a mile away of a fragment of a circular lead tank from the excavations east of Magna Castra Farm.[31] This tank was found in a deposit associated with a granary and possible mill of late second century date. The construction of the Kenchester tank was identical to the other known examples, but it was apparently not decorated. On this basis, its early date, and its location in a part of the site where there was some evidence for industrial activity, the excavators suggested that the tank was most likely used for industrial purposes. While this is an economical explanation for its presence here, it is not an entirely convincing one. This is because, for one thing, the building the tank came from featured carefully laid floors and elaborately painted walls.[32]

Most of the circular lead tanks have come to light in eastern England, and the nearest other examples to the Kenchester one are only as far west as Bourton-on-the-Water in Gloucestershire.[33] However, the stamped tile at the site east of Kenchester came from Gloucester and the Cirencester region, and the architectural stonework was carved from Cotswolds limestone. While we cannot argue from this meagre evidence that the tank from which the scrap piece came must have been used by a Christian community in Herefordshire, it should be noted that it has now been established that there were Romano-Britons using such tanks here.

There are no excavated Romano-British cemeteries in Herefordshire, although the existence of one has been inferred from roadside burials found in Jack and Hayter's second season of work, just south of the east gate at Kenchester. The presence of a church in close proximity to the west of the town may reflect the existence of cemeteries in this direction also, and may even hint at continuity from late Roman memorial structures.[34] The presence of churches in or very close to Roman towns in the county at Leintwardine and Blackwardine reinforces such possibilities, but this is a consideration for the part of this paper devoted to the British Church.

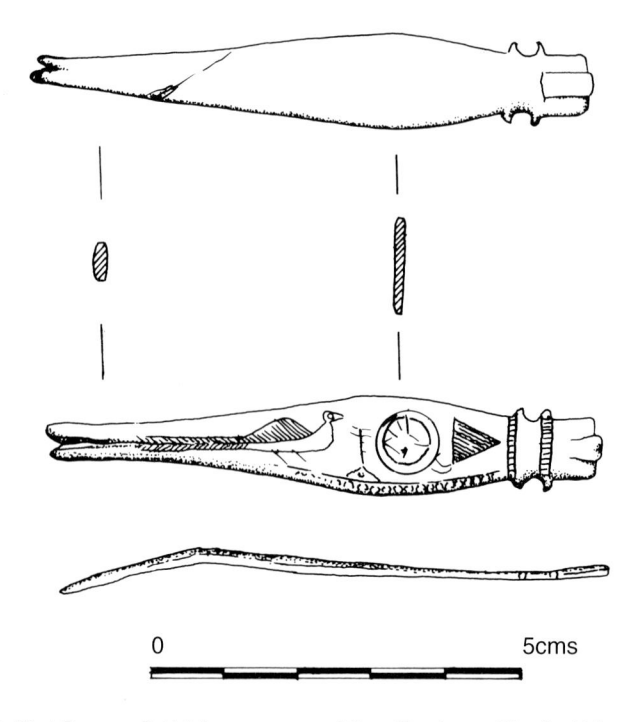

Fig 23 A Romano-British bronze strap-end from Kenchester (Hereford Museum). The peacock and tree-of-life are Christian emblems. © *Copyright Herefordshire Archaeology*

These vague indications need to be evaluated alongside unequivocal evidence for the presence of Christians at Kenchester, namely a strap-end found within the walled area in 1961, and now in Hereford Museum (Fig 23). This bronze belt-fitting bears incised geometric motifs accompanied by a peacock and a tree-of-life symbol.[35] It is worth emphasising both that Mawer regards this as one of the very few combinations of motif that represents unquestionable evidence for ownership of the objects concerned by Christians, and that the belts concerned were quite probably insignia of office. It is not surprising to find such an item within a late Roman walled settlement, since such defended centres were an integral part of the network of provincial administration represented also by the coastal forts.

The Upton Bishop frieze and its implications

At the beginning of this discussion it was noted that there are materials that although published long ago have not previously been considered at all closely. One such item is a carved fragment of finely-tooled red sandstone incorporated into the external face of the south wall of the chancel at Upton Bishop church near Ross-on-Wye. When first noted, this sculpture was identified as part of a tombstone.[36] Since it features a toga-wearing male figure set in a niche, this is ostensibly a reasonable interpretation. However, the way the toga folds are depicted, the treatment of the raised right hand, and the presence of another figure in an adjoining niche raise questions about the status of this carving as more than simply a piece of pagan funerary sculpture. The presence of a second niche indicates that the stone is likely to have been part of a panel or frieze. In itself, this reduces the likelihood of its being a tombstone. Closer inspection of the piece on site only serves to heighten the interest of these observations (Fig 24).

The formal banding treatment of the hair and the swept lines of the toga folds imply a fourth century date for the sculpture. Moreover, the right hand and forearm are represented in a manner exactly similar to the figures depicted on the wall-paintings at the Lullingstone villa in Kent, again of similar date. The treatment of the palm and the thumb is identical, as is the form of the elaborate cuffs or wrist-bands. The Lullingstone figures are unequivocally standing in the 'orans' open-handed position adopted in early Christian prayer, in front of a curtain draped across a colonnade.[37]

Unfortunately, the further piece of the Upton frieze is missing, but the flattened niches might just be interpreted as an intended colonnade. The very edge of the broken stone bears a representation of a left hand outstretched within a niche in exactly the same manner as the right hand of the surviving figure. The possibility needs also to be considered therefore that this adjoining figure had both hands held outwards, possibly as the central figure in a group of three. A high density of tripartite niched stone friezes exists in the Gloucestershire Cotswolds, and as such they are typical votive sculpture addressed to or invoking local deities. While a non-Christian votive function cannot be ruled out, a Christian frieze of this kind might after all have been a piece of funerary sculpture, or even part of a sarcophagus.[38]

The classicism of the treatment of every feature of the Upton figure (other than the face of the person depicted) is unusual in a late Roman sculpture in such a peripheral area. That it was locally produced is however certain, since the stone

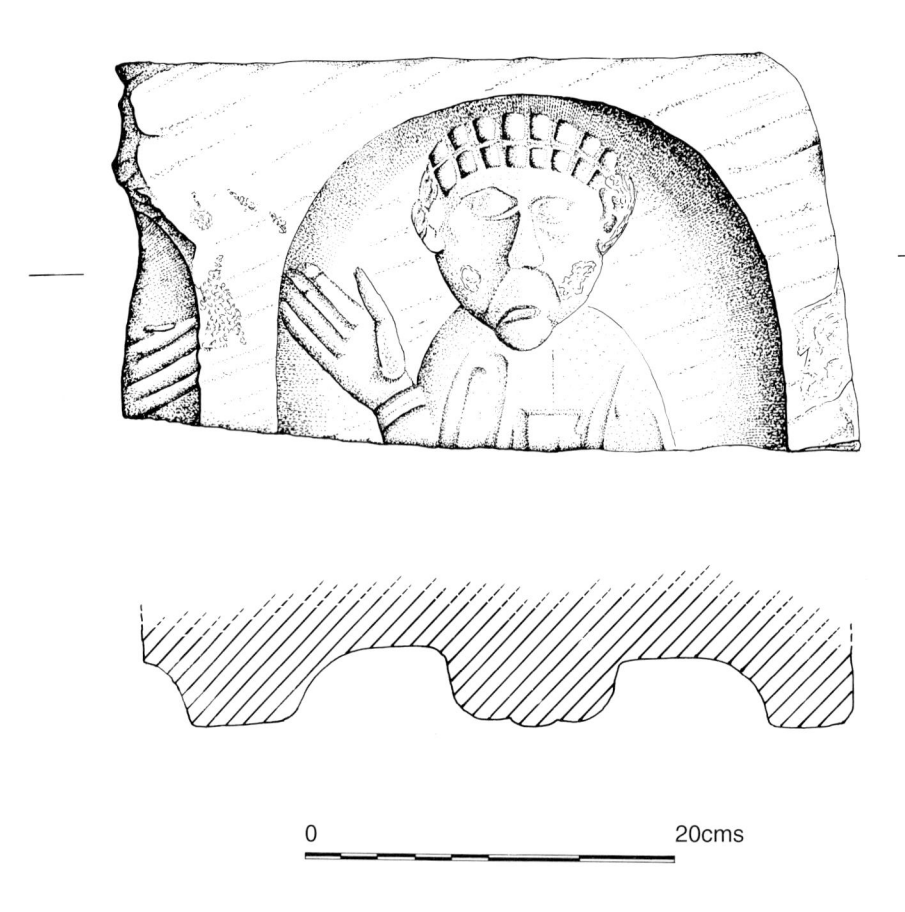

Fig 24 The sandstone frieze at Upton Bishop church. The uplifted hands of both figures echo portrayals of late Roman Christians at prayer.

© *Copyright Herefordshire Archaeology.*

For Upton Bishop church and frieze location see colour plates 8 and 9

is a fine-grained red sandstone, and this suggests moreover that the fragment has not travelled far from its place of initial deposition.

Nikolaus Pevsner recognised the importance of this piece of sculpture through a detailed description of its form in his *Buildings of England, Herefordshire* volume, but did not seek to interpret its significance.[39] We can now frame such significance not only in terms of a possible reference to Christian prayer or ritual, but also in reference to its geographical location. Upton Bishop is situated only two miles north of the Romano-British iron-working centre identified as

Ariconium, near Weston-under-Penyard. This centre is in turn located in an area that appears to have had a reasonably well-articulated tradition of a local church community with a named bishop, Dubricius, as its hierarch in the fifth century.[40]

As at Kenchester, it would be surprising if such a focal settlement had not supported a Christian community. The tradition of fine stone carving in south Herefordshire represented by the Upton Bishop frieze is not otherwise recorded. As such, the stone can only as yet be regarded as hinting at the presence here in the late Roman period of the organised Christian community of at least the sixth century attested in the later written sources.

The British Church

The background

After the end of the formal civil organisation of the Roman provinces of Britannia, a remarkable thing appears to have happened. While the state dissolved firstly into a series of local sub-Roman administrative units and then into reconstituted chiefdoms controlled by local war-lords, an evangelical fervour seems to have swept parts of the countryside. For the first time, much of Britain can be said to have become a Christian land. This widespread conversion of the rural population was not however only a British phenomenon: a similar process appears to have happened in parts of France and Spain.[41]

The ecclesiastical organisation to respond to, and perhaps even to have provoked, this development here was already in place, but in the fifth century, dynamic new ingredients were added. These were the cult of saints (which extended and effectively replaced the cult of martyrs), the raising of memorials, and the advent of monasticism. While the first two were a direct continuation and development of established practices in the Roman world, monasticism arose out of particular circumstances at the turn of the fifth century, and took two distinct forms. The first and earliest of these involved the grouping of clergy into metropolitan administrative centres. These were often based in former Roman towns, but they were also located at new sites. One such was probably the centre at Bangor-is-y-Coed on the River Dee near Wrexham. The second and later monastic form was eremitical, with groups of hermits living in remote places, sometimes in a dispersed manner, and following the practices of St Anthony and the 'desert fathers'.[42]

The British Church was not apparently a proselytising one and later English clerics like Bede berated it for its failure to convert the pagan Saxons. Aldhelm noted the disdain for the English voiced by the British clergy in what had by around 690 become south-west Wales. When addressing English visitors, and having declined to celebrate divine offices with them, these British clergy styled themselves *cathari*, that is, 'the pure ones', thereby distinguishing themselves from the parvenu English Christians.[43] This snobbery produced its own reaction, with both Bede and Alcuin regarding the British Church as degenerate, and dismissing its contribution to the wider achievements of Christendom in the later first millennium.

At the time of the mission of Augustine to the English from 597, the British Church was therefore considered from the outside to be insular in more than location. While in some aspects of practice this may have been true, it is also to a large degree an English myth in its own right. There had been direct contacts between British communities and the eastern Mediterranean, and it is this link that archaeology has so graphically demonstrated in the last thirty years. The evidence has come from early ecclesiastical sites, but more so from the contemporary 'courts' of the secular British leaders where it has taken the form of sherds from eastern Mediterranean and north African ceramic containers.[44] This should not surprise us, since late fourth and early fifth century Romano-Britons had been present in the far south of the Roman world. An example was an anonymous British correspondent writing from Sicily in the first decade of the fifth century.[45] What the pottery clearly demonstrates is that commerce and contacts continued in a very tangible way not only directly but also via Spain and south-west France throughout the fifth and sixth centuries.

The archaeology of the British Church

The archaeology of the early British Church has been defined by the pioneers Ralegh Radford and Charles Thomas as featuring enclosed circular burial grounds and churchyards, slab-lined graves, memorial-stones, reliquaries and altars.[46] Best known are the memorial stones bearing inscriptions of various kinds found in western and northern Britain through to the seventh century. More complex memorials existed, such as the small square or rectangular construction of boulders or slabs that in modern-day Ireland is called a *leacht*.[47] These cairns are capped by a masonry block, with a flat top, and sometimes a decorated standing stone or slab is affixed in the top. The C12th *Life* of St Illtud provides an account of the burial of St Samson which describes what sounds like a *leacht* in South Wales.[48] These structures are apparently insular versions of the better-documented Mediterranean altar-graves. The parallel practice of incision of crosses onto portable altars and altar slabs began in the seventh or eighth century, and continued, in some parts of Britain, into the thirteenth century. One development of the altar-grave appears to be an upright stone altar with decorated frontal stone.[49]

Such prestigious burials rarely occurred in isolation. Several cemeteries that have been examined archaeologically in western Britain in recent years betray some continuity of practice from late Roman Britain in the form of mausolea set amid rows of carefully ordered east-west oriented burials. Fourth century Christian cemeteries like those at Lankhills, Winchester, and Poundbury in Dorset contained such mausolea, and they occur in a remarkably similar form in fifth and sixth century contexts in Wales.[50] Excavated examples include those found in cemeteries at Llandegai (Caernarfon), Plas Gogerddan (Ceredigion) and Tandderwen (Denbigh).[51] None of these latter cemeteries were associated with extant churches, but traditions of such association are persistent throughout western Britain. One approach has been the search for the sites of early British churches by the identification of circularity in extant churchyards. This kind of approach has been examined critically in Cornwall, where it was found that while most circular or oval churchyards belong to what are likely to have been first millennium foundations, many of these are demonstrably tenth century or later.[52] The chief pitfalls of making an uncritical linkage between circularity and early foundation are a failure to include sites where churches no longer exist (and which cannot therefore form part of the sample), and the glossing of the complexities of site development.

That the situation can have been extremely complex has become appreciated through both aerial photography and excavation. In South Wales, for instance, the circular churchyard may represent only the latest phase in a long history of the site.[53] Meanwhile, excavation has demonstrated (for instance, at Capel Meulog, Llandrindod Wells), how such development can involve shifts in site focus, changes to churchyard boundaries and church location, and cemetery extensions and contraction.[54]

The context of the early British Church in Herefordshire

The early British church existed in a political framework that evolved rapidly. (Fig 25) In the north of the county, the literary evidence (such as it is) can be read to the effect that there is at least a possibility that St David founded a monastery at Llanllieni (Leominster).[55] This location was at the centre of a territorial unit that may have retained some cohesiveness throughout the later first millennium, and which could have approximated to an early small-scale British kingdom.[56]

1. Leominster	7. Llanveynoe	13. Peterstow
2. Buckenhill, Woolhope	8. Madley	14. Moccas
3. Canon Pyon	9. Bredwardine	15. Bolgros
4. Eccles Green	10. Abbey Dore	16. Whitchurch
5. Eccleswall	11. Dorstone	17. Llanfrother (Hentland)
6. Egleton	12. Llangarron	18. Hentland (Goodrich)

© *Crown copyright. All rights reserved. Herefordshire Council. LA09069L. 2001*
© *Copyright Herefordshire Archaeology*

Fig 25 The British church in Herefordshire: the location of some of the more important places mentioned in the text.

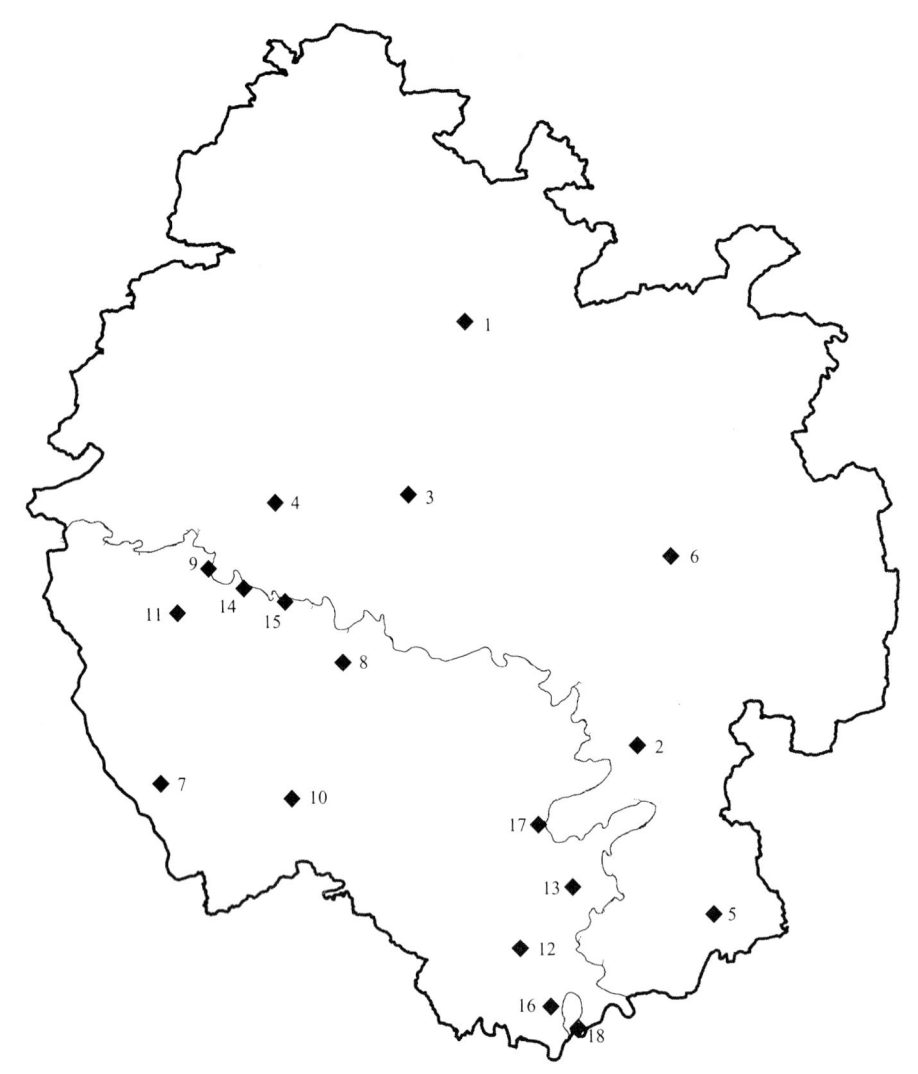

In the south of what later became Herefordshire at least two further identifiable British kingdoms developed in parallel. Firstly, the charters collected together and transcribed in the early twelfth century *Book of Llandaff* indicate the existence of a kingdom of Ercic during the sixth century.[57] This kingdom apparently became a client of the more powerful kingdom of Gwent from the seventh century, but retained its identity through to the tenth century. The second was what was likely to have been the kingdom of Ewyas. Although this seems to have been subject at various times to Gwent or to Brycheiniog, it retained an identity such that it was still regarded even beyond the Middle Ages as a Welsh province.[58]

Throughout the area of Herefordshire, it seems likely that this early British church had a diocesan organisation. Medieval Welsh sources record in south-east Wales the presence and seniority of an early cleric called Dubric (St Dubricius or St Dyfrig). The dedication of a number of churches in south Herefordshire today locates his presence quite specifically, and this is supported by several Llandaff charters which mention his name in reference to seventh century church dedications in this region.

The seniority of this Dubric to figures such as St Illtud and St Samson, recorded in several saints' *Lives*, indicates a likely fifth or early sixth century date for his activities, and this is supported by the one known version of his *Life*.[59] In these references, he is specifically denoted a bishop, his authority was clearly regarded as senior to other saints, and his birth and power were apparently based upon the kingdom of Ercic. The suggested (and plausible) etymological link to Ariconium at least raises the possibility that Dubric was the bishop of the sub-Roman community that developed in the region based on that Romano-British centre.

The Llandaff charters record the bounds of estates belonging to particular foundations, referred to as 'Lann', later 'Llan'.[60] It is important to note that this term refers both to the church enclosure itself, and to the (usually small) estate which had been gifted in order to support it. The gift of land was made either by a king or some other secular authority to a bishop or other church leader, specifically for the foundation of a small community with its church.[61] An example is the grant of land at Bolgros to Bishop Ufelwy by King Gwrfodwr of Ercic in 610 AD.[62] The text of this charter describes how the bishop made a perambulation of the bounds of the estate accompanied by his clergy, sprinkling holy water, while the holy cross and relics were carried in front of him. In the presence of the king he then consecrated the place for a church in the middle of the estate, dedicating it to the Holy Trinity, St Paul, St Dubricius, and St Teilo.

Apparently encapsulated in microcosm within this account, then, is the history of the sixth century British church in Herefordshire, in both liturgical practice and episcopal succession.

Each 'llan' is likely to have possessed a church dedicated in this manner to a variety of saints, perhaps with a later simplification to a principal saint, or to a more local one. It has often been claimed that church dedications are an indicator of the pattern of early ecclesiastical activity. What is perhaps more likely is that ancient patterns of gifting, association and allegiance are echoed faintly in the llan-names surviving today. So it is that saints well known from dedications elsewhere in Wales, such as Beuno and Tysilio, are remembered at Llanveynoe, and at Sellack and Llancillo, respectively. Meanwhile the cult of others, such as St Keyne (Kentchurch) extended yet further afield, for instance to Somerset. In parallel, more local figures such as St Cynfal (Llangunville) and St Wenarth (St Weonards) are also represented and commemorated.[63]

In addition to these British saints more universal dedications, such as to St Bride (Bridget), as at Bridstow, may nonetheless echo early practice. The place-names Peterstow and Martinstow indicate the active presence of the cult of these two saints from early on. Their familiarity to members of the Anglian church presumably led to the place-name translation in the second millennium. The cult of Martin is also attested through the traditional names of holy wells at Llanveynoe and Ewias Lacy, as well as by further church dedications at Hereford. One of these was the extra-mural suburb south of the Wye bridge and another was associated with St Guthlac's monastery north of the river. The possible connection with early ecclesiastical activity is explored later in the chapter.

The survival of the early British Church in north Herefordshire?

One issue that continues to interest many historians of the fifth century in western Britain is the question of continuity. What happened to the Christian communities of late Roman Herefordshire in the century following the cessation of Roman rule in Britain, around 410? In whatever light the occupation of fifth century Wroxeter is viewed, the late coin series at Kenchester, and the degree of wear evident on late fourth century coin issues, indicates that both exchange and economic activity continued there well into the fifth century.[64]

Moreover, the sequences of structures noted in places like Ilchester and Wells in Somerset has been used, however tenuously, to suggest some continuity of both urban and rural sites sacred to Christianity.[65] The location of early churches in the areas outside former Romano-British towns has been traced now for numbers of sites, from the better-known examples such as Canterbury and St

Albans, to less well explored cases such as Great Chesterford on the Cambridgeshire/Essex border. In Herefordshire, such a geographical association of later church and Roman town can be observed in the cases of Kenchester, Blackwardine and perhaps also Stretton Grandison.[66] However, as yet there is no material evidence, eg in the form of an excavated early ecclesiastical structure beneath or near the later church, to support the idea of an institutional link.

In the absence of definite archaeological information, recourse has frequently been made to place-names and church dedications, to try to locate continuities in early church sites or communities. Both types of data have their own attendant problems. An example of a place-name element frequently claimed as significant is 'Eccles'. Place-names containing this element have long been regarded as potentially referring to church buildings, or to early church communities, in sub-Roman Britain.[67]

There are apparently three of these 'eccles-' type place-names in Herefordshire, and the location of at least two of them could be taken to reinforce the idea of an early church connection. Eccleswall is immediately adjacent to the central area of the extensive Romano-British settlement at Weston-under-Penyard.[68] A second instance is Egleton, immediately north of Stretton Grandison.[69] The third, at Eccles Green, lies much further away from a major Roman settlement, being some seven kilometres north-west of Kenchester. There are hints of Roman sites here, however, since a north-south Roman road linking Sarnesfield to Portway passes through Eccles Green, and a possible piece of Roman stonework exists at Norton Canon church close by.[70]

Despite such propinquities, we have no way of determining what the significance of such 'Eccles' names was. In the case of the place-names close to the Romano-British town sites, it is just possible that they represent churches associated with former extra-mural cemeteries. Meanwhile, the status of the Norton Canon area in the Roman period is far from certain. The 'Eccles' place-name might suggest the persistent memory of the presence of an 'eglwys' settlement in the area. Moreover, just to the west a 'Stow' place-name (without an apparent remembered link to a particular saint's llan), and a 'merthyr' place-name, also exist in close proximity.[71] It seems reasonable to suppose, therefore, that some form of continuity is marked by these place-name associations, but it will be very difficult to establish their significance in relation to archaeological evidence.

The evidence of dedications is interesting, although since these can change, great caution is necessary. Some may be more persistent than others, and in this light the distribution of dedications to St Lawrence throughout the county is interesting. On the continent, these are found in several early church contexts, as

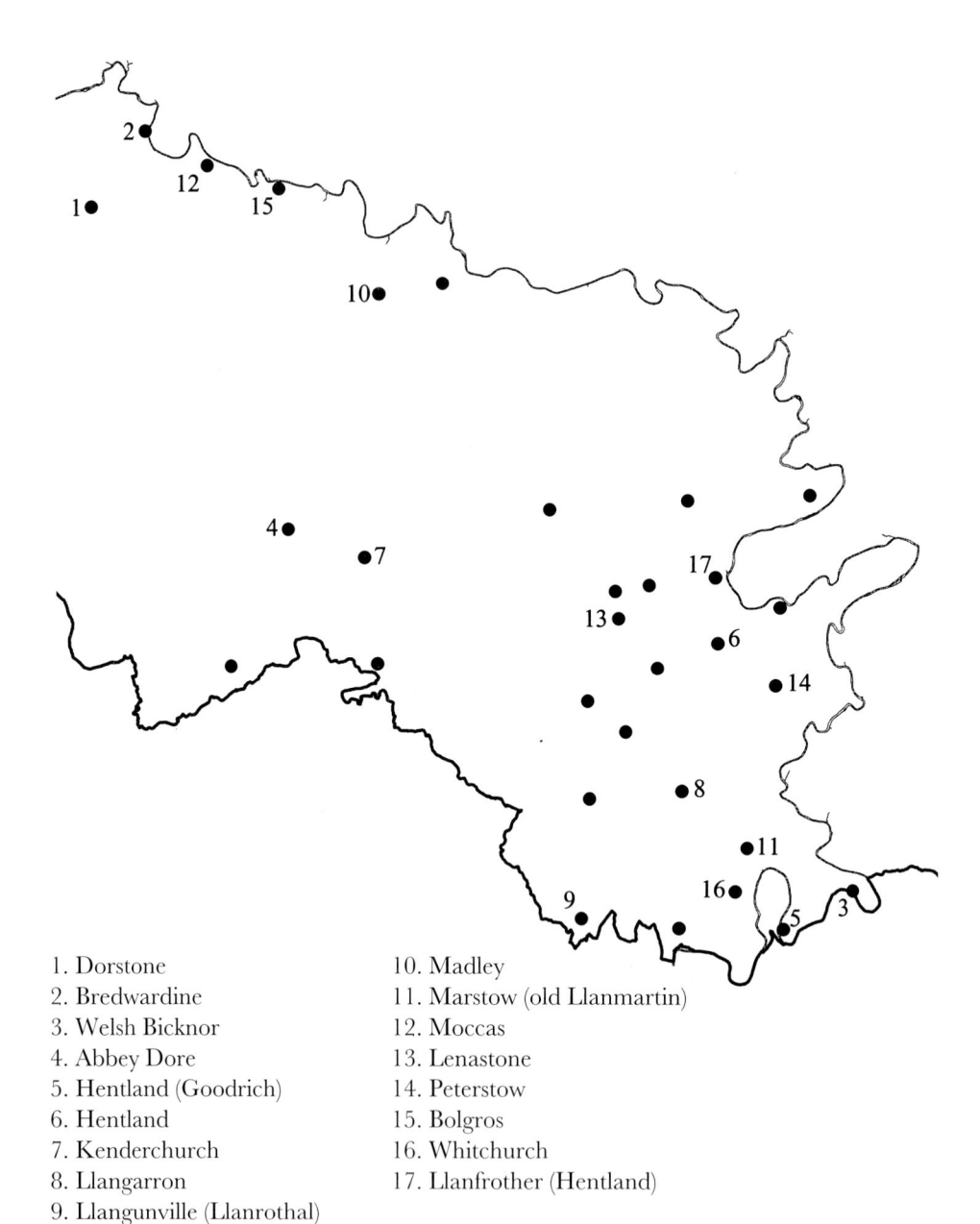

1. Dorstone
2. Bredwardine
3. Welsh Bicknor
4. Abbey Dore
5. Hentland (Goodrich)
6. Hentland
7. Kenderchurch
8. Llangarron
9. Llangunville (Llanrothal)
10. Madley
11. Marstow (old Llanmartin)
12. Moccas
13. Lenastone
14. Peterstow
15. Bolgros
16. Whitchurch
17. Llanfrother (Hentland)

© *Crown copyright. All rights reserved. Herefordshire Council. LA09069L. 2001*
© *Copyright Herefordshire Archaeology*

Fig 26 Church foundations of the mid first millennium in south Herefordshire attested in the Llandaff charters (after Coplestone-Crow)

at Trier. There are only five St Lawrence dedications among Herefordshire parish churches, at Weston-under-Penyard, Stretton Grandison, Bishopstone, Canon Pyon and Preston-on-Wye.[72] Added to the connection traced for two at least of the 'eccles' names, this distribution is potentially quite significant.

The same two settlements at Weston and Stretton account for two of these St Lawrence occurrences, and their proximity to Roman towns is striking. The Bishopstone example is moreover very close to Kenchester, and on its glebeland was discovered a major Roman villa. In the western part of Canon Pyon parish, there is a stream referred to around 1200 as Walshebrok. This area, between Butthouse Farm and Canon Pyon church, was apparently in the hands of Gruffydd ap Maredudd in 1086. We have recently noted here, some 400m southwest of that church, a circular ditched enclosure now bisected by the same stream, that is a possible candidate for an early circular church enclosure.[73]

It was moreover adjacent to the settlement that later became known as Preston-on-Wye that the early seventh century foundation at Bolgros was located, and this area too is less than four kilometres south-west of the Bishopstone-Kenchester area, albeit across the Wye. Such connections may simply be coincidental, but equally a case can be made for at least considering the possibility of tenurial and community links.

In north Herefordshire, in several cases Roman finds have been made at, or Roman material has been incorporated into, churches. The case of Norton Canon has already been cited. Further examples are Staunton-on-Arrow, where a statuette of the god Mercury is said to have been found in or near the graveyard, and Putley, where the church appears to occupy part of the site of a Roman villa. Again, such finds may be coincidental. They will, however, merit further enquiry.[74]

Other ways of tracing possible survivals will also need to be considered. For instance, it is often noted that the presence of a chapel at Buckenhill Farm, Woolhope, dedicated to St Dubricius, is an indication that Ercic once extended eastwards of the Wye.[75] No such necessity is required if instead it is allowed that there were British communities still able to dedicate churches to British saints in areas north and east of the Wye surrounded by Anglian English communities, well into the later first millennium.

British Church sites in south Herefordshire

It is inevitably difficult to be certain about the survival of British Christian communities in north Herefordshire beyond the early seventh century. In contrast there is documentary evidence for the communities south of the Wye from just this period, and in particular for the foundation of churches. This is not the place to rehearse in detail what can be pieced together about this series of church foundations from the Llandaff charters, and from other sources. The charters indicate the founding of churches as early as the late sixth century, either in new locations, or as re-dedications of old ones (Fig 26).

What exactly was located within early church 'llan' sites is of interest. Although it has been assumed that most of these sites comprised open graveyards without chapels, the documentary evidence for churches in Ercic at least is unequivocal. One of the most intriguing things that can be deduced from the Llandaff charter evidence is that in at least two cases, there is a formula that refers to two separate churches set 'in uno cimiterio' or 'in eodem cimiterio'. These are thought to be the sites at Hentland and at Welsh Bicknor. In one case the two churches in the same cemetery were dedicated to St. Dyfrig and to St. Teilo, and in the other to St. Constantine and to the twelve saints.[76]

As in the northern part of the county, for instance possibly at Canon Pyon, church sites may have moved. A number of llan- sites in the valley of the Garren Brook, for instance, are attested from place-names but must represent now lost church sites. One example is Llanfernach – now Llangunnock – in the south-east corner of St Weonards parish. Another is Lenastone, which is rendered in a Llandaff charter as 'ecclesiam henlennic'.[77]

The existence of at least two Hentlands indicates the presence of former church-settlements at these places.[78] One of these sites, within Goodrich parish on the banks of the Wye below Symonds Yat, now has no trace of either church or churchyard. It has been suggested that this later became united with the church at Welsh Bicknor. The second refers not only to the present Hentland parish church, but possibly also to the site identified at Llanfrother as that of Dyfrig's first and most important monastery, the 'Hennlan super ripam Gui' of one of the Llandaff charters.[79]

Mention of this 'monastery' raises the question of the status of these early churches in respect to one another. Monasteries will have been places with a number of priests and novices. They were potentially also places of retreat and scholarship, and some may even have hosted libraries and scriptoria. Some were no doubt senior in reference to their foundation-date, and it is quite likely that any site referred to as 'the old llan' was just such an early foundation (as the Constantine dedication at Henllan/Garthbenni may also imply). Other early or major foundations appear to have the status of monasteries from the documentary evidence. In particular, reference to 'cenubia' in the charters seems deliberately to confer a status on these places superior to the other church communities.[80] Two such sites are those at Abbey Dore (the area of 'Lann Cerniu'), and Dorstone (the area of 'Cum Barruc').[81]

Other sites in south Herefordshire that could have been monasteries are Whitchurch, Llanveynoe, and Llangarron. The latter two will be discussed at greater length below. At Whitchurch, the church dedicated now to St Dubricius is probably that referred to in one charter as Lann Tiuinauc.[82] In the twelfth to fourteenth century, this site was known by four different names. Landeuenok (St Gwynnog, 1334), St Tiburcius (St Dubricius, 1325), Wytechirche (1320) and Albo Monasterio (1291). Coplestone-Crow reconstructs this to suggest that an early dedication to St Gwynnog (who is also the subject of a dedication at Llanwonog in Clodock parish) was replaced by one to St Dubricius. However, it seems most likely that this was another multiple dedication. The oldest fabric in the church still bears traces of the white plaster that correlates with the 'white church' name, and the former existence of a high-status structure here is also indicated by the presence of what is possibly a late first millennium font.[83]

Some church sites are immediately recognisable from the documentary sources because their topography is distinctive. An example is Kenderchurch, whose charter entry 'Llancinitir lann icruc' referring to the church of St Cynidr on top of the mound, is an accurate description of the hilltop on which the church now dedicated to St Mary stands.[84] Interestingly, this early dedication recurs in reference to a hermitage on an island near the Wye at Winforton, and this too may originally have been a monastic site.

Archaeology and the British Church in south Herefordshire

In contrast to this essentially documentary and topographical information on church sites, the specifically material and archaeological evidence remains sparse. So far the only indication that these communities were participating in the world of contacts (however tenuous) with the eastern Mediterranean is the recorded presence of a sherd of imported pottery from Goodrich.[85] This is of course very close to the ecclesiastical sites at Hentland and Whitchurch noted above, as well as being in the same general area as the concentration of early church sites in the Garren valley.

Although south Herefordshire is outside the area in which most inscribed stones of fifth to seventh century date are found, at least one inscription links the Ewyas area into the same world.[86] This is an inscribed stone found beneath the church of St. Clydog at Clodock. The inscription translates: 'To the dear wife of Guinddo, a resident of this place', and is clearly therefore a memoria. The form of such sites is nonetheless difficult to reconstruct. An ecclesiastical community at

Clodock presumably occupied a valley-bottom site close to the Monnow, if not actually on the site of the present church, then very close by. However, the present churchyard enclosure is no longer circular or oval, as llan-enclosures are generally assumed to have been. In contrast, the site of Martinstow church considerably southwards on the Garren, and abandoned in the nineteenth century, does conform to type. This is because although the later churchyard featured straight lengths of stone walling, the earlier boundary was clearly curvilinear. The same is manifestly the case at Llangarron nearby.

Another question to be considered is whether any early fabric can be identified within the builds of these south Herefordshire churches. It is generally presumed that British churches were built in timber, and that stone structures were rare, despite both the excavated examples in Wales already noted, and plentiful evidence from the western seaboard of the British Isles.[87] The presence of megalithic boulders upon which part of the north wall of Peterstow church is built suggests a possible early, and British Church, origin for this structure. An archway forming part of the north entrance of Upton Bishop church is also unusual. This has similarities to the building traditions of Anglo-Saxon church building, as does the north doorway at Michaelchurch. The presence of tufa in the fabric of some churches south of the Wye will be noted later.

No memorial altars, *leachta*, or early crosses have so far been recorded in Herefordshire. However, one site in Ewyas features stones clearly in the same tradition. This is the site of St Beuno's, now St Peter's, church at Llanveynoe. There are a series of three stones at this site that indicate that an ecclesiastical centre of some importance once existed here.

The first two stones are cross-incised slabs, and have been assumed to be late commemorative stones. However, at least one of these, featuring an unusual crucifixion representation, is closely similar to other such representations as at Phillack in Cornwall, that Charles Thomas has interpreted as frontal panels of stone altars. The second stone bears an incised Latin cross with pendant alpha and omega signs. Along one edge it bears a dedicatory inscription. The name formula and script of this inscription is almost identical to one on another cross-incised slab from the early monastic site at Ardwall Isle in south-west Scotland. This may also be a frontal stone, or one of the quadrangular stones set in the top of a *leacht*-type altar. Alternatively, it may be a fragment of a larger decorated stone cross. These stones have been attributed stylistically to the late eleventh century. However, although the Latin form of the crosses could be taken to support at least a late first millennium date, the earliest dated examples are of the seventh century.[88]

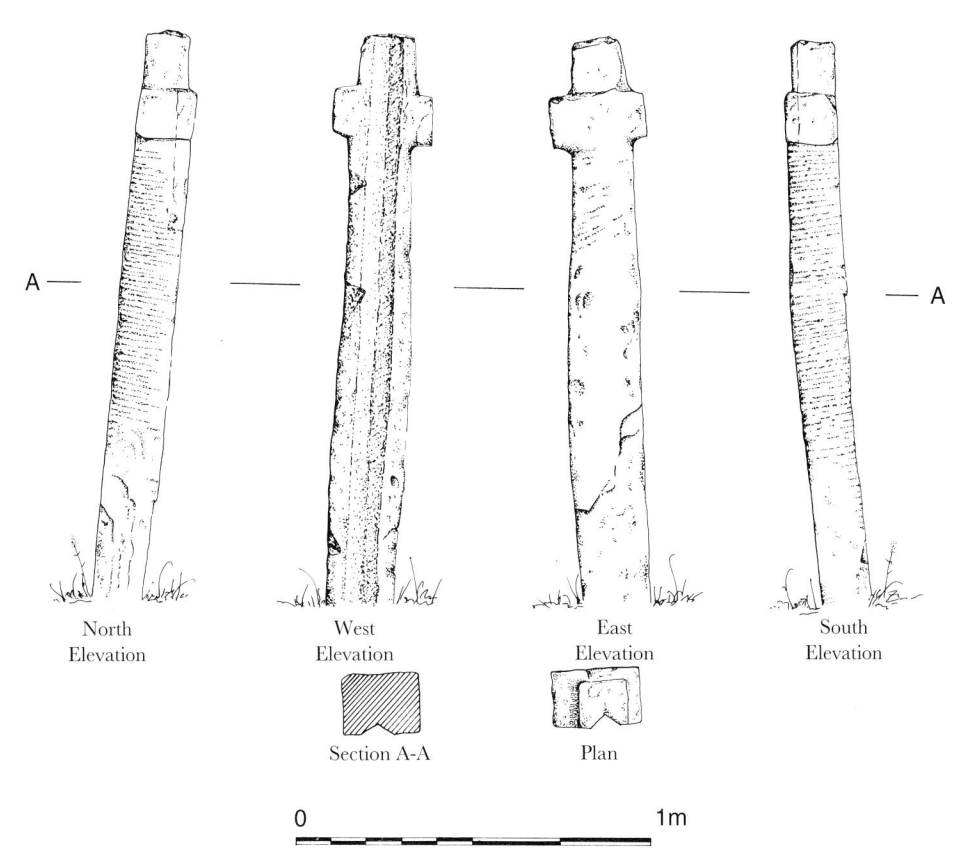

ARCHAEOLOGY AND THE THREE EARLY CHURCHES OF HEREFORDSHIRE 121

Fig 27 The short-armed cross in the churchyard at Llanveynoe. The arms and 'ledge' at the rear would probably have supported an elaborate timber cross-superstructure.
The groove in the front of the stone was possibly used for libations.
© *Copyright Herefordshire Archaeology*
For Llanveynoe church and cross see colour plates 5 and 6

The third stone at Llanveynoe has largely escaped previous notice, but comprises the best evidence presently observable on the site, for its former importance. The stone is an example of a classic form of the short-armed cross known from all over western Britain, but especially associated with sites like Ardwall Isle in Galloway, and those on the Isle of Man.[89]

In the year 2000 this stone, which stands 1.6m high from present ground level was recorded by *Herefordshire Archaeology* staff.[90] The short-arm form is thought to have been designed for the support of a wooden cross superstructure, and the stone step or 'saddle' visible on the back of the Llanveynoe stone is explicable in these terms (Fig 27). Of greatest interest is the fact that the lower part of the shaft of the cross clearly tapers, from about 0.4m above present ground-level. This, together with the form of a curious groove down the front face, and the apparently deliberate incline backwards, of the upper part of the cross, have important implications for its original setting and use. The cross can confidently be identified as a memorial stone cross the lower tapered end of which was inserted into a *leacht* or similar structure.

It is even possible that the stone marked a burial-place or memorial of St Beuno himself. The version of the *Life* of St. Samson noted above recounts the ritual surrounding Samson's burial: 'the body was taken and honourably carried by the clergy and buried in the midst of quadrangular stones standing upright in the cemetery, a stone cross being placed above and the insignia of a bishop inscribed below.' The cross at Llanveynoe is, therefore, exactly one such cross. The tapering of its lower portion would appear to have been created deliberately to facilitate its 'hafting' within the cairn of stones surmounting a grave of a pre-eminently saintly personage.

The Life of St Beuno records that King Ynyr of Gwent granted lands in Ewyas to Beuno around 600, and it has been deduced that he therefore founded his first church and monastery at Llanveynoe.[91] The king is said then to have enrolled in the monastery. Beuno nonetheless left on a further and protracted circuit of church founding in Wales, dying at Clynnog in the Lleyn peninsula around 648. It would have been quite within the normal practice of the time for relics of St Bueno's body to have been returned to Llanveynoe for burial either immediately, or some years afterwards when his cult had grown.

The frontal groove cut on this stone cross merits further explanation. It is undoubtedly an original feature of the stone, and is unlikely to have been purely decorative. One possibility is that it was cut for the pouring of libations downwards into the tomb. This would explain why the groove begins from the very top of the stone, and extends down even along the tapering part of the shaft. As such it may provide a not altogether surprising instance of the persistence of aspects of religious belief and practice from Romano-British times. A libation conduit consisting of a lead pipe leading from above ground down into a lead tank containing a cremation is recorded from a late Roman cist grave at Caerleon, in just the area that was later central to the kingdom of Gwent.[92]

The Llanveynoe stones are stated to have come from the field next to the churchyard, and recent survey by *Herefordshire Archaeology* staff has located and mapped the presence of an earthwork complex here, into which the later churchyard has been inserted. It may simply be that the survival or recovery of such stones has been better here at Llanveynoe, but the link to the cult of St

ARCHAEOLOGY AND THE THREE EARLY CHURCHES OF HEREFORDSHIRE 123

Beuno puts this site squarely within the wider tradition of early Christian monastic centres throughout the western seaboard of Britain.

Coming face-to-face with the British Church: the Llangarron figure

After all these tantalising hints of locations aassociated with the British Church, it comes as something of a shock to be brought literally face-to-face with

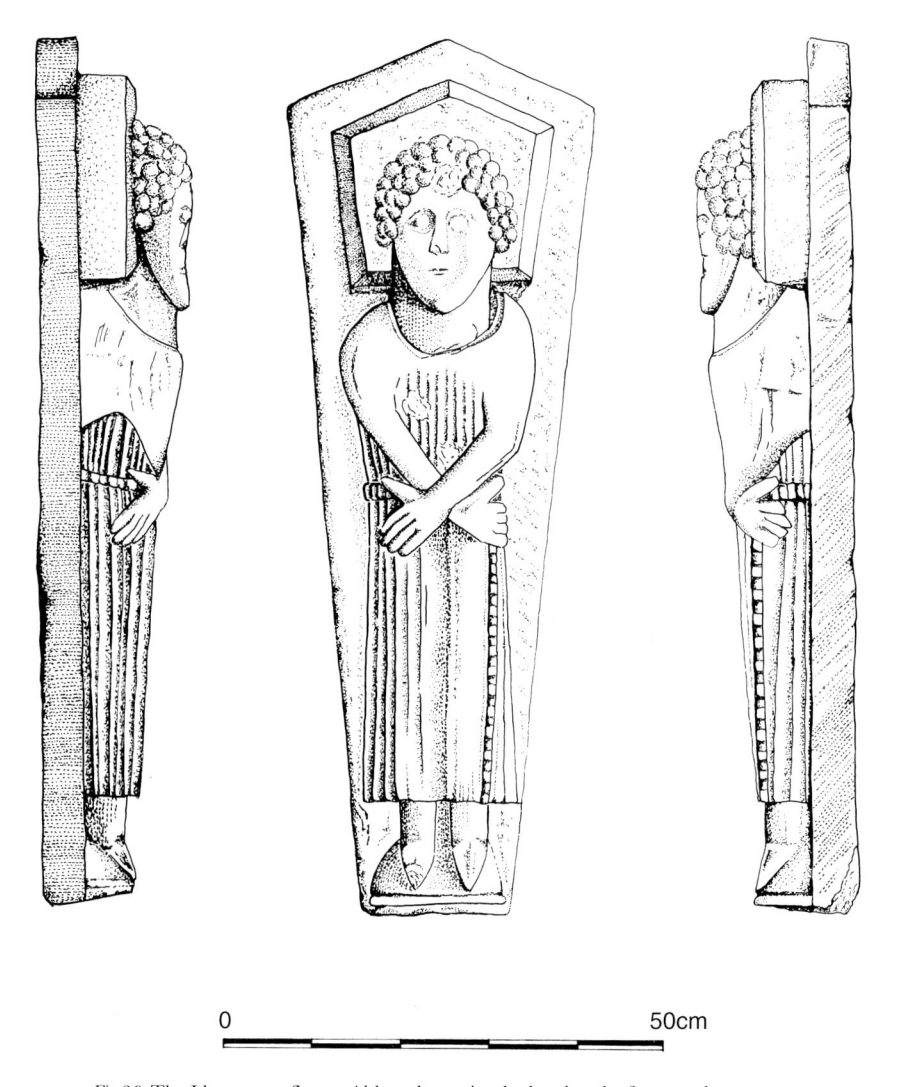

Fig 28 The Llangarron figure. Although previously dated to the fourteenth century, the origins of the stone carving could be first millennium.
©*Copyright Herefordshire Archaeology.*
For Llangarron church see colour plate 7

a sculpture in the church at Llangarron that may represent a member of that Church in the fifth or sixth century. This encounter is experienced inside another of the churches in the centre of the Garren area of south Herefordshire discussed earlier. The sculpture concerned features a representation of a figure in stone that bears attributes characteristic of pagan insular sculptural traditions, together with some from the late Roman world (Fig 28). The stone carving has been interpreted in the past as the cover from a fifteenth century child's coffin.[93] This seems to have been adduced from the shape of the edges of the stone. However, the possibility has not been considered that these were formed when the figure as now surviving was cut from a larger stone.

Detailed examination of the figure itself indicates the extreme unlikelihood of a high medieval date.[94] Firstly, the representation fits well within known traditions of Iron Age and Romano-British figure sculpture. The half-round figure sculpting, the tapering proportions of the body (with a disproportionately-sized head reducing to tiny legs and feet), the triangular-cut jaw, and the protruding lentoid-shaped eyes are the key attributes. The main classical and late Roman feature is the representation of the hair, depicted as a covering of raised dots. The feet are treated summarily. A near-identical form for the feet of a half-round figure sculpture is to be seen on the tombstone of Philus from late Romano-British Cirencester, for instance.

What could be ascribed only to the British church is the garb the figure is depicted as wearing. This is in effect a simple clerical gown tied at the waist with a cord. Its simplicity stands in stark contrast to the vestments usually depicted on medieval grave-slabs. This therefore appears to be a representation, whether from an altar frieze or a memorial stone, of a priest of the early British church. The lack of obvious parallels is worrying, but if it is indeed a stone of this kind and of this date, it is a remarkable survival.

It is perhaps worth asking what it is doing at this particular location. The church not long ago was set within a circular churchyard, which, as we have seen from other places such as Llangan and Capel Meulog, may simply have been the last in a series of such ecclesiastical enclosures here. The dedication of the church is interesting, to St Deinst, one of the local saints whose activities or cult occurred only within the immediate polity of Ercic and Gwent, since the only other known dedication is at Itton in Monmouthshire.

However, of greater interest is the name of the settlement. There are probably upwards of twenty llans in the valley of the Garren brook and its northern branch the Gamber (in Welsh, Amyr), and some of them were noted above. Of all these, only one is termed Llan-garron, the church-enclosure or settlement on the Garren, and one might wonder why this is so. One possibility is simply that it was the largest settlement in the area. Another now conceivable is that it was because here there once existed a monastic community, wealthy and important enough to have sponsored figure carvings of its priests.

The Anglian Church

The earliest history of the English settlement of the western areas of the West Midlands at present remains somewhat obscure.[95] The sources are meagre, but there is every indication that the first westward movement into Herefordshire did not occur until late in the sixth century. The most plausible recent reconstruction views this first as a westwards push into the Forest of Dean area, from Gloucestershire and following the Battle of Dyrham in 577. Welsh annals record that this was repulsed. A less perceptible 'folk' penetration from the Midlands is inferred from place-name evidence, taking place perhaps in the early seventh century.[96] It is possible that the migration was peaceful, but this cannot simply be assumed to have been the case.

What appears certain is that this movement of people on a significant scale had occurred early in the seventh century. By that time there may have existed a recognisably Anglian polity centred upon north-central Herefordshire. Place-names provide some indication that any such grouping probably represented a political fusion of people of British and of Anglo-Saxon origin. Such a situation certainly seems to have obtained in the kingdom of the Hwicce in the Gloucestershire-Worcestershire region, based upon Winchcombe. There seems no reason to suppose that the Herefordshire situation was significantly different, except, perhaps, for the presence of a yet larger British element.[97]

The field evidence for the migration, and the establishment of this 'Magonsaetan' kingdom, is currently in effect non-existent. However, the distribution of early dykes is interesting, suggesting a complex process of exclusion (including self-exclusion) of those north Herefordshire communities unwilling to consider themselves part of a new hybrid culture.[98]

Much of what we know about the early English church comes from the writings of the Northumbrian monk, Bede. Perhaps due to distance, but more probably because of the preponderance of the British element, we nonetheless learn little from Bede's 'Ecclesiastical History' about the origins of the Anglian Church in Herefordshire. The story of the early formation of this new church organisation in the county is therefore, if anything, even more obscure than that of either the Romano-British or the British Church.

Much of the evidence for the development of ecclesiastical institutions in Herefordshire particularly towards the end of the first millennium has already been rehearsed in this volume and elsewhere.[99] Elsewhere, such as in Oxfordshire and Worcestershire, the documentation is relatively extensive, and consists of charters granting land to monasteries, and for the late Saxon period, of wills, as well as the records of the proceedings of Church councils.[100]

Fundamental to the organisation of the Anglian Church was its network of minsters. This term covers a variety of size and kind of church establishment, but the majority were in effect local canonries, from each of which a small band of priests ministered to the local population. In parallel, the population often from wide areas were buried at the minster churches.[101] Other kinds of ecclesiastical centre existed, however, and three in particular deserve mention. Firstly, there were the cathedrals and their monastic establishments. Secondly, there were smaller monasteries founded for or by the Mercian nobility. These were sometimes located in relatively remote places, such as is documented at Breedon-on-the-Hill in Leicestershire. Thirdly, there were the estate churches and chapels, which it is assumed were served by clergy attached to the households of local lords.

The archaeology of Anglian Christianity

The question of how the earliest Christians can be recognised has been a major issue for those studying the material evidence for Anglo-Saxon Christianity. Where is the evidence for the conversion of the Anglian population in the seventh century? John Blair has suggested that it may exist at the sites and in the burial grounds of minster churches and their dependent chapels. In west Oxfordshire, for instance, he has noted that in female graves of the period there have been found pendant crosses and brooches, and bronze so-called thread-boxes.[102] He thinks that these latter can more convincingly be interpreted as personal reliquaries, and that they mark a point of transition in personal beliefs.

Structural evidence for the major churches of what became the Anglian Church in Mercia has come from a series of excavations at ecclesiastical sites in the Midlands. Prominent among these is Repton, the site of a monastery and the reputed burial place of several Mercian kings.[103] The archaeology of the sites of residences and monasteries not only comprises the remains of the structures themselves, but also the residues of major building operations, as at St Peter's church in Northampton, and at Eynsham Abbey in Oxfordshire. At both sites, circular mortar mixers have been found in quantity.[104] Building in stone anywhere is still thought to have been unusual through much of the Saxon period, and appears to have been reserved in many cases for religious buildings.

Considerable effort has been devoted in central and southern England to the study of the standing fabric of existing churches, to look for pre-Conquest evidence. Much of such fabric probably dates to the eleventh century, and the establishment of the parochial system.[105] In some cases, the standing structural evidence can be related to the former existence of monasteries, and survival of their major churches. Cases in point are Breamore in Hampshire and Brixworth in Northamptonshire.

Our current understanding of the internal arrangements of Anglian churches is limited by the number of sites that have been extensively investigated. An example of a fully excavated minster church is that of St Peter's at Barton-upon-Humber in Lincolnshire. Here the sites of the font, altar and screen have been located, showing some remarkable continuities of practice.[106] The investigation of Mercian churches of more modest proportions has been very limited so far. What has been claimed as the entire plan of St Bertelin's church at Stafford was recovered through salvage excavation in the 1950s.[107]

Churches attached to major manorial centres have been located through excavation at North Elmham in Norfolk (the site also of an East Anglian bishopric), Raunds in Northamptonshire, Wicken Bonhunt in Essex, and Flixborough in Lincolnshire. This latter site was excavated between 1989 and 1991 and gave an indication of the kinds of material present at such sites. The site was in use between the seventh and tenth centuries, and up to seven large hall buildings at first thought to be monastic and now considered to be domestic buildings were present.[108]

A mortuary chapel with infant and four adult burials inside it was in use between 750 and 850, before being rebuilt as a domestic structure. Finds from the site included seven styli and an inscribed lead plaque, a variety of jewellery, a hanging-bowl mount, and bronze vessels. An iron bell and carpentry tools were found in a lead tank, and there was evidence for textile manufacture, leather working, bone working and metalworking. Imports included Ipswich ware pottery, lava quernstones, silver coinage and glass vessels. Fine ceramics included imports from France, Belgium and Germany.

It is salutary that even a site with such rich and scriptorial material as this was not accepted as a major ecclesiastical centre, in part due to its lack of secure documentation historically. Definite traces of the form of Mercian middle and late Saxon monastic establishments continue to be elusive.

The Anglian Church and the early Diocese of Hereford

The first evidence for the existence of the bishopric at Hereford is the reference in a Council of Canterbury in 803 to Wulfheard, bishop of the Church at Hereford.[109] Mention was made in the same Council that certain monasteries had been given to Hereford 'in ancient days'. This could be taken to substantiate the tradition that the first incumbent was Bishop Putta, presiding between 670 and 680. Wulfheard was accompanied to Canterbury in 803 by an abbot, three priests and deacons, and this gives an indication of the extensive establishment that existed at that time in Hereford. The dependent monasteries of 803 probably included Bromyard, which was mentioned in a grant of land in the Frome valley by the church at Hereford in the 840s. Further minsters in the county for which similar subsidiary monastic status might be inferred, and for which charter or other historical evidence exists, are Lye near Lingen, Leominster, Ledbury, Acton Beauchamp and St Guthlac's, Hereford.[110]

The identification of individual minster churches is far from easy. The best we can often do is use retrospective arguments from later information. In Herefordshire, much of this comes from the Domesday survey, a document clearly not intended for the purpose of reviewing the nature and extent of the Anglo-Saxon church in the county. John Blair has undertaken this retrospective task, using the mention of two or more priests to indicate the location of superior churches.[111] This produces what looks like an unrealistically small number of minsters in Herefordshire, with minsters only at Leominster, Bromyard, Hereford, Ewias Harold, Fownhope, Ledbury, and Linton. It has been suggested that by adding in all Domesday mention of priests and churches, a more believable and denser pattern emerges, with a further 34 potential sites locatable.[112]

Church fabric and Anglo-Saxon churches in Herefordshire

The material evidence for the existence and form of structures associated with the Anglian Church in Herefordshire is at present restricted to the results of quite limited studies of fabric survival (Fig 29). The Taylors in their monumental and country-wide survey of church architecture initially identified seven cases in the county where they thought Saxon fabric was likely to have survived. On reconsideration, and relating this to documentary sources, they later included only Tedstone Delamere.[113] This singular evidence comprised a strip-work gable, forming an inverted V-shape, surviving as a relict feature in the fabric of the north nave wall. Such features mark the former existence of transepts (as can be seen at former monastic churches such as Breamore in Hampshire already mentioned), or of porches. The Tedstone gable is located above a blocked

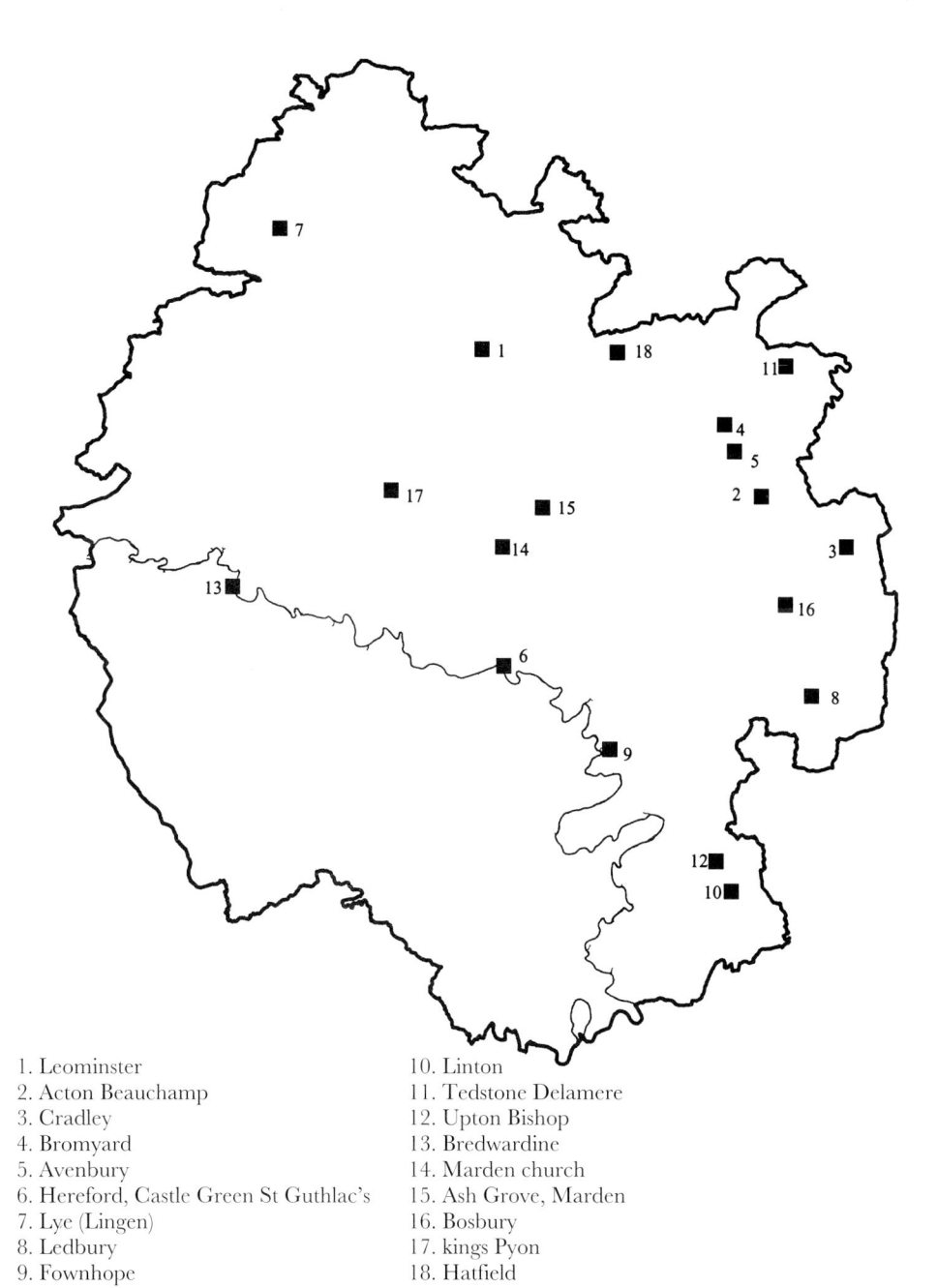

ARCHAEOLOGY AND THE THREE EARLY CHURCHES OF HEREFORDSHIRE 129

1. Leominster
2. Acton Beauchamp
3. Cradley
4. Bromyard
5. Avenbury
6. Hereford, Castle Green St Guthlac's
7. Lye (Lingen)
8. Ledbury
9. Fownhope
10. Linton
11. Tedstone Delamere
12. Upton Bishop
13. Bredwardine
14. Marden church
15. Ash Grove, Marden
16. Bosbury
17. kings Pyon
18. Hatfield

© *Crown copyright. All rights reserved. Herefordshire Council. LA09069L. 2001*
© *Copyright Herefordshire Archaeology*

Fig 29 The Anglian church in Herefordshire. The map shows the location of key minster churches and monasteries, and other sites mentioned in the text.

doorway on the north side of the nave, and is therefore most likely to represent the former existence of a porch here.

In the last two decades of the twentieth century there has therefore been some dispute over how much of the structural fabric of existing churches can be regarded even as transitional Saxo-Norman in Herefordshire. In the less sceptical direction, it has been argued that some combinations of features can be taken as indicative of the likely former existence of a pre-Norman structure.[114] These features are counter-pitched masonry (producing a 'herring-bone' effect), tufa stone blocks, and the presence of some other structural evidence for the former existence of a pre-Conquest church (chiefly, the presence of possible early stone carving or a particular architectural feature).

A theoretical maximum of 38 churches in Herefordshire have thereby been considered to feature at least one of these three indicators of early structures.[115] In contrast, only Bredwardine, Hatfield and Wigmore are seen to possess all three. If two of the three indicators is deemed sufficient, Munsley, Mathon, Edvin Loach, Tedstone Delamere, King's Pyon, Letton, and Llancillo can be added. Such an approach has its shortcomings.[116] Future work needs to be directed to the investigation of whole churches. At Michaelchurch and Upton Bishop, for instance, as well as at Tedstone Delamere and Bredwardine, likely late Saxon archways or doorways provide a starting-point for such investigation.

The case of Bredwardine, located on a high bluff overlooking the south bank of the Wye, offers a glimpse of the potential. Like nearby Moccas, this structure possesses indisputably Romanesque features, and there has been much use of tufa for architectural detailing. Both churches appear to have had the west ends of their naves entirely remodelled, while featuring elaborate north and south doorways built very close to the west end of the nave in each case. At Bredwardine, the infilling of the dismantled west door reveals this to have been of monumental proportions.

Several authorities have deduced that the original chancel at Bredwardine was incorporated into an enlarged nave and was replaced around 1300 by a later chancel on an entirely different orientation.[117] There is however no plausible reason why such a sequence would have produced such an odd arrangement as is now evident. The three distinct 'cells' of the church here each have different orientations, the most eccentric of which is the eastern-most. Doubts about the claimed sequence of development are compounded when the extent of the use of tufa in the 'new' chancel is appreciated.

The presence here of a doorway in the south elevation close to the junction with the supposed former chancel is the piece of evidence that begins to require the entire unravelling of the former interpretation. This doorway, which is integral with the build of this eastern-most cell of the church and again built from tufa, features an inverted V-shape pointed arch. This arch is of a distinctive style that has elsewhere (such as at St Peter's church, Barton-upon-Humber, previously mentioned) been identified as a clear indicator of Saxon date (Fig 30).

We can now outline a different explanation for the otherwise uncomfortable orientations of the walls of the putative 'earlier' chancel at Bredwardine. Rather than simply reflecting a superseded chancel, they become explicable as the consequence of linking up two formerly separate structures. The possibility exists that two separate structures at Bredwardine are present because the most easterly, 'new' chancel, was in fact the earliest of the structures now on the site. Moreover, this structure stands within the southern part of an early earthwork marked by a bank extending around the whole hilltop overlooking the Wye, and through which the original route to the river crossing passed. The western end of the nave has its formerly monumental west front standing actually upon the western bank of this enclosure. I suggest that what is represented here is a complex succession starting with an early (presumably British) church enclosure, and then followed by a succession or grouping of church structures built within its bounds.[118] One, and conceivably both, of the two apparently earliest elements among these structures, the present chancel and the nave, can be said now to possess indications of a pre-Norman (if only very late Saxon) date, and Anglian architectural form.

Fig 30 The south doorway in what is now the chancel of St Andrew's church, Bredwardine. Note the distinctive Saxon pointed-arch form
© *Copyright Herefordshire Archaeology.*

From fabric to bells

A footnote to this discussion of fabric, and of possible continuity from the British to the Anglian Church in northern Herefordshire, is provided by the story of two bells. Both are similar to large cow-bells, and are of iron coated with bronze. One of them is of a typical simple tapered form with handle. It was recovered in 1848 from a pond close to Marden church (Fig 31). The second is of a more squared form, and was ploughed up in a field at Bosbury in 1890. Both conform to a type dated between the seventh and ninth centuries, and common in Ireland, and to some extent also Scotland and Wales.[119]

These so-called 'Celtic Bells' were used instead of bells hung in a belfry, to summon people to church services. They were also used (if the tradition recounted to Giraldus Cambrensis at Glascwm in the twelfth century is to be believed) in funeral processions to toll the dead back to the churchyard. What their provenance suggests is that there were minsters at Marden (which has already been noted as likely), and at Bosbury (otherwise undocumented) in the first millennium, and that these institutions continued the practices of the British church.

Fig 31 An ecclesiastical hand-bell from Marden (Hereford Museum). This object neatly attests the synthesis of British and Anglian traditions. Ht 40cm

© *Copyright Herefordshire Archaeology*

The whole status of Marden, and of nearby Sutton, in the Anglo-Saxon period is currently under discussion. The existence here of an ecclesiastical centre in association with the likely royal centre might explain why the manor of Marden was a royal estate with unique ties to Hereford. It might also explain why St Guthlac's monastery owned so much land in the vicinity by the eleventh century.[120]

Cemeteries and chapels

So far, the amount of below-ground archaeological investigation of churches in Herefordshire has been minimal. No excavations designed specifically to understand the sequence of development have taken place, except for limited trenching at old Llanwarne church.[121] Few early burials within churchyards have been excavated and none dated. However, a radiocarbon determination was obtained from a skeleton excavated within Lower Sapey churchyard northeast of Bromyard and just over the border in Worcestershire. This church is also, co-incidentally, a structure featuring counter-pitched stone and tufa in its fabric, and the radiocarbon sample indicated a probable tenth century date for the skeleton.[122]

Another burial has been found during drainage works just to the east of the enclosure wall of St Mary's church at King's Pyon. A north-south ditch some 30m further to the east, and a pit containing pottery of unusual form about the same distance southwards were undated. However, if this burial was among the early interments here, we may suppose that, as at Shipton-under-Wychwood in Oxfordshire (where Saxon burials were similarly found some distance from the church), this indicates a likely minster status of the church here, in accordance also with the documented Domesday presence of a priest.[123]

In reference to Oxfordshire, John Blair has suggested that it was very unlikely and perhaps impossible that the whole population was buried in the cemeteries of minster churches. Where, he therefore asked, are the rural cemeteries that were not located alongside such churches? The answer is that these cemeteries do exist, as indicated in that county by the evidence from Beacon Hill, Lewknor, and Chimney near Bampton.[124] The latter is of especial interest, since it can be shown from documentary evidence to have been dependent on the minster at Bampton, some five kilometres away.

We do have the emergent possibility of just such a situation in Herefordshire, perhaps significantly again at Marden. Here, burials were found over an extended period of time, at a quarry on a prominent ridge overlooking the Lugg valley, at a place called Ash Grove. Part of the extensive cemetery was investigated in the early 1950s. The burials were apparently without grave-goods, and were carefully oriented. The location of the cemetery on this hilltop within the parish of Marden, but 3.5km away from the likely mother church, is thought to mark the site out as a possible dependent cemetery which nonetheless failed to become the focus for an independent parish.[125]

The archaeology of Anglian monasteries in Herefordshire

The relation of the British church communities to the Anglo-Saxon churches that succeeded them in Herefordshire is at this stage far from clear. However, examples where continuity can plausibly be argued include Leominster, Canon Pyon, and Bredwardine already mentioned. Another example that may also be added is Stanford Bishop, where a circular churchyard is complemented by traces of an outer ditch, and by a standing stone at the lych gate.

The only likely monastic church that we have any physical information about from excavation so far in Herefordshire is St Guthlac's in Hereford, located within the outer ward of the later castle. In 1973, a graveyard with a very great density of burials was located and partly excavated there, with the earliest apparently going back to the seventh century. Part of a possible stone church was examined near to the south-eastern corner of the present park, while a smaller church with a timber predecessor had been examined to the north of this, in an excavation of 1960.[126]

This smaller structure was re-interpreted during the later excavation as originally an Anglo-Saxon structure. However, it was not apparently realised at the time that this was most likely the chapel of St Martin, which it has been assumed on the evidence of medieval documentation must have been of twelfth century origin.[127] If the identification is correct, then the chapel could have been rebuilt on the site of an earlier (and perhaps British) foundation.[128]

Meanwhile, it also seems most probable that the larger structure was part of the monastic church of St Guthlac. Parch-marks noted in grass northwards of the excavated structure could be taken to indicate that a large associated monastic complex existed here. As at Leominster, the conventual buildings were apparently located to the north of the church. The evidence of the two oriented structures does not give a point of origin for the monastery here, but the location next to the Wye is, as we have seen, typical of some of the most important of the likely early British ecclesiastical sites, including Hentland, Whitchurch, Bolgros and Bredwardine.

Acton Beauchamp and Anglo-Saxon monastic crosses

This is not to say that the material evidence for Anglian monasteries in Herefordshire is limited to Hereford city. Of most immediate significance here is the cross-shaft fragment that survives re-used as the lintel for the doorway into the tower of St Giles' church, Acton Beauchamp (see Blair, this volume). King Aethelbald of Mercia had granted land here to his associate, Buca, early in the

Fig 32 The Acton Beauchamp cross-shaft. This version of the inhabited vine-scroll ornament is considered to date to the early ninth century. Length 1.5m © *Copyright Herefordshire Archaeology*

For Acton Beauchamp church see colour plate 3

eighth century, 'to be a perpetual dwelling for the servants of God'.[129] The stone has a square-cut but tapering form, and features a panel with inhabited vine-scroll ornament which is aligned along the axis of the stone (Fig 32).

The vine-scroll makes three loops from the base of the panel, narrowing slightly towards the top. The lower loop contains a bird, and the upper two loops each fail to entirely contain leaping fantastical beasts. This form of decoration is regarded as typical of a characteristically Mercian style influential throughout the ninth century, and found not only on sculpture, but also in metalwork and on manuscript decorations. The style of the Acton Beauchamp panel has been compared closely to that of the decoration on a cross-head from Cropthorne in Worcestershire (also a documented site with royal and monastic associations). Both are considered to be early examples of the Mercian inhabited vine-scroll style.[130]

The Acton Beauchamp piece has so far been considered in isolation, and has not always been recognised as a cross-shaft fragment. However, not only can such an identification be confirmed, but it can also be seen as part of a series of such monuments in the region, with reference to a similar fragment surviving at St. Andrew's church at Wroxeter. Here there is late historical evidence that the shaft was part of a freestanding cross (Fig 33).[131]

the North Side Wroxeter   the West Side Wroxeter

Fig 33 The cross that once stood in St Andrew's churchyard Wroxeter. The upper tapering section mirrors the Acton Beauchamp shaft. After White, R and Barker, P, *Wroxeter: Life and Death of a Roman City*, page 141, Tempus, Stroud, 1998, by courtesy of the authors and publishers

This cross may also have been similar to the one seen by William of Malmesbury at Hereford in c 1125 (see Hillaby, this volume).[132] An inscription on this cross was commissioned by Cuthbert, who was bishop between 736 and 740. The cross was erected to commemorate the new burial place of three of Cuthbert's predecessors and the local prince, Milfrith, whose name links him back to the Magonsaetan royal family of the seventh century. The date of the cross is slightly earlier than that suspected for the Acton one, but the latter may also have been set up by the abbot of the monastery and have carried a dedicatory inscription.

Built into the fabric of the church of St James at Cradley are parts of what may be yet another such stone cross. The piece there that has received most notice so far is what is identified as a frieze with crockets in alternating directions.[133] This may be from the central band of a Wroxeter-type cross. However, other fragments are also built into the fabric, including the south wall of the chancel. A rebuilt doorway is also similar to those we have already noted at Upton Bishop and at Michaelchurch. These clues raise at least the possibility of an otherwise undocumented monastery here.

Conclusion

Herefordshire was part of that area of the country that remained British for as much as two centuries after the economic collapse of 'Roman Britain'. Although this is a major reason why the study of early church communities in this county is of more than local interest, it is not the only one. Another is the location of the county at the margin of, though largely within, the area of denser settlement in Roman Britain. Yet others are the evidence of continuity of religious organisation and institutions through the two centuries 400 – 600 and (in the south of the county) beyond, and, perhaps the most important, the likelihood that the character of the emergent Anglian-English Church was influenced to an unknown but substantial degree by that of the British population that absorbed the incoming settlers.

Archaeology can provide but a faint register of the lived historical complexities of such a dynamic period of British history, especially given the greater use of organic (rather than inorganic) materials for artefacts then. Even when the traces and materials are relatively abundant, as in the Romano-British period, evidence of early Christian communities is elusive. Archaeology does have three critical advantages over the meagre historical record for the period, however. The first is the relative ubiquity of material traces, and the insights into very local circumstances it provides through those remains. The second is its evidence for succession: both in very local sequences of activity, and across very considerable spans of time. The third is the impartiality of its evidence. While wealthier establishments are likely to have given rise to more robust constructions, archaeology has no more to say, inherently, about the fate of British as of Anglian communities. Before closing this contribution, it is therefore perhaps worth summarising some of its key insights.

For the Romano-British period, up to two-thirds of the land area of Herefordshire could be considered to lie within the 'civil zone'. This latter part of Britain was not so much a 'lowland zone' topographically, as one characterised by the same dense pattern of roads, farms, and major settlements located at nodal points on the communications network. The indications of the presence of a Christian community at Kenchester are as slight as at most other places within this 'lowland' part of the country. However, the presence of rich villas in the immediate hinterland of Kenchester indicates that conditions locally were not necessarily very different from those obtaining in, say, the hinterland of Dorchester in Dorset.

The discovery that the known Romano-British settlement by Stretton Grandison in the Frome valley was walled, and that the circuit of these defences was no shorter than that around Kenchester, reinforces the impression of a settled affluent farming community.[134] Not only was building stone and other material being imported from the Cotswolds, from Oxfordshire, and beyond: ideas travelled westwards, too. The likely late Roman frieze incorporated into the fabric of the church of St John the Baptist at Upton Bishop may well have derived from a building complex nearby. Such a settlement would have been one of several representing the fourth century phase of the Romano-British centre at 'Ariconium', whose wealth was founded on an iron producing industry originating before the Roman invasion.

There are many indications of continuity into succeeding centuries, and these include ecclesiastical ones. Many strands of evidence have been examined here, some more robust than others. Archaeologically, these are more numerous and more tangible in the south of the county. Place-names, coincidences of Romano-British remains with church sites, and to some extent also church dedications, provide no more than circumstantial clues.

Sites such as that surrounding the church of St Peter at Llanveynoe give in contrast very tangible expression to the first millennium Christian community detectable here otherwise only by the place-name link to St Beuno. Here more than anywhere else in the county, with its three early memorial stones and clearly-traceable *llan* enclosure, the presence of the early British Church as a once-living entity is most vividly felt. This should occasion no surprise, of course, since historically nowhere better expresses the lived ambiguities of 'Welsh' Herefordshire. Nonetheless, what that site also represents is an untapped archaeological potential shared throughout the county. This is perhaps most sharply brought to mind when standing within the circular hilltop enclosure at Stanford Bishop by Bromyard in which St James' church also stands. The British church was noted as possessing as its memorial in stone also the likely early medieval, first millennium AD, figure of a cleric at Llangarron.

The material evidence, such as it is, for the Anglian/earlier English Church in the county, was considered. Here again, though meagre, this evidence has yet to be examined as closely as it merits. Attention switches, almost for the first time, to the fabric of church buildings. However, this is at present of very limited utility. With less than a handful of exceptions, standing fabric will currently provide clues for the built form of late tenth or early eleventh century parish churches. Excavation has been limited so far to sites on the Castle Green at Hereford. However, a documented monastery at Acton Beauchamp south of Bromyard finds tangible expression in part of the shaft of a stone memorial cross.

The existence of a similar cross at St Andrew's church at Wroxeter in Shropshire, and its documented form as standing, from a drawing, enables us to envision what this cross at Acton looked like. This enables us to envisage the possibility that stones in the fabric of St James' church at Cradley came from a similar cross, and to infer, in turn, the presence of another, undocumented, monastery there. Yet it was minster churches and not monasteries (if such a clear distinction is indeed possible) that typified the organisation of the Anglian Church in Herefordshire. These may have had both large 'parishes' and dependent chapelries, the latter associated with burial grounds. It may therefore be that the as yet undated cemetery at Ash Grove in Marden has the greatest potential at the start of the third millennium to bring us into direct contact with the first millennium Anglian Christians in the county.

Acknowledgements

I would like to record my thanks to Tony and Ann Malpas for inviting me to contribute to 'The Early Church in Herefordshire' local history day school in June 2000, and for their forbearance in seeing the present chapter through to publication. I am also pleased to acknowledge the help of Tim Hoverd, Archaeological Projects Officer at *Herefordshire Archaeology* with the fieldwork reported here, and in preparing the line drawings for publication. Paul White produced the distribution maps. The Kenchester strap-end and Marden bell are illustrated courtesy of Hereford Museum, with thanks to Judy Stevenson for facilitating access. I thank the editorial group for this volume, for detailed comments on the manuscript draft of the chapter, and extend these also to Dr. Paul Stamper for kindly reading and commenting upon a penultimate draft version. Errors of fact and omission remain my responsibility. Finally, I wish to acknowledge the dedication of Peter Holliday, the Leominster librarian, and his staff, in providing a service conducive to the kind of research that is essential for the production of surveys, however preliminary, of the kind I have written here.

Notes and References

1. By the term 'early Church' I mean here the early organisation of a Christian community. This is not meant to imply that the communities concerned were either homogeneous or centrally organised. 'The Church' throughout the first millennium in Britain comprised a series of interrelated and interconnected, but sometimes quite antagonistic, groups. The intention is to convey rather that their sense of identity was not only Christian, but also (to them) recognisably ordered.

2. The Royal Commission on Historic Monuments, England, *An Inventory of the Historical Monuments of Herefordshire*, I (South-West, 1931), II (East, 1932), III (North-West, 1934).

3. Morris, J, *The Age of Arthur*, (repr 1995), 343, 346-50, 45.

4. The cult of Alban was sufficiently well-established for Gildas to have referred to 'sanctum Albanum Verolamiensem', and he also mentioned Aaron and Julian 'of the legionary town' (usually taken to mean Caerleon). For discussion of the date and character of the persecutions see Thomas, C, *Christianity in Roman Britain to AD 500*, (London, 1984) 46-50; and Frend, W H C, 'The Christianisation of Roman Britain' in Barley, M W & Hanson, R P C, *Christianity in Britain, 300-700*, (Leicester, 1968) 37-49.

5. The composition of these delegations is discussed in detail in Frend, (1968) see note 4, 38-9. See also Esmonde-Cleary, S, *The Ending of Roman Britain*, (London,1989) 121. For speculations about the location of diocese, Thomas (1981) see note 4, 197-200.

6. On Pelagius and Pelagianism Thomas (1981) see note 4, 53-60; Morris, J (1995) see note 3, 71-2; 338-45.

7. Esmonde-Cleary, (1989) see note 5, 121.

8. Esmonde-Cleary, (1989) see note 5, 162-8; Morris, (1995) see note 3, 343-4.

9. Germanus' apparent failure to call a synod was taken by Morris (1995, see note 3, 344-5) to indicate a general lack of success in stemming the tide of Pelagianism.

10. For the most detailed exegesis and documentation for this view see Thomas (1981) see note 4, especially 96-142.

11. For the last-mentioned, see Painter, K S, *The Water Newton Early Christian Silver*, British Museum (1977). More recently, the corpus has been further expanded by the Thetford Treasure, now also on display at the British Museum.

12. Mawer, C F, *Evidence for Christianity in Roman Britain: The small-finds*, British Archaeological Reports, British Series 243, (Oxford, 1995).

13. Mawer, see note 12, 136.

14. Thomas included these in his survey (see note 4, 101-2), but with clear caveats. The arguments for rejecting a Christian association are rehearsed in Mawer, see note 12, 39-40.

15. Henig, M, *Religion in Roman Britain* (London, 1985, 120-1), has made the point that 'it is worth making the effort in order to imagine what sort of faith it (that is, Christianity) would have seemed to a neutral observer in the time of Constantine'; he concluded that it was very much a minority and highly syncretistic faith, many of whose adherents would have been equally comfortable with the beliefs and conventions of rural paganism.

16. For a discussion of the sophisticated spiritual allegory deducible in the Brading representation, see Henig, (1985) see note 15, 220-1.

17. Green, C J S, 'The cemetery of a Romano-British Christian community at Poundbury, Dorchester, Dorset' in S.M. Pearce (ed), *The Early Church in Western Britain and Ireland*, British Archaeological Reports, British Series 102, (Oxford, 1982) 61-76. Green also suggested that the clustering of burials around important graves at Poundbury represented a quasi-pastoral or familial organisation.

18 Radford, C A Ralegh, 'Christian Origins in Britain', *Medieval Archaeology* (1971), 15, 1-12, was the first full survey of such sites. The most detailed recent account of the Silchester structure remains Thomas, (1981) see note 4, 169, 195, 214-17. Henig, (1985), see note 15, 222, regards it as 'a possible purpose-built urban shrine', in other words, not uncommon in a pagan context, but here with an alleged Christian use assumed rather than proven.

19 The evidence so far adduced is from the results of gradiometry and ground-penetrating radar survey south of the baths-basilica complex. These indicate the late presence of a rectangular structure 30m long (cf Silchester 20m long, including 'baptistery') and 13m wide (Silchester 10m) oriented east-west and with an apsidal eastern end, and located adjacent to a major street intersection. White, R, & Barker, P, *Wroxeter - Life and Death of a Roman City*, (Tempus, Stroud, 1998), 74, 107-8, Colour Plate 14.

20 Mawer, see note 12, 138-9.

21 Dark, K & Dark, P, *The Landscape of Roman Britain*, (Tempus, Stroud, 1997) provides an overview; McWhirr, A, *Roman Gloucestershire*, (Gloucester County Library Series, 1986), gives a more local perspective.

22 Frend, (1986) see note 4, 42; Painter, (1977) see note 11; Todd, M, *Roman Britain 55 B C - A D 400*, Fontana, 1981, 227-230.

23 Henig, M, See note 15, 123-7, 219, observed that feasting and secrecy were shared with many other 'mystery' cults of the later Roman world. Also the reasons for the rural provenance of much of the rich paraphernalia was that the wealthy patrons of the cults had no incentive to keep them in urban temples, whose treasures were at several points in the fourth century susceptible to confiscation by Imperial order.

24 Mawer, see note 12, 137; sites such as Brancaster and Richborough are prominent in the record.

25 Guy, C, 'Roman Circular Lead Tanks in Britain', *Britannia* XII, (1981) 271-6. The apparent predominance of chi-rho decorated examples may need to be reviewed, but was represented by seven out of then twelve known examples of lead tanks in Guy's survey. See also Watts, D J, 'Circular lead tanks and their significance for Romano-British Christianity, *Antiquaries Journal*', (1988) 68, 210-22.

26 Mawer, see note 12, 86-7.

27 Green, see note 17, 73; Mawer, see note 12, 93-4.

28 Jack, Col G H, & Hayter, A G K, jointly carried out the excavations (Reports of the Research Committee of the Woolhope Club, I and II, 1916 & 1926).

29 Regarded as such by Mawer as a result of her review of the evidence.

30 Henig, (1985) see note 15, 223.

31 The excavations were carried out in advance of quarrying, between 1977 and 1979, Wilmott, A R, & Rhatz, S P Q, 'An Iron Age and Roman Settlement outside Kenchester (Magnis), Herefordshire: Excavations, 1977-79', *Transactions of the Woolhope Naturalists' Field Club*, (1985), XLV, 36-185.

32 The apparently early date provides the best evidence, at present, against a Christian use for the tank.

33 Guy, (1981) see note 25, 271.

34 For the east gate cemetery see Jack & Hayter, see note 28. Morris, R, *Churches in the Landscape*, (Phoenix, 1989, 17ff) describes several cases, including Ilchester (Somerset) and Gloucester, where such continuity can be related to the sites of later churches located in the suburbs of Romano-British towns.

35 Mawer, see note 12, 63, 124.

36 RCHME, (1932) see note 2, II 45; Plate 78.

37 It was these stylistic similarities, and the colonnaded setting, which first raised the possibility to me that the piece could have a strong Christian connection. While preparing this paper for publication, I inspected the reconstructed wall-painting

at the British Museum. At one end of the painted frieze, there is a figure with only one arm so raised.

38 A representation of an 'orant' figure of this kind on a fourth century tombstone from Egypt, and a sixth century one from Overkirkhope, Selkirk, are cited by Thomas, (1981) see note 4, 94, along with the example of a row of such figures on an early fifth century sarcophagus from Tarragona, Spain.

39 Pevsner, N, *Buildings of England: Herefordshire*, (1963), 304, noted that 'The surviving portion depicts the head and shoulders of a man with right hand raised, inset in a round-headed recess. Alongside this figure is a second fragment, again in a recess, and now represented only by a fragment of the left hand'. Ray, K, 'A Romano-British stone frieze at Upton Bishop church', Herefordshire Archaeology Report, 25, 2001.

40 Fenn, R W D, 'Early Christianity in Herefordshire', *Transactions of the Woolhope Naturalists' Field Club*, (1968) 333-47; Thomas, (1981) see note 4, 267; Doble, G H, *St. Dubricius*, (Welsh Saints, No.2), (Guildford, 1943); Davies, W, *Wales in the Early Middle Ages*, (Leicester 1982).

41 For a recent vivid account of this period in its European context see Knight, J, *The End of Antiquity: Archaeology, Society and Religion AD 235-700*, (Tempus, Stroud, 1999).

42 No recent comprehensive survey of the form and archaeology of the early Christian church exists; the best general study remains Thomas, C, *The Early Christian Archaeology of North Britain*, (Oxford 1971).

43 Morris, R, see note 34, 10, quoting Lapidge, M & Herren, M (eds), *The Prose Works of Aldhelm* (Ipswich,1979) 158.

44 For a recent summary, see Campbell, E., 'The archaeological evidence for external contacts: imports, trade and economy in Celtic Britain AD 400-800' in Dark, K R, (ed) *External Contacts and the Economy of Late Roman and Post-Roman Britain* (Boydell, Woodbridge, 1996) 83-96.

45 Morris, J, see note 3, 340-2.

46 Radford, C A R, 'The Early Church in Strathclyde and Galloway', *Medieval Archaeology* (1967) 11, 105-126; Thomas, C (1971) see note 42.

47 The word is derived from the Latin 'lectus', a bed. In Ireland as in Wales (bedd), this was a term often used to denote a grave. Thomas suggested that these constructions might rather have been altars (1971, see note 42, 169-73), and this appears to have become an orthodoxy (cf. Laing, L, *The Archaeology of Late Celtic Britain and Ireland c 400–1200 AD*, (Methuen, 1975, 382).

48 Wade-Evans, A W, *Vitae Sanctorum Britanniae et Genealogiae*, (Cardiff, 1944, 217) quoted in Thomas, C (1971) see note 42, 173-5 and fig 84 which illustrates a 'ruined leacht' surviving into the early years of the C 20th, at Marown on the Isle of Man.

49 Thomas, C, (1971) see note 42, 181f. Stone altars with incised crosses are recorded in Herefordshire, (eg Wigmore church), and have been generally regarded as medieval in date (J. Tonkin, pers comm).

50 Esmonde-Cleary, S, (1989) see note 5, 126, 133.

51 James, H, 'Early Medieval Cemeteries in Wales', in Edwards, N, & Lane, A (eds) *The Early Church in Wales and the West* (Oxbow, 1992) 90-103.

52 Preston-Jones, A, 'Decoding Cornish Churchyards' in Edwards & Lane, (1992) see note 51, 104-124.

53 As at Llangan, Carmarthenshire, where earlier permutations of the enclosure have been revealed from the air (James, T A, 'Air Photography of Ecclesiastical sites in South Wales', 62-76 in Edwards & Lane, (1992) see note 51, figs 84 & 85).

54 James, (1992) see note 51, 98-9.

55 Hillaby, J, 'Leominster and Hereford: The Origins of the Diocese', in Whitehead, D, (ed), *Medieval Art, Architecture and Archaeology at Hereford*, British Archaeological Association, 1995).

56 The projected area was the district of Leen, the bounds of which are suggested in Coplestone-Crow, B, *Herefordshire Place-Names* British Archaeological Reports, British Series, 214, (Oxford, 1989) 6-9. The likelihood that integrity of various British territories was maintained, and perhaps even locally defined by dyke systems, needs to be kept in mind. Ray, K, 'Marking the Magonsaete? Herefordshire's post-Roman dyke systems', (in preparation).

57 This name can be rendered as 'Ergyn' in its early Welsh form, and is Anglicised as 'Erging'. Coplestone-Crow (1989, see note 56, 2-5) suggests former bounds to this kingdom (centred upon Ariconium) of the Monnow and Dore to the west, the Wye and the Frome valley to the north, the Malverns and the lower Leadon to the east, and the Severn to the south (following the pre-Conquest southern boundary of the Diocese of Hereford, and taking in Dean and the 'Cantref coch').

58 Coplestone-Crow (1989) see note 56, suggests that it was only ever a commote and not a former kingdom. If a distinction is made between church dedications that have parallels in Breicheiniog (St Cadog, St Clydawg, St Cynidr & St Cynog) and those with associations with St Dyfrig, it can be suggested that the former mark the territory of Ewyas and the latter Ercic; Wedell, N, 'St Ailworth: A Celtic Saint in the Black Mountains?' *Archaeologia Cambrensis* CXLVI (1997) 2000, 79-100. This might reflect the situation only in the later first millennium, reinforcing a potentially early date for the St Beuno dedication (see notes 63 & 88-91).

59 Fenn, (1968) see note 40, 334-9.

60 Davies, W, *The Llandaff Charters*, (Aberystwyth, 1979); Davies, (1982) see note 40.

61 Davies, (1982) see note 40, 164-6; These communities were sustained both from the wealth of these estates, and from gifts and fines, but not from tithes, which were unknown in 'Welsh' Herefordshire until the second millennium, see Pryce, H, 'Ecclesiastical Wealth in Early Medieval Wales', in Edwards & Lane, (1992) see note 51, 22-32.

62 Bolgros has been identified as Bellimoor, Preston-on-Wye, see Davies, (1982) see note 40, 144-5. Coplestone-Crow, (1989, see note 56, 169) has made a better identification of this site, described in the charter as 'super ripam Gui', as at present-day Bycross.

63 Some dedications may reflect an early development of the cult of these saints but some may belong to a later first millennium wave of re-dedication, eg in Cornwall (Preston-Jones, 1992, see note 52, 109) and in Carmarthenshire (Evans, J W, 'Aspects of the early church in Carmarthenshire' in James, H, (ed) *Sir Gar: Studies in Carmarthenshire History*, Carmarthen, 1991, 239-53).

64 For Wroxeter see White & Barker, (1998) see note 19, 118f. For Kenchester, see Wilmott, A R, 'Kenchester (Magnis): a reconsideration', *Transactions of the Woolhope Naturalists' Field Club*, XLIII, 1980,117-34.

65 Morris, R, (1989) see note 34, 31-4.

66 At Leintwardine, the later church stands actually within the walls of the former Roman settlement.

67 Ekwall, E, *The Place-Names of Lancashire*, (Manchester, 1922) 257; Jackson, J, 'Eccles in English Place-Names', in Barley & Hanson, (1968) see note 4, 87-92.

68 Coplestone-Crow (1989 see note 56,130) renders this without questioning as 'Spring at a Celtic Christian centre'.

69 Today, this is a small civil parish.

70 The potential difficulties of using place-names in this way are illustrated by the apparent presence of another 'eccles' name at Eccles Alley near Almeley, only a kilometre from Eccles Green. The medieval spelling of this name, Eckeley ('Ecca's wood or clearing'), bears out no 'eccles' link, and could even call into question the Eccles Green derivation. The suggestion has been made that the stone underpinning the south transept of

St. Nicholas' church at Norton Canon was possibly of Romano-British origin (RCHME, (1934) see note 2, III, 154, which states: 'large square stone with part of a setting-out line on the surface, probably Roman'). Dr Paul Stamper, English Heritage regional Inspector of Ancient Monuments, has recently visited this site with me, and has raised the interesting possibility that the object may instead represent a squared stone block with an incised tympanum upon it. This presumably would once have formed the head to one of the main doorways into the church.

71 At Whitney-on-Wye and Brilley, respectively. 'Stow' can have a multiplicity of meanings (as can 'eccles'), including a re-named llan- site, and also a place where a shrine existed (Gelling, M, 'Some meanings of stow' in Pearce, S M, ed, *The Early Church in Western Britain and Ireland*, British Archaeological Reports, 102, Oxford, 1982, 187-96). 'Merthyr' can mean 'place where a saint's relics are stored'. However, in Cornwall at least, it is now thought that these are late first millennium namings of dependent chapels located in an earlier enclosure (Preston-Jones, 1992, see note 52, 113-4). This would certainly fit the location in Brilley.

72 It was objected during the conference, that at least one of these churches, at Stretton Grandison, had a clear record of historically recent re-dedication. However, the 'dedication-change' reason for dismissing potential continuity can be very circular: a dedication may 'return' by the same token. It is worth re-iterating that for the churches south of the Wye, several noted in the Llandaff charters had multiple dedications that routinely included Dubricius among both 'metropolitan' and very local saints. These 'multiples' have obviously become simplified through time, with further changes among the suite of saints represented, and yet some local continuity is clearly evident.

73 Tyler Bell, who has researched the association between Romano-British material and later churches for his Oxford University D. Phil thesis, has informed me that there are a surprising number of Roman sites on former glebeland. He considers that it must be of some interest how so many such sites came into the possession of the church. The significance of the name Walshebrok at Canon Pyon dated to around 1200 AD, and of a 'Villa Wallensica' reference of c 1250 is noted in Coplestone-Crow, (1989), see note 56, 172.

74 For Staunton-on-Arrow see RCHME, (1934) see note 2, III, 183. At Putley, Romano-British tiles were discovered when the foundations for the new north annexe of the church were being dug, around 1876. (*Victoria County History, Herefordshire*, I, 1906, 193). During a site visit by *Herefordshire Archaeology* staff in May 2000, it was noted that the church appears to stand in the north-east corner of a large earthwork terrace.

75 Stanford, S, *The Archaeology of the Welsh Marches* (2nd edition, 1991),112.

76 Coplestone-Crow (1989), see note 56, 33, 92-3 & 98-100, infers combinatory re-dedication rather than the co-existence of two separate church structures, but the latter cannot be discounted.

77 Coplestone-Crow, (1989), see note 56, 162. Another site likely to have been abandoned is that echoed in the name 'St Ailworth's chapel', now convincingly identified by Wedell as the site of an early church dedicated to St Eilewedd within the northern annexe of Walterstone Camp between Clodock and Llancillo (Wedell, N, 1997, see note 58). Duncumb J, *Collections Towards the History and Antiquities of the County of Herefordshire* II, (London 1812) 315-316, noted not only the correct site of this chapel but also the removal of a large cross-inscribed stone from the site within (then) living memory.

78 'Hentland' is an Anglicisation of Welsh 'hen' (old) and 'llan' (church enclosure).

79 Coplestone-Crow, (1989) see note 56, 92-3 & 98-100. He suggests that a later charter reference to two churches 'in one cemetery' implies a union of Llanfrother (?old place of the brethren) with a 'lann teliau' at present-day Hentland in the eleventh century.

80 The significance of this distinction has, I think, previously been missed. Huw Pryce ('Pastoral Care in early medieval Wales', in Blair, J & Sharpe, R, eds, *Pastoral Care Before the Parish*, Leicester, 1992, 57-61) has noted a pattern of small local churches, larger church foundations (eg Bolgros), and monasteries.

81 Coplestone-Crow (1989), see note 56, 20 for Lann Cerniu & 73-4 for Cwm Barruc. 'Cerniu' is taken to refer to 'Cenubia Cornubium' since the early C8th charter states 'Cenubia Cornubium id est Lann Cernui super ripam Dour'. The 'monastery of the Cornishman' is in turn thought to have been one founded by Digain, son of Constantine Gorneu, king of Dumnonia. Cwm Barruc has previously been conflated with the Lann Cernui and assumed to be at Abbey Dore because of its location in the same valley. However, he is surely right to stress the significance of reference to the 'lech' (Arthur's Stone) in the Cwm Barruc bounds.

82 Coplestone-Crow, (1989) see note 56, 205.

83 The place-name 'Whitchurch' is widely taken to refer to a site of early veneration, or a place which contained a saint's relics and was subject to pilgrimage (as at Whitchurch Canonicorum in Dorset; see Rollason, D, 'The shrines of saints in later Anglo-Saxon England: distribution and significance', in Butler, L A S, & Morris, R, eds *The Anglo-Saxon Church*, Council for British Archaeology Research Report 60, 1986, 32-43). The situation of the site on the banks of the Wye is no doubt significant, in view of the sites of other early churches. Also there are indications that the church was sited further to the east, with its original location now eroded away in part by the Wye.

84 Coplestone-Crow, (1989) see note 56, 109.

85 Stanford, (1991) see note 75, 110.

86 For a recent synthesis of information about such stones in south and south-central Wales as well as in Cornwall see Thomas, C, *And Shall These Mute Stones Speak? Post-Roman Inscriptions in Western Britain*, (University of Wales, 1994). A second early inscribed stone, drawn for Edward Lhuyd c 1698 and alleged to have been found near Olchon House in the valley below Llanveynoe church to the west, has since been lost (Wedell, 1997, see note 58, 89). This has been dated stylistically to the sixth century (Nash-Williams, V E, *The Early Christian Monuments of Wales*, Cardiff, 1950, No 409), but was not noted by Thomas, whose concern in the 'Mute Stones' book was only with central Brycheiniog.

87 Edwards, N & Lane, A, 'The archaeology of the early church in Wales: an introduction', in Edwards & Lane, (1992) see note 51, 1-11.

88 RCHME, (1931) see note 2, I, 173. These two stones are illustrated in Stanford, (1991) see note 75, 111, Plate 17. The face depicted on the larger of the two stones is very similar in treatment to that depicted upon a cross shaft fragment from Bardsey Island, Caernarvonshire, a place with traditional connections with St Dyfrig. The incised Latin cross on the smaller stone is of exactly the same form and proportions as that on the back of Enniaun's Cross at Margam in Glamorgan (see Laing, 1975 see note 47, Figs 27A and 27B, respectively). The stones have also been dated stylistically to the ninth or tenth century (Nash-Williams, 1950, see note 86, nos 410 & 411).

89 Thomas, C, (1971) see note 42, 195-7.

90 Ray, K, 'The church enclosure and crosses at Llanveynoe', Herefordshire Archaeology Report 26, 2001. Watkins, A, *The Old Standing Crosses of Herefordshire* (London, 1929, for the Woolhope Naturalists' Field Club); he noted it as the oldest standing stone cross in the county, and pointed out its early Christian affinities. It was he who, assisted by the vicar, re-erected the stone where it now stands.

91 Baring-Gould, S, Lives of the British Saints, (ed. Bryce, D, Llanerch reprint, 1990).

92 Hope, V M, 'The Iron and Roman Ages, c 600 BC to AD 400', in Jupp, P C &

Gittings, C, (eds) *Death in England: An Illustrated History*, (Manchester University Press, 1999), 58 fig 25, 40-64. An alternative possibility is that the groove was cut into the Llanveynoe stone in recent times to turn the cross into a drain. Given the easily fractured nature of the stone it is difficult to see how this could have been done without breaking it.

93 RCHME, (1931) see note 2 I, 167-8.

94 Ray, K, 'A stone figure carving at Llangarron Church', Herefordshire Archaeology Report 24, (2001).

95 Pretty, K, 'Defining the Magonsaete' in Bassett, S, (ed), *The Origins of the Anglo-Saxon Kingdoms*', (1989) 171-83; Gelling, M, *The West Midlands in the Middle Ages*, (Leicester University Press, 1992).

96 Bassett, S, 'Church and diocese in the West Midlands: the transition from British to Anglo-Saxon control', in Blair & Sharpe, eds, (1992) see note 80, 13-40.

97 Hooke, D, *The Anglo-Saxon Landscape: the kingdom of the Hwicce*, (Manchester University Press, 1985).

98 Ray, K, 'Marking the Magonsaete? Herefordshire's post-Roman dyke systems', in preparation.

99 Blair, J, this volume. Bassett, (1992) see note 80.

100 For the use of charter evidence see Blair, J, *Anglo-Saxon Oxfordshire*, (Stroud, 1994,) and Hooke, (1985) see note 97.

101 There has been much debate in recent years concerning the status of the term 'minster' in Anglo-Saxon England, and how it relates to the British system of pastoral care. The model of a minster church surrounded by a pastoral territory (rendered as 'parochia', and in some limited contexts as 'hyrnesse') is developed most fully in Blair & Sharpe, (1992), see note 80. Usages before the tenth century are very difficult to interpret, and the distinction between pastoral centre and monastery often seems to have been blurred. Morris, (1989), see note 34, 129-133, gives a very useful practical summary of what the term 'minster' could mean, and how by the ninth century the terminology was becoming codified.

102 Blair, (1994) see note 100, 70-3.

103 Morris, (1989) see note 34, 130-1, 256-7.

104 For Northampton, see Blair, J, 'Palaces or Minsters? Northampton and Cheddar Reconsidered', *Anglo-Saxon England*, 25, (1996) 97-121. For Eynsham Abbey, see Blair, J, (1985) see note 100, 114-16.

105 Morris, R, (1989) see note 34,140-67.

106 Rodwell, W J & K, 'St. Peter's church, Barton-upon-Humber: excavation and structural study, 1978-81', *Antiquaries Journal*, 62, (1982), 283-315.

107 Oswald, A, *The Church of St. Bertelin at Stafford and its Cross*, Birmingham City Museum and Art Gallery, (1956) quoted in Thomas, (1971) see note 42, 71.

108 Loveluck, C, 'Uncovering an Anglo-Saxon 'royal' manor', *British Archaeology*, No 28, (1997), 8-9.

109 Stenton, F M, 'Pre-Conquest Herefordshire' in RCHME, *Herefordshire*, III, (1934), lv-lxi.

110 Parsons, D, 'Early Churches in Herefordshire: Documentary and Structural Evidence' in Whitehead, D, (ed), (1995) see note 55, 61-2.

111 Blair, J, 'Secular minster churches in Domesday Book', in Sawyer, P, (ed), *Domesday Book: a reassessment*, (1985), 104-42.

112 Parsons, (1995) see note 110, Figure 2.

113 Taylor, H M & J, *Anglo-Saxon Architecture* (two volumes), (Cambridge, 1965), 727; Taylor, H M, *Anglo-Saxon Architecture*, III, (Cambridge,1978), 767-72.

114 Parsons, (1995), see note 110, 67.

115 From the data summarised in Parsons, (1995) see note 110, Figures 3-5.

116 eg 'weighting' of the significance of the presence of only one indicator-feature. Another problem (admitted by Parsons) is that of the longevity of building practices, such that some counter-pitched masonry is of even later medieval date. Another is the specificity of a source for materials, producing a localised tradition of use; eg

Parsons notes the Shelsey Walsh source as the likely reason for the concentration of structures featuring tufa blocks in the north-east of the county, while the Bredwardine - Moccas - Tyberton source (not noted by Parsons) explains the middle-Wye concentration.

117 RCHME see note 2, I, (1931), 25-7. Pevsner (1963, see note 39, 83) elaborated the idea by suggesting that the chancel was rebuilt c 1300, but equally failed to explain the contrasting orientation, except to suggest that the tower of 1790 north-east of the nave might have replaced a Norman tower.

118 The British church enclosure could well be that identified by Coplestone-Crow (1989, see note 56, 42-3) as the 'Lann Iunabui' of one of the earliest of the Llandaff charters. The church was documented as being located near to the river Wye. An early church settlement also links well with the unpublished archaeological evidence for a Romano-British settlement here. The scenario of a series of roughly aligned but separate churches on one site is documented widely for the Irish church, but also for several places in Anglo-Saxon England, Blair, J, 'Anglo-Saxon minsters: a topographical review', in Blair & Sharpe, eds, (1992) see note 80.

119 Leather, E M, *The Folklore of Herefordshire*, (1912 repr 1992), 169-70, where the account of their funereal use is given. The type is described in Laing, (1975) see note 47, 371-2. The Marden bell survives at Hereford Museum, while the Bosbury bell is in the Horniman Museum in London.

120 A *Herefordshire Archaeology* research project has been underway at Sutton and Marden since 1999. An early estate administrative centre has been discovered at Freen's Court, a series of fortified enclosures near Sutton St. Michael church, and another complex at Marden: Ray, K & Hoverd, T, 'Archaeological Works at Sutton St. Michael, Herefordshire, 1999: An Interim Statement', Herefordshire Archaeology Report 1, 2000; Ray, K & Hoverd, T, 'The Sutton St. Michael-Marden Project: An Interim Account of Works in 2000', Herefordshire Archaeology Report 19, 2001. Excavations by Worcestershire County Archaeological Service staff in July 2000 at a quarry site in Wellington parish but just across the river Lugg from Marden church have revealed the base timbers of a Saxon water-mill that was probably in royal ownership.

121 Shoesmith, R, 'Llanwarne Old Church', *Transactions of the Woolhope Naturalists' Field Club*, XLIII, (iii), (1981), 267-97. Several successive floor levels were revealed, dating back to before the thirteenth century. No traces of a pre-Conquest structure were found.

122 Hoverd, T, 'Old St. Bartholomew's Church, Lower Sapey, Worcestershire: A re-interment', Hereford Archaeology Series 326, 1997.

123 Wichbold, D, 'Salvage Recording at a Medieval Barn, King's Pyon' Hereford and Worcester County Archaeological Service, Report 267, 1995; For Shipton, see Blair, (1994), see note 100, 66.

124 Blair, (1994) see note 100, 72-3.

125 This failure stands in contrast to the twin parishes of Sutton which appear to have once formed part of Marden. Bone samples from two of the documented skeletons at Ash Grove have been submitted for radiocarbon accelerator dating. Records of early discoveries of skeletons have come to light at Sutton Hill near Burmarsh, at some distance from Marden church but probably still within its former parochia.

126 Shoesmith, R, *Hereford City Excavations, 1: Excavations at Castle Green*, Council for British Archaeology, Research Report 36, (1980). For the excavation of the smaller church, see pp 45-8.

127 Speed's map of 1610 places the chapel of St. Martin in the centre of the outer ward of the castle, in exactly the location in which the smaller structure was found.

128 As suggested by Whitehead, D, (1980) see note 126, but for different reasons.

129 Finberg, H P R, *Early Charters of the West Midlands*, (Leicester, 1972); cf. Morris, (1989) see note 34,123.

130 This style is regarded as having been influential throughout the ninth century and was evident in metalwork and manuscripts as well as in sculpture, see Cramp, R, 'Schools of Mercian Sculpture' in Dornier, A, (ed) *Mercian Studies*, (Leicester University Press, 1977), 191-233. The Cropthorne cross-head and the Acton Beauchamp shaft are thought to be the earliest examples of the style (ibid, 225).

131 White and Barker, (1998) see note 19, Plate 25a, Figure 70. A mid-eighteenth century engraving shows this cross as a freestanding churchyard structure, immediately before its dismantling and incorporation into the church fabric in the 1760s. The cross featured a lower shaft segment, only the upper part of which carried a decorative panel. There was then a narrow central horizontal projecting stone band, surmounted by an upper panel of Acton Beauchamp type. It is this panel that most prominently survives at Wroxeter, but parts of the central band also appear still to be present. Above this, there was presumably once a cross-head of Cropthorne type.

132 In the *Gesta Pontificum*, noted by Stenton, (1934) see note 109, lvi; Whitehead, (1980) see note 128, 3.

133 Pevsner, (1963) see note 39, 106.

134 Ray, K, 'The defended Romano-British town at Canon Frome/Stretton Grandison', Herefordshire Archaeology Report No. 15, 2000.

Glossary

List of Illustrations

Index of the churches and other places
in Herefordshire referred to in this book

Index of Names

Glossary

abacus – (pl abaci) flat rectilinear section surmounting a capital

abcedary – primer, table or book containing the rudiments of anything in alphabetical order

ambulatory – a walkway (often an extension of the aisles) which went around the choir and presbytery. Chapels were commonly built opening off an ambulatory

breviary – liturgical book containing the service for each day to be recited by those in orders

cartulary – a place where papers or records are kept, whence the collection of charters relating to a church's property or the book in which they are entered

cenubia – (Latin) Monasteries referred to as such in the Llandaff charters

chi-rho – the first letters of the Greek word *Christos* ΧΡΙΣΤΟΣ

chrism – oil mingled with balm, consecrated for use as an unguent in the administration of certain sacraments in the Eastern and Western Churches

commote – a sub-division of a neighbourhood locality or cantref (in Wales a territorial and administrative division)

crockets – decorative carved features placed on the sloping sides of spires, pinnacles, gables etc, in Gothic architecture, usually in bud or leaf shapes

diapered – decorative surface work composed of square or lozenge shapes

ealdorman – West Saxon form of alderman

eglwys – (Welsh) church. Source for the anglicisation, 'eccles'

epigrams – short poems with witty endings or sayings/maxims

gloss – a footnote or comment (accidentally) incorporated into text

gradual – a psalm or hymn sung between the readings at the eucharist; liturgical book containing all the choral chants for the Proper of the Mass

hagiography – biography of a saint

hermeneutic – for the purposes of preaching

herneys – obedience, a jurisdiction, a district obedient to a single jurisdiction (Old English heran to hear or obey)

hide – variable unit of land, enough for a household

impost – angular top course of a pillar supporting an arch or arcade

leacht – (Irish) a memorial cairn purportedly built over a saint's grave

leam – a glow or glint (now dialect or northern)

memoria – (Latin). a memorial formula inscribed on a stone marking a Christian burial of the immediate post-Roman centuries in western Britain

merthyr – (Welsh) related to Latin, 'martyrium'. Used for a place where a saint's relics are stored. Could also mean a dependent chapel within an early parish

noetic – of or relating to the mind or intellect

orans – a figure in the attitude of prayer, arms outstretched and open handed; early Christian

palaeography – the study of writing and documents from the past

parch marks – areas of grassland or crop which, becoming drier than the surrounding areas, produce indicative markings seen from a distance

parochia – (Latin) the territory served by monks or canons from an Anglo-Saxon minster church

polity – form of political organization, body of people organized under a system of government

polyander – a burial place or enclosure

presbytery – the part of the church reserved for ordained clergy; in medieval churches the part of the church east of the choir, including the high altar

pulpitum – screen, sometimes stone, shutting off the choir from the nave

reveal – the internal side surface of a recess, or of the opening for a doorway or window between the frame and the outer surface of the wall

sequence – music for a liturgical procession accompanying the Gospel Book

small-finds – individual objects, usually recovered through archaeological excavation

springer – in an arch, the lowest curved stone (it absorbs the lateral forces)

stemma – diagram showing the relationship between a text and the various manuscripts

synchretistic – belief or religious practice that draws upon a combination of traditions

triforium – the second level of arcading (often without windows) in the nave (and choir) of a church building above the main arches and below the clerestory; often at the height of the aisle roofs

use – the variant form of the Roman Rite used in a particular region diocese or monastic order

virgate – an early English land-measure, varying greatly in extent, but in many cases averaging thirty acres

List of Illustrations

Figures

    The Llangarron Figure *frontispiece*

1. Two pieces of ecclesiastical sculpture of c 800 from the same West Midlands workshop. Cross-head at Cropthorne (Worcestershire) and cross-shaft at Acton Beauchamp (Herefordshire)   7
2. The context of Leominster, Hereford and Sutton St Michael. Map showing all directional place-names within its area and the known boundary of the residual mother-parish of Leominster   10
3. The legend of St Etfrid, extract from BL Harley MS 2253 f132r   16
4. The Mercian and Kentish Royal families   42
5. The Leominster Parochia as listed in the 1123 charter, with places otherwise known as dependent   43
6. Leominster: the minster precinct   49
7. Canterbury: King Ethelbert's Church of St Peter and St Paul, c 613 and King Eadbald's Chapel of St Mary c 618   54
8a. Christ Church Canterbury: the Cathedral with Archbishop Cuthbert's Chapel of St John the Baptist. A tentative reconstruction after H M Taylor   55
8b. Hereford: the first Cathedral with Bishop Cuthbert's burial Chapel. A hypothetical reconstruction dependent on analogy   55
9. Bromyard Parish Church: the re-set stone carving of St Peter above the south portal   61
10. The Episcopal Parochiae of Bromyard and Ledbury   63
11. Cropthorne, Worcestershire: arm of cross shaft c 800   66
12. Cropthorne, Worcestershire: arm of cross shaft c 800   66
13. Bird carved on the Gloucester cross-shaft   66
14. Bird carved on the cross-shaft set as a lintel over the south doorway at Acton Beauchamp   67
15. Bird carved on the west portal at Leominster Priory Church   67
16. Diagrammatic plan of Leominster Priory Church, as it may have been c 1150, showing the location of the monastic choir, the principal space for worship   80
17. Diagrammatic plan of Leominster Priory Church, as it may have been c 1250, showing the new South Nave, an additional space for worship   82
18. Diagrammatic plan of Leominster Priory Church, as it may have been c 1350, showing the new Lady Chapel, South Aisle and Forbury Chapel   84
19. Plan of the Priory Church of S S Peter and Paul, Leominster   88
20. Existing wall painting of the Wheel of Life, Leominster Priory Church   91
21. Reproduction of the Wheel of life painting at Leominster by C J Praetorius   93

22	Roman roads and major Romano-British settlements in Herefordshire	103
23	A Romano-British bronze strap-end from Kenchester	106
24	The sandstone frieze at Upton Bishop church	108
25	The British church in Herefordshire: the locations of some of the key places mentioned in the text	112
26	Church foundations of the mid first millennium in south Herefordshire attested in the Llandaff charters.	116
27	The short-armed cross in the churchyard at Llanveynoe	121
28	The Llangarron figure	123
29	The Anglian Church in Herefordshire. The map shows the location of key minster churches, monasteries and other sites mentioned in the text	129
30	The south doorway in what is now the chancel of St Andrew's church, Bredwardine	131
31	An ecclesiastical hand-bell from Marden	132
32	The Acton Beauchamp cross-shaft	135
33	The cross that once stood in St. Andrew's churchyard Wroxeter	136

The illustrations accompanying the legend of St Etfrid on pages 16-31 have been reproduced from lino-cuts made by Hugh Pawsey

Front Cover: A montage of images from the six papers

Back Cover: Two arms of the Cropthorne Worcester Cross

Colour Plates

1. The Summer Canon, 'Sumer is icumen in'/'Perspice Christicola', British Library MS 478, f 11b
2. Wheel of Life wall painting on the north wall of the nave, St Mary's Church, Kempley, Gloucestershire
3. Acton Beauchamp, St Giles, from the south. The Anglo-Saxon cross-shaft forms the lintel over the doorway at the base of the tower
4. Modern interpretation of the Wheel of Life painting in Leominster Priory Church by Arthur Davis
5. Llanveynoe, St Beuno and St Peter, from the south east. The short-armed cross stands in the churchyard near the porch
6. The Llanveynoe cross
7. Llangarron, St Deinst, view from the bridge over the Garren brook
8. Upton Bishop, St John the Baptist, from the south east. The sandstone frieze is set in the south wall of the chancel next to the hexagonal vestry
9. The Upton Bishop sandstone frieze set between two other stone fragments

Index of the churches and other places in Herefordshire referred to in this book

For details of these places reference may be made to the many books on the subject, of which the following are recommended:-

The Royal Commission on Historic Monuments, England, *An Inventory of the Historical Monuments of Herefordshire*, I (South-West, 1931), II (East, 1932), III (North-West, 1934)

Pevsner, N, *The Buildings of England; Herefordshire* (1963)

Salter, M, *The Old Parish Churches of Herefordshire* (1990)

Leonard, J, *Churches of Herefordshire and Their Treasures* (2000)

Abbey Dore 47, 112, 116, 119
Acton Beauchamp 5-7, 12, 65, 128-9, 134-5, 139
Almeley 44
Avenbury 64, 65, 129
Aylton 69
Aymestrey 44

Bache 44
Bishops Frome 58
Bishopstone 117
Blackwardine 103
Bosbury 58, 69, 129
Bredenbury 68
Bredwardine 47, 112, 116, 129-31, 134
Bridstow 114
Brockhampton 58, 64
Bromyard 5, 58, 61-4, 128, 129, 133
Bromyard parochia 63

Canon Pyon 58, 112, 117, 118, 134
Cholstrey 50
Clodock 119
Coddington 58, 69
Collington 64
Colwall 58, 69
Cradley 58, 69, 129, 137, 139
Croft Ambrey 44

Dewchurch 4, 47
Donnington 58, 69
Dorstone 112, 116, 119

Eardisley 44
Eastnor 58, 69
Eaton Bishop 47, 58
Edvin Loach 64, 130
Edwyn Ralph 64
Ergyng 4, 12
Ewias Lacy (Longtown) 114

Fownhope 128, 129

Garway 4
Goodrich 116, 119
Grendon Bishop 64
Grendon Warren 64

Hatfield 129, 130
Hentland 112, 116, 118, 119, 134
Hereford Cathedral 8
Hereford St Guthlac's 8, 10, 59, 114, 128, 129, 132, 134
Hereford 9, 10, 14, 53, 55, 56
Holme Lacy 58
How Caple 58

Ivington 44

Kenchester 103-6, 115, 138
Kenderchurch 116, 119
Kentchurch 114
King's Pyon 129, 130, 133

Ledbury 11, 53, 56, 58, 61-4, 69-70, 128-9
Ledbury parochia 63
Leintwardine 103, 106
Lenastone 118
Leominster 5, 9-12, 14, 33-37, 41-2, 44-8, 57-61, 65, 77-87, 98, 111, 128-9, 134
Leominster Forbury Chapel 83
Leominster parochia 43
Letton 130
Lingen 128
Linton (Lye) 128-9
Little Cowarne 64
Little Marcle 69
Llancillo 114, 130
Llancloudy 47,
Llangarron 112, 116, 119, 120, 123-5, 138
Llangunnock 118
Llangunvill 114
Llanrothal 116
Llanveynoe 112, 114, 119, 120-3, 138
Llanwarne 4
Lyde 9, 53, 58

Madley 47, 58, 112, 116
Marden 129, 132, 133, 139
Marstow 116
Martinstow 114, 120
Mathon 130
Michaelchurch 120, 130, 137
Moccas 4, 47, 112, 116
Moreton Jeffries 68
Much Marcle 58, 69
Munsley 130

Norton Canon 115, 117

Orleton 14

Peterchurch 47
Peterstow 112, 114, 116
Pixley 69
Preston-on-Wye 47, 58, 117
Putley 117

Risbury 44
Ross-on-Wye 58

Saltmarsh 64
St Weonard's 4, 114
Sellack 114
Shelwick 9
Shobdon 53, 65, 69
Stanford Bishop 58, 64, 134, 138
Staunton-on-Arrow 117
Stockton 44
Stoke Lacy 64
Stoke Prior 44
Stretton Grandison 103, 115, 117, 138
Sutton 9, 132
Sutton St Michael 9, 12

Tedstone Delamere 64, 128, 129, 130
Tedstone Wafer 64
Thornbury 64
Titley 44
Tyberton 58

Ullingswick 58, 68
Upper Sapey 64
Upton Bishop 58, 107-9, 120, 129, 130, 137, 138

Wacton 64
Walford 58
Wapley 44
Welsh Bicknor 116, 118
Weobley 44
Weston-under-Penyard 115, 117
Whitbourne 58, 64
Whitchurch 112, 116, 119, 134
Wigmore 69, 130
Winforton 119
Wolferlow 64
Woolhope 58, 117
Wormsley 58

Index of Names

Aaron, 100
Abbo of Fleury 34
Adam of Orleton 14, 37, 46
Aelfstan 61
Aelfthryth 9
Aethelbald 6, 8, 42, 65, 134
Aethelberht 8, 9, 10, 41, 51, 53, 54, 57
Aethelflaed 59
Aethelmod 8, 46
Aethelred 35, 46, 50, 59
Aethelwig, Abbot 68
Aethelwold 34
Aidan 45
Alban 100
Alcuin 110
Aldhelm 109
Alfred 33, 34, 59, 68
Alkmund 59
Aquablanca, Peter D 62
Athelstan 60
Augustine 36, 54, 110
Augustine of Hippo 100

Balbulus, Notker 15
Bannister, Henry 62
Bede 4-6, 36, 50, 52, 53, 59, 60, 68, 109, 110, 125
Benedict, St 79
Beorhtwulf 65
Beorngyth 51
Berhtferth 9
Berhtwald 54, 55
Berhtwulf 61
Bertha 41, 54
Bethune, Robert de, Bishop 34
Beuno, St 114, 120, 122
Birinus 56
Biscop, Benedict 59
Bride (Bridget), St 114
Buca 6, 7, 65

Canterbury, St Augustine's 32, 41
Cantilupe, St Thomas 37, 62
Cenwalh, 56
Ceollach 45
Chad, St 45, 56
Clydog, St 119
Coenred 57
Coenthryth 9
Colman, Abbot 4
Columba, St 46, 47, 68
Constantine, St 118
Cropthorne (Worcs) 7
Crowland 8, 9
Cuenberg 52
Cuthbert 52-56, 136
Cuthwulf 61
Cyneberht 6
Cynegils 56
Cynfal, St 114

David, St 33, 47, 48, 111
Deinst, St 124
Diuma 45
Domneva 14, 33, 35
Dubricius (Dubric, Dyfrig) 109, 113, 117-9
Duns Scotus 34
Dunstan 34
Durham 32

Eadbald 54, 55
Eadfrith 4, 8, 41, 42, 45, 46, 56, 57,
Eadgifu 57
Eafe 41, 42
Ecgberht, Bishop 5
Ecgfrith 35, 51
Ecgmund, 20
Edberg 37
Edburga, St 32
Edgar 32, 34
Edith, Queen 33

Edouart, A G 81, 92
Entferth 46
Etfrid 14-38
Ethelbert 14
Ethelmund 46
Ethelred 35
Ethelwald of Deira 35

Fastidius 100
Freeman, A E 92
Foliot, Bishop Gilbert 53
Foliot, Bishop Hugh 69

Germanus, Bishop 99, 100
Giraldus Cambrensis 132
Godwin, Earl 33
Goscelin 32
Gregory 33, 36, 53, 54, 68
Grimm, Brothers 9
Guthlac, St 8, 58, 114, 132, 134
Gwrfodwr 113
Gwynog, St 119

Haedddi, Bishop 56
Haemme 8, 46, 57
Hanbury (Worcs) 4
Henry I 60, 79, 89
Hygeberht 51

Iambert 56
Illtud, St 110, 113
Ithel ap Morgan 58

Jaenberht 52
Jerome, St 60

Kempley, St Mary's 91, 93
Kenelm, St 51
Keyne, St 114

Laurence, St 54, 115, 117
Leofric, Bishop 45
Lisle, Robert de 93
Liuthard 54
Lydbury North 11

Magonsaete 4, 10, 41, 52, 57, 125, 136
Maildubh 45
Martin, St 114
Merchelm 41, 56
Merefin 41
Merwald 14, 32-35, 41, 42, 46, 56, 57
Milburga, St 14, 32-38
Mildburg 41, 42, 46, 57, 60
Mildfrith 41, 42, 52, 57
Mildgith 41
Mildred 41, 42
Mildrith 32, 35, 36
Milferth 9
Milfrith 136
Milred 52, 54

Neale, J M 15
Nothelm 55

Offa 8, 10, 14, 20, 51, 52
Oftfor 45
Old Radnor 86
Osfrith 52
Oshelm 52
Oswald 34, 53, 59, 60
Oswiu 35
Oswy 45

Patrick, St 99
Paul, St 113
Pecham, John, Archbishop of Canterbury 77, 83
Pelagius 100
Penda 35, 45
Peter, St 114, 120
Prophete, John 62
Prosper of Acquitaine 99
Putta 50-56, 128

Ramsey Abbey 34
Reading Abbey 77, 79, 81, 83, 89
Rhigyfarch 33, 35, 48
Richard de Capella 60
Robert de Bethune 53, 69, 89
Robert de Melun 53

Samson, St 110, 113, 122
Scott, G G 78, 92
Seaxwulf 52, 57
Stoke Orchard, St James the great 90
Sweyn 33
Swinfield, Bishop 62
Sweyn, Earl Godwin 3

Tatwine 54, 55
Teilo, St 113, 118
Theodore, Archbishop 55-57, 59
Torthere 52, 65
Trumhere 45
Tyrhthil 52
Tysilio, St 114
Urse d'Abitot 68
Ufelwg, Bishop 113

Waerferth 68
Walhstod 52, 53, 57
Wealdhere 52
Wenarth, St 114
Wenlock 14
Werburg, St 37, 59
Winberht 9
William of Malmesbury 52, 136
William of Winchester 77
Wistan, St 14, 15
Wistanstow 14
Wlpher 35
Wulfheard 128